More Praise for
The Three Tensions

"Business, like the rest of life, is all about managing tensions. It's rare to find a business book that deals head-on with that challenge and even rarer to find one that offers practical ideas for what managers can actually do about it. *The Three Tensions* does both."
—Matthew Barrett, chairman, Barclays plc

"The three tensions resonate with me. Companies have to overcome the compromises embedded in conventional leadership thinking. At Textron, we found the actions the authors recommend to be important elements in helping us achieve our goal of becoming the premier multi-industry company."
—Lewis B. Campbell, chairman, president and CEO, Textron Inc.

"An insightful window into the real world of leading the modern corporation."
—Tom Glocer, chief executive, Reuters Group plc

"The tension BBVA worries about as a company has changed over time. We are now concentrating on addressing the inevitable conflict that all large companies face between whole versus parts. Getting this right is our route to the next level of performance."
—José Ignacio Goirigolzarri, president and COO, Grupo BBVA

"Some business books get stuck in orbit at 60,000 feet. Others start in the weeds and never hack their way out. This is that rare thing, a book about big ideas, but with very immediate, concrete, and immensely valuable lessons and applications."
—Chris Jones, former chairman and CEO, J. Walter Thompson

"The authors explore some themes that we hold dear here at Nordstrom: the overriding need to build your business around a focus on customer benefit and the importance of growing sustainable earnings rather than merely sustaining earnings growth. This is an important and useful book."

—Blake Nordstrom, president, Nordstrom Inc.

"This is a book that makes you think. Brimming with new ideas, it takes a fresh look at the main reasons standing in the way of growing company value—and comes up with a wealth of solutions."

—Sir Brian Pitman, former chairman, Lloyds TSB Group

"Avoiding unnecessary compromises is the mark of good management. The authors explore the central imperatives for meeting this standard. In particular, I find the concept of sustainable earnings to be both valid and powerful."

—Sir John Sunderland, chairman,
Cadbury Schweppes plc

"A welcome book about the ever-present difficulties of business leadership. While it doesn't pretend that attaining superior performance can be reduced to a formula, it provides an accessible framework and some useful new concepts for improving the odds."

—John Varley, group chief executive, Barclays plc

"To be a great basketball player, you have to be able to go left and right. It's the same in business. You have to be able to grow the quantity of earnings and their quality, to be an entrepreneur and a part of the company. If you can only go in one direction, you'll never win. *The Three Tensions* is a very helpful guide to leaders in thinking about—and finding ways through—the apparent conflicts of running an institution."

—Robert D. Walter, chairman and founder,
Cardinal Health Inc.

JB JOSSEY-BASS

THE THREE TENSIONS

Winning the Struggle to Perform Without Compromise

Dominic Dodd

Ken Favaro

BICENTENNIAL
1807
WILEY
2007
BICENTENNIAL

John Wiley & Sons, Inc.

Published by Jossey-Bass
A Wiley Imprint

The quotation in the box on p. 86 is from Ludwig von Mises, *Human Action,* 4th ed. (Irvington-on-Hudson, NY: Foundation for Economic Education, 1996), p. 654. The quotation on p. 91 is from Lewis Carroll, *Through the Looking Glass* (London: Puffin Books), p. 66.

Readers should be aware that Internet Web sites offered as citations and/or sources for further information may have changed or disappeared between the time this was written and when it is read.

Jossey-Bass books and products are available through most bookstores. To contact Jossey-Bass directly call our Customer Care Department within the U.S. at 800-956-7739, outside the U.S. at 317-572-3986, or fax 317-572-4002.

Library of Congress Cataloging-in-Publication Data

Dodd, Dominic, date.
  The three tensions: winning the struggle to perform without compromise / Dominic Dodd, Ken Favaro.
    p. cm.
  Includes bibliographical references and index.
  ISBN-13: 978-0-7879-8779-4
  ISBN-10: 0-7879-8779-4
  1. Success in business. 2. Executives. 3. Leadership. 4. Industrial management. I. Favaro, Ken. II. Title.
  HF5386.D547 2007
  658.4'092—dc22   2006029102

Printed in the United States of America
FIRST EDITION
PB Printing   10 9 8 7 6 5 4 3 2 1

Contents

In memory of Dr. Bill
1925–2006

FOREWORD

Great performance rises above compromise. It doesn't come with some surrender elsewhere, it comes without concession. It is not the product of making the best choices, but of avoiding the need to make unnecessary choices in the first place.

The discipline of management has quietly made a virtue of compromise. It has made heroes of trade-off, of balance, of today's priority objective.

We wrote this book because we believe that management should aim higher. The manager's first task should not be to arbitrate between competing objectives but to reconcile them into great performance on many fronts at the same time. Management should be the art of overcoming compromise.

To meet this challenge, managers must step onto a new path. Sports teams stand a greater chance of winning the championship if players concentrate as much on getting better at building the skills that count-for example, passing the ball-as they do on winning today's game. Similarly, organizations stand a greater chance of meeting their many performance objectives, without compromise, if they concentrate on strengthening the capabilities that help knit them all together. This book is about those elusive connecting capabilities.

We write for practitioners and scholars alike-particularly practitioners who are students of management thinking and scholars who have a close interest in the everyday practice of management. We hope that what follows makes a small contribution to a new direction for the discipline of management: helping managers win the struggle to perform without compromise.

INTRODUCTION

A manager argued that he could either increase his business unit's margins or its sales, but not both. His chief executive reminded him of the time when people lived in mud huts and faced the stark choice between light and heat: punch a hole in the side of your hut, and you let the daylight in, but also the cold; block up all the openings, and you stay warm, but sit in darkness. The invention of glass made it possible to overcome the dilemma—to let in the light, but not the cold. How then, he asked his manager, will you resolve your dilemma between no sales growth and no margin improvement? Where is the glass?

The central challenge for business leaders is how to achieve many objectives at the same time. The problem is not to become more profitable or to find new revenue growth; the problem is to do both at the same time. It isn't the need to produce better performance in the short term that makes the job hard, but the need to produce results today *and* build for tomorrow simultaneously. The real puzzle is how to strengthen each individual part of the company *and* increase the benefits of belonging to a larger whole, not how to do the one at the expense of the other. Every leader and every company constantly faces the problem of how to make progress on seemingly conflicting objectives at the same time.

Of all the competing objectives, three pairs stand out: profitability vs. growth; short term vs. long term; and whole vs. parts. On each of these three tensions, companies often make progress on one objective, only to fail on the other. They seek strong growth, only to find poor profitability; then they chase profitability, but find that growth eludes them. They build for tomorrow, but lose sight of performance today; then they squeeze out earnings today at the expense of profits tomorrow. They free up each part of the company to be more successful, but see the benefits from coordinating across the parts slip away; then, in the effort to create one-company benefits, they undermine the performance of the individual parts. As priority shifts to one place, performance elsewhere declines. As performance elsewhere declines, priority shifts once more. Companies may hope for a glass window, but they end up punching a hole in the side of the hut, then blocking it up again. This is not some caricature of the most egregiously managed companies. As we will see, most companies struggle in this way.

In contrast, the companies that master the three tensions are the corporate winners. Growth with profitability, earnings today that endure tomorrow, and high-performing parts within a valuable whole—as we will see, all these are worth far more to a company's success than performance that is trapped in trade-offs. The better the answers that companies find to the mud-hut conundrum, the better they perform.

However, that conundrum is very real. Tensions between objectives are due to powerful forces to which no company is immune. Some spring from how competitive markets work, some from how organizations work. They are as difficult to avoid as competition and human nature themselves.

But escape is possible. Some of the forces behind each tension are the unintended product of management practices. They are self-inflicted.

BATTING AVERAGE

This book is about the three tensions that pull business and its leaders in different directions, and what can be done to escape their influence. It is therefore a book about the struggle to meet many objectives at the same time. In it we address three questions. How much do the three tensions matter? Why do companies get trapped within them? And what can leaders do to escape from them?

Central to our case is a concept we call *batting average,* a term we borrow from baseball. It is a measure of how often a company is able to achieve two performance objectives at the same time in a given year. So, for example, a company that succeeded in earning a positive profit margin and in growing revenue *at the same time* in three out of ten years has a batting average of .300 or 30 percent on the profitability vs. growth tension.

You might ask "So what?" Aren't we talking about the natural rhythm of business? Doesn't it make sense to grow and then consolidate and work on profitability, and then go for the next phase of growth? Isn't accepting losses now part of creating profits later? Isn't there a time for giving priority to the performance of the parts and a time for putting first the performance of the whole? Isn't it total company performance *over time* that matters—regardless of whether or not that performance is built on compromises between multiple objectives at any particular point in time?

The evidence says otherwise. As you'll see in the chapters that follow, one of the main findings of this book is that batting averages correlate closely with total shareholder returns (TSR). The higher a company's batting average—the more it escapes from the three tensions—the higher its TSR. The lower the batting average—the more the company is trapped by the three tensions—the lower the returns. In fact, as we explore further in Chapter One, batting average is a better predictor for TSR *than any other single measure of operating performance.*

This is a striking finding. *A company with years of booms and busts in profitability and growth—even many big boom years—is less likely to have high share performance than a firm that reliably meets both objectives of positive profitability and real growth at the same time most of the time.* Far from being the natural path to high performance, this "natural rhythm of business" stands in its way.

Business Is a Different Game

There are a few important differences between batting average in baseball and batting average in business. First, in baseball, many other measures of performance matter as much or more—for example, "on base percentage." In business, however, batting average is much more important. Second, whereas in baseball a batting average of .300 is more than respectable, the bar is set much higher in business. Companies in the top quartile of total shareholder returns typically hit above .500. A final difference is presentational: in this book, we use percentages to express batting averages.

Some managers might believe that a company's batting average is determined by its environment. In their minds, some industries present managers with stark choices between performance objectives, whereas others do not. For instance, companies in capital-intensive industries are forced to accept short-term losses for long-term gains more than companies in low-capital industries. The headroom to grow and be profitable at the same time is surely limited in low-growth and unprofitable industries. Even if it is valuable, hitting for a high batting average is not something managers can control, the thinking goes.

There is an important element of truth to this position. Industry context *does* affect a company's ability to meet many objectives at the same time. But batting averages don't behave as you might expect them to. They vary more *within* an industry than *across* industries. It is possible to have a high batting average in every industry, even the most challenging. And companies can get stuck with low batting averages even in the most promising industries. By implication, escape from the three tensions is not just desirable—it's within management's control.

THREE COMMON BONDS

In resolving the mud-hut conundrum, the common bond that made two conflicting objectives possible—light and warmth—was glass. With glass, the two objectives could be met at the same time; without it, they could not. Likewise, for each of the three tensions there is a common bond: a necessary ingredient for the two objectives in a tension to act as complements rather than substitutes. If this bond is absent, the two objectives become substitutes: good performance on one will lead to poor performance on another. But if the bond is strong, then good and mutually reinforcing performance on both objectives is possible.

Customer benefit is the common bond between profitability and growth. Customer benefit is different from what the product or service is or can do. It is the reward that customers receive through their experience of choosing and using a product or service. It varies by customer and by context. But if both revenue management and cost management are rooted in high or growing customer benefit, profitability and growth are much more likely to coexist than if one or both are not. When managers divorce the management of revenue and cost from customer benefit, profitability and growth become divided from each other. But this is no clarion call for more "customer focus." As we will see, increasing customer focus is often the surest way to lose touch with customer benefit.

Sustainable earnings are the common bond between today's performance and tomorrow's. They are earnings that are not influenced by borrowing or lending between timeframes. They are neither borrowed from the future by cutting necessary long-term investment, nor are they borrowed from the past by clinging to a business that is past its time. They are repeatable. If the management of today's performance and of tomorrow's are both designed to grow sustainable earnings, then companies will be much more likely to avoid unnecessary choices between the short term and the long term. But "grow sustainable earnings" is not the same as "sustain earnings growth." Although the former often results in the latter, the reverse is all too often not the case.

A company's *diagonal assets* form the common bond that allows it to increase the individual performance of its parts and capture one-company benefits at the same time. Diagonal assets are resources and capabilities—ways of working, cultural norms, and other often intangible factors—that allow the company to act both as a single company and as many different businesses at the same time. A company with few or weak diagonal assets will find that there are many barriers to making this feat both possible and relatively painless. A company with strong diagonal assets will find that it really can be more than just its parts.

How strong a company can make these three common bonds—customer benefit, sustainable earnings, and diagonal assets—determines whether it can overcome the three tensions to enjoy performance without compromise. All too often, these bonds sit in an organization's blind spot. They are hard to measure. You can't touch or feel them. Even customers, let alone marketing departments, find it difficult to articulate customer benefit. The difference between sustainable earnings and unsustainable earnings is often hard to know. You won't find a company's diagonal assets on its organization chart. All three are easily overlooked.

Furthermore, what leads companies to lose sight of these common bonds are perfectly sensible management practices: increasing customer focus; managing costs to achieve earnings targets;

working hard to sustain annual earnings growth; using "net present value" to manage investment; increasing autonomy, especially to stimulate growth; and centralizing operations, especially to reduce costs. All these are part of the conventional wisdom of management. But, as we will see, these practices can lead companies to weaken the three common bonds that turn opposing objectives into mutually compatible objectives. They are well-disguised traps that hold companies back and prevent them from performing to their potential.

Overcoming the three tensions requires keeping the organization's attention squarely trained on the three common bonds. Leaders have a number of tools at their disposal: standards, strategy, structure, process, culture. All can be called on to help. As we will see, the answer is not in designing new tools but in combining and using familiar tools in different ways.

Together the three tensions form a tangled web of interdependencies. Addressing all three at once can be a formidable task—perhaps too formidable, especially for larger, more complex companies. And often one tension is more important to resolve than others in order to improve company performance. A final challenge, then, is judging which tension to pay most heed to and when. The answers are not as obvious as might at first be imagined.

THE BOOK AHEAD

In Chapter One, we explain the three tensions and why they matter for every company. We show how they act in concert to form what we term "the corporate cycle"—a self-defeating path of behaviors that limits company performance. We put batting average forward as an important measure of corporate performance, showing how it correlates with TSR.

The core of the book is found in Chapters Two, Three, and Four, which explore each of the three tensions in turn. We follow the same structure in each chapter. We look at the forces that make the tension hard to resolve, and we identify the traps companies fall into that make things worse. We examine the common bond that ties together the competing objectives and that must be the focal point for addressing the tension. Then we discuss and illustrate approaches leaders can take to strengthen that bond and thus master the tension.

Chapter Five looks back at the lessons of earlier chapters to suggest new ways for managers to tackle the old struggle to achieve many performance objectives at the same time. We consider circumstances in which one tension is more important to resolve than another and discuss how you can decide the right "lead tension" for your company.

One final set of forces gives extra momentum to the corporate cycle. Although achieving many apparently conflicting objectives at the same time is central to the challenge of management, it is not yet central to the *literature* on management. Much of the "management ideas industry" dances to the same rhythm as the corporate cycle. That is, there are many techniques for how to improve company performance on one objective that are silent on how to do so for the other. It is this one-sidedness that permits—even encourages—fashion in management. In the final chapter, we argue that management as a professional discipline must break out of its own cycle of ideas by building greater consensus on its purpose, scope, and method.

Our Research and Groundwork

The research for this book is based on the performance of more than one thousand public companies between 1983 and 2003. We chose so many companies and so many years in order to iron out the effects of different economic cycles. Doing so also allowed us, where appropriate, to look meaningfully at different industries and other subsets of our data. We therefore believe that our findings are not a function of our decisions on which companies to include or what timeframe to use. Others wishing to replicate our results with similarly robust data should be able to do so.

To ensure a practitioner's perspective, we talked in depth with twenty chairmen and chief executives from different companies in different industries. They feel different tensions and wrestle with them in different ways. Some of these companies (for example, Alcan) want to improve profitability without sacrificing growth; others (for example, Cadbury Schweppes and Xerox) are seeking a higher growth rate without sacrificing profitability. Some (for example, LaSalle) are aiming at higher short-term earnings without sacrificing long-term profits; others (for example, BP, Dow Jones, and Reuters) are working to build for long-term profits without taking their eyes off short-term performance. Some (for example, Cardinal Health and ABN AMRO) are trying to increase one-company benefits without undermining the individual performance of their major business units. Others (for example, BBVA) are trying to increase business unit performance without sacrificing one-company benefits. They are all seeking to achieve high standards of performance on many objectives, but they start from different positions. They also have many different views about how to get there.

AUDIENCE AND CAVEATS

This book is written for anyone with an interest in business or management. We have tried to keep it as accessible as we can and to use our appendixes to deal with more technical matters, such as the link between batting average and TSR, and our research methodology.

Although the context in which we write is the management of large companies, the book's findings are relevant to companies of any size. They should also be of interest to managers of nonprofit organizations. The tensions of today vs. tomorrow and whole vs. parts have obvious application. The same principles for managing the tension of profitability vs. growth also apply to the tension of service quality vs. service cost with which nonprofit organizations must contend.

Although there are many ways of using this book, there are also many ways of misinterpreting it. We would like to warn against a few of them. The first is to confuse examples for evidence. On average, the twenty leaders we met and their companies have scored higher batting averages and earned higher TSR than their peers. But that is not why we chose them. We chose them for the more prosaic reason that we know them and they know us. You should resist the temptation to think that we are holding these companies up as evidence. We are not claiming that these companies and their performance prove our point, and we are not presuming to explain their performance.

It would have been easy for us to have selected the top companies by batting average and looked for common themes across their management approaches. Many of the companies whose leaders we interviewed would have made the cut. Unfortunately, the path between individual management practices and total company performance is long and complex. This makes "argument by exemplar" a risky business. We have avoided it. Where we feel that evidence is possible and useful, we use large sets of data.

Second, we are not arguing that overcoming the three tensions is always possible or even always desirable. Difficult choices cannot always be avoided. A start-up will see growth before it sees profitability. It would be nice never to have to choose between short-term earnings and investment for the long term, but often managers must do so. And when such choices must be made, some objectives will be more valuable than others. Our position is simply that *unnecessary* choices between objectives should be avoided wherever possible. The standard we have in mind for each tension is to achieve a batting average of above 50 percent—meeting both objectives at the same time *more often than not.* As we will see, this standard is usually the minimum necessary to finish in the top quartile of an industry's TSR.

We argue that the common bond within each tension is simple in concept. But we don't believe that keeping an organization's attention trained on it is simple in practice. We agree wholeheartedly with one chief executive, who said, "It may be simple, but it's bloody hard." We know as much from our own company. Superior performance cannot be reduced to a formula. So, rather than a recipe for business leaders and managers to follow, this book puts forward a new way of thinking about the struggle for superior performance. We invite you to convert that way of thinking into the practical experimentation in your company that is the true source of better performance.

Finally, a desire for "both" should not be mistaken for a desire for "balance." We are concerned with the pursuit of performance without compromise: both profitability *and* growth; both good performance today *and* good performance tomorrow; and both more benefits across the whole *and* better individual performance for each part. This is not the same as advocating balance as a philosophy of management. Balance soon becomes a case of "a bit of each," not "a lot of both." It is to poke a small hole in the hut to let in a bit of light and keep things a bit less cold. Or to build a village full of huts, some with holes in them and some without. The right aspiration—no matter how difficult—is to invent glass instead.

THE THREE TENSIONS

CHAPTER ONE

THE CORPORATE CYCLE

'tis wisdom to beware;
And better shun the bait, than struggle in the snare.
JOHN DRYDEN, EPISTLE 13

Growth becomes the new imperative. The leaders of the company look to the future and set demanding goals for market share and new revenue. They know that they must invest and that long-term gain may mean some short-term pain for earnings. But "no change" is not an option. To grow, the company must take greater risks and encourage more experimentation. So the leaders push more authority down the organization. Central intervention in day-to-day management is reduced. They sharpen individual incentives for growth. The emphasis is on building: brands, new businesses, alliances. The company reaches out into new markets and adopts new ways of doing things. The watchwords of the day are ambition, innovation, initiative, change. It's an exciting time to be around.

But the results are mixed. Revenue does grow, but margins fall. Large investments in the name of future potential haven't translated into higher earnings today. The new energy that was unleashed within the organization seems to have ebbed. Duplication and complexity are widespread. People fear that the company has moved into areas too distant from its real skills. No one seems to have paid enough attention to the details, to the everyday tasks. Standards for investment approval and for financial discipline have slipped. There is "slack" in the system everywhere. The sense that things aren't working comes to a head. Pressure for better results—now—is bcoming intense.

A drive for efficiency follows. People start to say that what the company needs is "better execution, not more strategy." Company leaders place a moratorium on new acquisitions and shelve some of the recent new ventures. They set goals for costs, margins, profitability. Budgets tighten. Peripheral businesses are sold. Some operations are centralized to reduce duplication and waste and to instill more control. Everyone recognizes the need to act as one well-coordinated company. Where before there was local initiative, now there is top-down guidance. The priorities are to standardize, share "best practice," and avoid "reinventing the wheel." The new words on everyone's lips are discipline, coordination, standards, and "payback." The going is tough, but there's a new sense of realism. Determination is high.

Soon, however, it feels as if the company is backing itself into a corner. Earnings growth has started to become ever more reliant on delaying investments, cutting into costs that customers care about, pulling tactical levers. People start to worry that the company is starving the future to feed the present. The existing business doesn't have enough headroom to secure future prosperity. Growth is as elusive as ever. The company has become too rigid, too distant from its customers, too inward focused, too obsessed with numbers. Everyone knows "we can't shrink ourselves to greatness." And so growth becomes the new imperative. . . .

THE THREE TENSIONS AND THE CORPORATE CYCLE THEY CREATE

A path of least resistance lies in front of every company. It's not always easy to see that the path is turning inward in a circle. There's one sure way to tell, though: more progress on one front always seems to come at the cost of less progress on another. More growth damages profitability, and more profitability slows growth. Efforts to build for tomorrow distract everyone from producing results today; but when managers shift focus to results for today, they compromise the future strength of the company. Attempts to create one-company benefits hold back individual business units; then attempts to unleash the individual potential of the business units bar the way to capturing the benefits of being one company. It's like squeezing a balloon in one place only to find that it expands elsewhere.

These are the three tensions that act on every company: profitability vs. revenue growth; results today vs. results tomorrow; and the performance of the company as a whole vs. the performance of each part of the company. The tensions usually act in concert. When the priority is today's earnings, companies tend to push for higher profitability rather than faster revenue growth because they are confident they can increase profitability more quickly and with less investment than they can influence revenue growth. Companies that give greater priority to revenue growth often seek it by freeing up the individual parts of the company to stimulate new ideas, more experimentation, and greater adaptation to local markets. Conversely, a desire for improved profitability usually sits alongside greater emphasis on improving the performance of the company as a whole by coordinating across common activities to reduce costs.

Because of these affinities, priority and performance on some objectives sit more comfortably together than priority and performance on others. On the one side sits growth, tomorrow's performance, and the individual parts; on the other sits profitability, today's earnings, and benefits across the whole. Together they create the corporate cycle: an interaction of the three tensions that causes companies to cycle between two phases: the "Brave New World" phase, where the focus is on growth, long term and parts; and a "Back to Basics" phase, where the focus is on profitability, the short term and the whole (Figure 1.1). In between these two phases, the company attempts to deal with its failure to achieve adequate performance on the other three objectives. The completion of each phase is quite often marked by the decision of the chief executive to spend more time with his family.

It isn't hard to find companies that have been caught in the corporate cycle—swinging back and forth between seeking their brave new world and going back to basics. The history of General Motors (GM) over the last twenty years is as good an example as any.

General Motors, 1983–2003

In the 1980s, the company went on an $80 billion spending spree to build for the future. It took a 50 percent stake in Saab to expand its international presence and pushed into new markets by buying Electronic Data Systems and

FIGURE 1.1. THE CORPORATE CYCLE.

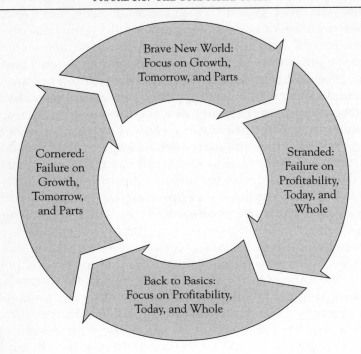

Brave New World:
Focus on Growth,
Tomorrow, and Parts

Stranded:
Failure on
Profitability,
Today, and
Whole

Cornered:
Failure on
Growth,
Tomorrow,
and Parts

Back to Basics:
Focus on Profitability,
Today, and Whole

Hughes Aircraft. GM formed a car-manufacturing joint venture with Toyota to experiment with Japanese production techniques. The company launched its Saturn car division as a "greenfield" operation. Between 1984 and 1990, GM's revenue grew at an average annual rate of 6–7 percent.

But by 1991, its profitability had suffered. GM's economic profit margin fell from 1.2 percent to −7.4 percent. (Economic profit margin is net profit after tax and a notional charge for capital, expressed as a percentage of revenue. We use it here and elsewhere as our measure for profitability because it includes all costs, operating and capital.) In 1992, the company came within forty minutes of bankruptcy. A boardroom coup put a new CEO in charge. He closed plants, cut the workforce, sold poor-performing component operations, centralized purchasing, and combined engineering operations across the company's car brands. He sold off noncore divisions, including National Car Rental and the recently acquired EDS. By 1999, GM's economic profit margins were up again to 2.5 percent.

But revenue growth in the years between 1991 and 1999 had slowed to an average annual rate of 4 percent, with GM's share of the world automobile market continuing to fall. And its earlier layoffs had saddled GM with nearly three retirees for every active worker. By the turn of the century, their generous pensions and health care terms had generated "legacy costs" amounting to over $1,000 a car, a cost that many of its foreign competitors didn't have. The company responded in 1999 and 2000 by redoubling its efforts to increase volumes to cover these fixed costs, launching aggressive marketing and discounting programs. It also bought the part of Saab it didn't own, acquired stakes in Fiat and Fuji Heavy Industries, and expanded its commercial finance business. Annual revenue growth returned to a healthier 6.5 percent in 1999–2000.

But by 2001, GM's economic profit margin turned negative again to −1.4 percent. With market share in its car business still sliding, the company embarked on a new phase of belt tightening to get costs in line with volume. GM cut a further thirty thousand jobs and identified ten plants for closure. It jettisoned another round of businesses, such as the defense and locomotive divisions. Its European subsidiaries centralized functions to reduce costs.

The current CEO, Rick Wagoner, is now in the uncomfortable position of walking the tightrope between keeping volumes up to cover GM's enormous legacy costs and trying to maneuver those costs down to lessen the need to chase volume at whatever price.

GM's BATTING AVERAGE

Between 1983 and 2003, GM achieved both positive real growth in revenue *and* a positive economic profit margin in only six years. In the other fourteen years, the company either didn't grow in real terms, was unprofitable, or failed on both fronts. To use a baseball analogy, a batter who gets six hits in twenty at bats would have a batting average of .300. GM's batting average on the tension between profitability and growth was .300, or 30 percent. (In this book, we use batting average as a measure of how frequently a company achieves two competing objectives at the same time.)

GM's performance on the tension between results today and results tomorrow painted a similar picture. In five of the years between 1983 and 1999, the company achieved higher earnings than the previous year and at the same time was on the path toward positive economic profit growth over the *next* five years. (Because economic profit includes a charge for the capital invested in the business, it is more relevant to judging long-term performance than earnings.) In the other years, either single-year earnings fell, or the company was on the path to negative economic profits over the next five years, or both. This gave GM a batting average on the today vs. tomorrow tension of five out of fifteen, or 33 percent.

These two batting averages are indicators of the degree to which a company is trapped in the corporate cycle. Companies that have broken out of the cycle will tend to achieve both objectives within each tension at the same time—at least more often than not. Companies trapped within the cycle usually achieve one objective at the expense of the other, or achieve neither. With performance of 30 percent and 33 percent, respectively, GM was clearly trapped within the cycle over the final two decades of the last century.

How Prevalent Is the Corporate Cycle?

It is tempting to think of companies like GM as rarities. But it isn't only such famously difficult-to-manage companies that behave this way. In a survey we conducted with the Economist Intelligence Unit of two hundred business executives in the United States, Europe, and Asia, 52 percent said that their company swings between objectives within at least one of the three tensions. One in four said they swing between a focus on profitability and a focus on growth. One in three reported swinging between a focus on short-term earnings and a focus on long-term investment. And one in three said that they swing between focusing on the stand-alone performance of the parts and focusing on benefits across the company as a whole.

The evidence is all over the business news. Companies go for scale, often through acquisition and diversification, and then they retrench, divest "noncore" assets, and manage down their costs. They make large "strategic" investments for the future and then cut back to concentrate on improving "execution" in the current business and squeezing out earnings today. They organize to stimulate local initiative and then they reorganize to achieve "one-company" benefits. Many management teams swing between pushing for one objective in each tension and then pushing for the other. The amount of time over which these changes occur, whether they are dramatic or evolutionary and whether in coordination or isolation, differs from company to company. But few companies can justly claim to be free from any trace of the influence of the corporate cycle.

Batting Average

Batting average is a measure of how often a business achieves both of the two objectives in a tension at the same time. It indicates whether and how much a company is overcoming the tension. Together, batting averages on the three tensions tell you how much a company is succeeding in breaking away from the corporate cycle.

Profitability vs. Growth Batting Average

The proportion of years that a company achieves *both* positive real revenue growth *and* a positive economic profit margin. For example, a company that achieves both positive revenue growth and a positive profit margin in three out of five years has a profitability vs. growth batting average of 60 percent.

Today vs. Tomorrow Batting Average

The proportion of years that a company has positive single-year earnings growth *and* is on the path to positive multiyear economic profits growth. We use five years for multiyear performance because it is a planning horizon for many companies. It is also not far off the average tenure for chief executives of large public companies.[1]

Whole vs. Parts Batting Average

The proportion of years that a company improves the performance of each part of the company irrespective of its relationship with the other parts *and* creates net positive one-company benefits from coordinating across them. For reasons we cover in Chapter Four, this batting average is very hard to measure from the outside. So for our thousand-company analysis, we have looked at the first two types of batting average instead. In Chapter Four we estimate batting averages for whole vs. parts by looking at the performance of a smaller set of five hundred companies.

See Appendixes A and B for more details.

In fact, many companies are as trapped in the corporate cycle as GM has been. We looked at the performance of all one thousand companies in our database over the twenty years between 1983 and 2003. In the same way as for GM, we calculated batting averages for each company. The batting average on profitability vs. growth across the sample was 38 percent. The batting average on earnings today vs. economic profits tomorrow was 44 percent. On both tensions, most companies hit the two objectives at the same time only two years in every five.

The probabilities of achieving both, either, or neither objective in each of the two tensions are shown in Figure 1.2. The average company is much more likely to achieve either or neither objective in each tension than it is to achieve both at the same time. At any point in time, at least three in every five companies are trapped somewhere in the corporate cycle by one or more of the three tensions.

This result was consistent with another finding from our survey (Figure 1.3). We asked executives to rate their company's capabilities on the three tensions. For each, fewer than one in four said their company was good at both objectives. Three-quarters said their companies were better at one than the other or were good at neither. Most companies have great difficulty in mastering the conflicts within the three tensions. Our conclusion is that the corporate cycle is not some curiosity that is relevant to a few aberrant companies. Most companies are trapped somewhere within it.

THE ECONOMIC AND POLITICAL FORCES BEHIND THE CORPORATE CYCLE

None of this is surprising. For all three tensions, the economic forces that act on companies serve to divide performance on one objective from performance on the other. Growth invites competition by imitation or substitution, leading to pressure on prices, costs, and therefore profitability. High profitability attracts new entrants, depressing market shares, prices, and therefore growth. Because competitors relentlessly introduce new products and services, what determines today's performance will be different from what determines tomorrow's performance. And good long-term

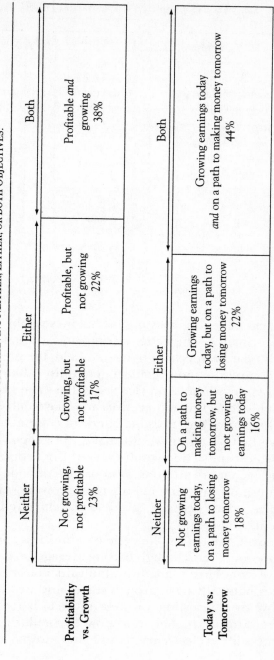

FIGURE 1.2. PROBABILITIES OF ACHIEVING NEITHER, EITHER, OR BOTH OBJECTIVES.

FIGURE 1.3. PERCENTAGE OF EXECUTIVES SAYING THEIR COMPANY IS . . .

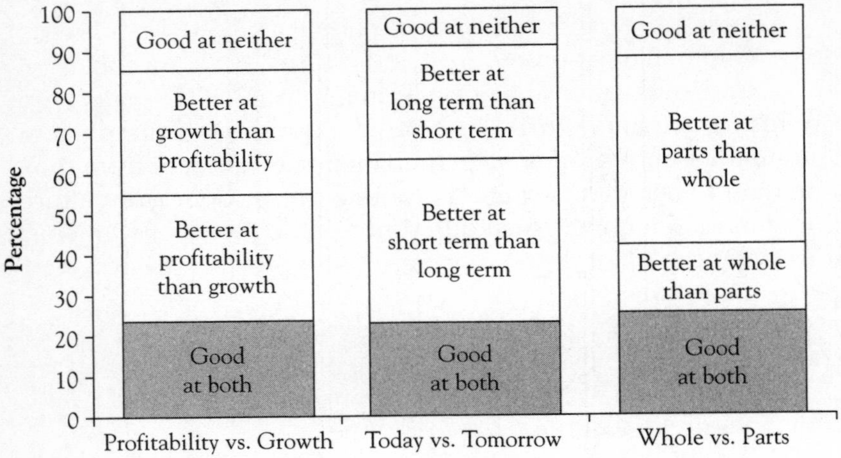

Good at neither	Good at neither	Good at neither
Better at growth than profitability	Better at long term than short term	Better at parts than whole
Better at profitability than growth	Better at short term than long term	Better at whole than parts
Good at both	Good at both	Good at both
Profitability vs. Growth	Today vs. Tomorrow	Whole vs. Parts

(Vertical axis: Percentage, scaled 0 to 100 in increments of 10.)

performance relies on investments that inescapably depress short-term performance. The better a company is at making each of its constituent parts a specialist in its own field, the greater the attraction for competitors to provide a generalist "all-under-one-roof" offer across the whole. And vice versa. For each of the three tensions, trade-offs between objectives are unavoidable. They almost seem to be part of the "invisible hand" of competitive markets.

These factors alone would make the corporate cycle hard enough to escape. The overall cycle of the economy makes the challenge even more arduous. Periods of economic prosperity create the funds for investing in long-term growth, which can lead to overcapacity, which depresses profitability, which reduces long-term investment. And so on.

Moreover, the typical life cycle of a business conspires against those who would score a high batting average on each tension. As they move from birth to maturity, individual businesses and whole industries naturally have growth stages and profitability stages. They move from investing for their future to harvesting and reaping the rewards in the here and now. Particularly at each end of the business life cycle—start-up and close-down—achieving both short-term and long-term results and both profitability and growth is just not possible.

What is more, different types of people are suited to different tasks. The manager suited to the task of finding growth is different from the manager suited to boosting profitability; explorers of the future are made differently from exploiters of the present; autonomous entrepreneurs are fundamentally different from those who want to belong to a larger corporate whole. Company cultures find it hard to embrace such different types of manager with equal warmth at the same time, hence the difficulty in achieving many performance objectives concurrently. A culture of risk taking and experimentation does not sit well alongside a culture of standardization and best practice; a culture of execution sits unhappily with a culture of vision; and a culture of autonomy does not fit well with a culture of working in teams.

The political behaviors inside companies push and pull across the tensions as well. What has been termed "the institutional imperative"[2] to protect and increase the scope and scale of the activities in your ambit or empire competes with the pressures to produce profits. The desire for new resources leads managers to promise future performance in exchange for permission to forgo earnings today. The suspicion that managers are "sandbagging" their resource requests—asking for more than they know to be necessary—leads their bosses to insist on a rapid return from those investments. Managers value their independence and freedom from interference, but their bosses feel they cannot justify the existence of the company as a whole or their roles in it without adding something beyond the summation of parts. And it is only human nature for new leaders to assert themselves by swinging the pendulum in the opposite direction from the last guy. The laws of politics are just as effective in dividing one objective from the other as are the laws of economics.

The pull of the corporate cycle will always be strong, some may argue. It is the natural rhythm of business. And it's not at all clear that making choices between objectives is always a bad thing. Good performance on one objective will be worth more than good performance on the other. It makes sense to grow and then consolidate and work on profitability, and then go for the next phase of growth. Accepting losses now is part of creating profits later. There is a time for giving priority to the performance of the parts, and a time for putting first the performance of the whole. Such choices, it is argued, are vital to the natural development of high-performing companies.

Furthermore, choice gives you that most precious of management commodities: focus. With a clear focus on growth, for example, managers can shape measures, targets, remuneration, structure, vision, processes, culture, and all the other tools at their disposal in a common direction. Choices between performance objectives are not just inevitable. The right choices are good business. Good management is all about making the right choices. Right?

THE LINK BETWEEN BATTING AVERAGE AND TOTAL SHAREHOLDER RETURNS

Well, perhaps not. A test of good management is what happens to the performance of the company on the capital markets over time: what happens to total returns to shareholders (the change in the value of investors' money through share price appreciation with dividends reinvested). If making choices between performance objectives were good business, you might expect there to be no correlation between batting averages—a measure of how often such choices are sidestepped—and total shareholder returns (TSR).

But, in fact, what you see is the opposite. Our main finding from our research is that *there is a close positive relationship between batting average and TSR*. The higher a company's batting average, the higher its TSR. The lower the batting average, the lower the returns. This is true for both of the tensions we can measure directly: profitability vs. growth and today vs. tomorrow (Figure 1.4).[3]

In fact, we found that batting average is a better proxy for TSR than revenue growth, economic profit margin, short-term earnings growth, long-term growth in economic profits, earnings-per-share growth, price-to-earnings (P/E) multiple, return on capital, or any other single measure of performance you might care to mention.

Companies with batting averages below 50 percent have lower economic profitability (c. −1 percent vs. c. +3 percent) and slower revenue growth (c. 6 percent vs. c. 11 percent) than companies with batting averages above 50 percent. And companies that bat less than 50 percent generate half the TSR of companies that bat over 50 percent.

This is a strange result, on the face of it. Students of capital markets generally agree that over the long run, the market value of a company gravitates toward its economic value: the sum, in today's money, of all future cash flows or, equivalently, of all future economic profits plus current capital.[4] Movements in a company's share price reflect changes in market expectations of *prospective* profits. But batting average is a *retrospective* measure, and it does not take account of the *amount* of profits expected over time.

That batting average correlates with TSR, despite these differences, suggests that a track record of avoiding performance compromises is much more important to the assessment of a company's future profit potential than at first would be imagined. Perhaps this should not be so surprising. After all, the two objectives in each of the three tensions are not independent of each other: poor performance on one objective will drag down performance on the other. Growth without profitability eventually stalls because it cuts off the reinvestment needed to keep growing. Profitability without growth eventually undermines profitability because it denies managers the scope and scale needed to fuel further efficiencies. Earnings in the short term eventually dry up without investment to keep them going into the long term. And long-term viability and health can be undermined by poor performance in the short term. The ability to get the most out of each part of the business ultimately relies on the ability to share and coordinate learning and talent across the whole; the ability to benefit from coordination across the whole relies on having high-performing parts with which to share.

The opposite is true as well. With the appropriate management, the better the performance you achieve on one objective, the better the performance you can achieve on the other. Higher growth brings with it the potential for using the benefits of scale to improve profitability; higher profitability increases the funds for

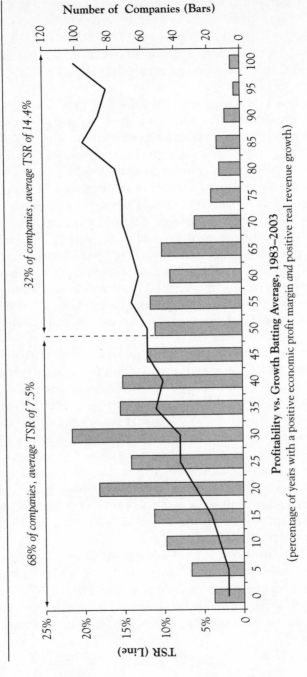

FIGURE 1.4. THE LINK BETWEEN BATTING AVERAGE AND TOTAL SHAREHOLDER RETURNS.

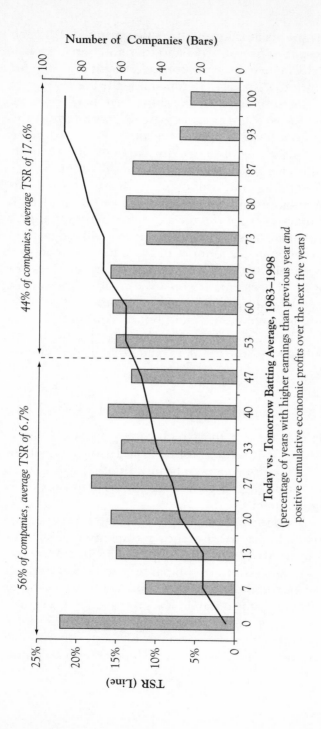

Number of Companies (Bars)

44% of companies, *average TSR of 17.6%*

56% of companies, *average TSR of 6.7%*

Today vs. Tomorrow Batting Average, 1983–1998
(percentage of years with higher earnings than previous year *and* positive cumulative economic profits over the next five years)

TSR (Line)

new growth investments and lowers the sales volumes at which those investments start to be justified—and therefore pursued. Better short-term performance increases the investment available for the long term; a business that is in better shape for the long term will have more opportunities for better short-term performance. Better-performing parts of the company create more opportunities across the company as a whole because there are more strengths to share. Good performance on one objective naturally creates opportunities for good performance on the other.

This interdependence may well explain why we observe this very clear positive relationship between batting average and TSR. What the capital markets prize the most are companies that provide evidence of *sustainable* performance. Investors will judge good performance on one objective as more likely to last if it is accompanied by good performance on the other. The capital markets just don't believe that good performance on any one objective will last if it is accompanied by poor performance on another.

By implication, management should not be considered just a science of making the right choices among many performance objectives. It should also be the art of avoiding the need to choose in the first place.

How Batting Averages Vary by Industry

Which companies manage to achieve high batting averages? Surely they must be in industries that are profitable and growing, that are attractive, stable, and not prone to cyclicality. In other words, they must be in *industries* with high batting averages. Well, the answer is not what you might expect.

Some industries do indeed have higher batting averages than others. For instance, the batting averages in the natural resources sector are much lower than those in the pharmaceuticals sector. But high- and low–batting-average companies can be found in all industries. For example, between 1985 and 2000 Nucor Steel scored a batting average on profitability vs. growth of 50 percent— double the 25 percent long-term average of the natural resources sector. Nucor's performance was considerably better than pharmaceutical firm Aventis, which scored only 25 percent in an industry that averages 53 percent. In fact, in every industry and on both measures, there is a bigger difference between the performance of the worst company and the best company than there is between the performance of the worst industry and the best industry (Table 1.1). When it comes to batting average, differences *within* industry dominate over differences *across* industry.

Ranked seventeenth, the automotive sector is trapped in the corporate cycle more than most. GM's performance was actually about average for the sector on both batting averages (30 percent vs. 34 percent for profitability vs. growth; 33 percent vs. 28 percent for today vs. tomorrow). Here too, the differences within the industry are striking. For instance, German carmaker BMW achieved both positive economic profitability and real revenue growth in ten years out of the twenty—a batting average of 50 percent. On the other end of the scale, Japanese automotive company Daihatsu managed to achieve both at the same time in only half as many years: a batting average of 25 percent. These differences in batting average line up with the differences in TSR: BMW earned the highest TSR returns at 14 percent, Daihatsu earned 4 percent, and GM stood in the middle with annual average returns of 8 percent.

Despite some important industry differences, batting average is much more tied to individual companies than to the industries in which they operate. There are companies that are able to escape the corporate cycle in the industries you would least expect it to be possible, and there are companies in the most promising industries that score very low batting averages.

ESCAPING THE CORPORATE CYCLE

The corporate cycle is the result of economic and political forces and management practices that make it difficult for a company to achieve many performance objectives at the same time. Batting average is our measure for how trapped a company is in the cycle. By this measure, around three-fifths of companies are somewhere in the corporate cycle at any point in time.

Yet escape is the path to superior performance. Our finding is that batting averages correlate with TSR. TSR reflects how far a

TABLE 1.1. BATTING AVERAGES BY INDUSTRY.

Industry	Rank Order	Profitability vs. Growth		Today vs. Tomorrow	
		Industry Average (%)	Industry Range (%)	Industry Average (%)	Industry Range (%)
Pharmaceutical and biotech	1	53	15–85	65	13–100
Retail	2	52	0–100	57	0–100
Business support	3	46	15–75	61	33–100
Health care	4	52	25–85	54	0–93
Consumer goods	5	43	5–100	60	0–100
Publishing, printing, and photo	6	43	5–70	55	0–87
Banks	7	46	0–100	51	0–100
Utilities	8	36	10–75	56	7–93
Other financial services	9	42	0–85	48	0–100
Insurance	10	42	0–90	45	0–93
Telecom	11	40	10–85	43	7–87
Construction and property	12	38	0–85	41	0–87
Electrical equipment	13	34	0–70	43	0–100
Manufacturing	14	34	0–80	40	0–100
Chemicals	15	31	5–85	43	0–100
Diversified industrials	16	32	0–95	40	0–100
Automotive	17	34	0–80	28	0–100
Oil and gas	18	33	0–60	28	0–73
Entertainment	19	30	0–90	27	0–93
Transport	20	26	5–65	27	0–87
Computing	21	29	0–70	22	0–87
Natural resources (not oil and gas)	22	25	5–50	25	0–73
All 1,000 companies		38		44	
Difference across industries		28		43	
Difference within industry			76		91

Note: Rank order is based on both batting averages.

company manages to break free of the three tensions that set the corporate cycle in motion.

To be sure, many of the forces that make the cycle so powerful are outside of management's control. They come from how markets and economies work and from human nature itself. The cycle will always be difficult to escape; its gravity will always work to pull you in. The cycle and the tensions that form it are shaped by powerful forces to which no company is immune.

But companies in the same industry share the same environment, the same external competitive forces, the same phase of industry life stage, and the same basic struggles of human nature within their organizations. Yet differences in batting averages *within* industry dominate over differences *across* industry. There are companies who are able to escape the corporate cycle in all industries. If general economic and political forces are so dominant in explaining the cycle, why is it that different companies in the same industry achieve such markedly different performance?

The only explanation is that some of the forces that trap companies in the corporate cycle are avoidable. Some companies are falling into traps of their own making; others are managing to step around them.

In the next three chapters, we consider each of the three tensions that form the corporate cycle. For each, we identify what can make compatible the pair of objectives within each tension—the common bond. We look at the traps that managers can fall into that break these bonds and what leadership teams can do to sidestep these traps. If leaders remain unaware of both those common bonds and those traps, their companies are unlikely to be able to break out of the snare of the corporate cycle. Struggling will only make it worse.

CHAPTER TWO

PROFITABILITY VS. GROWTH

*If management lets itself drift, it invariably drifts in
the direction of thinking of itself as producing goods
and services, not customer satisfactions.*
THEODORE LEVITT, "MARKETING MYOPIA," *HARVARD
BUSINESS REVIEW,* JULY–AUG. 1960

The new chief executive declared that never in his life had he come across such
an inward-looking company. His mission was to turn the organization around
to face its customers. For years under the old regime, the business units had
been made to leap through internal hoops to justify the smallest investment in
growth. Determined to change this, the new leader launched a "Go for Growth"
program with ambitious goals for revenue and market share. Acquisitions that
would previously have defied approval took the firm into new "adjacencies":
products, services, channels, and geographies. All around the company, new
energies and resources poured into line extensions, promotions, selective price
cuts to push up market share. The fastest-growing markets got the lion's share
of new investment. The slower-growth businesses were asked to improve profitability and cash flow.

For the most part, however, the new revenue came at lower margins than
that of the existing business. The faster-growth markets also turned out to be the
higher-cost markets. Acquisition and innovation costs piled up, and management became distracted from tending its traditional business. The result: a big
fall in company profit margins. Although some executives called for more time

to allow the various investments to bear fruit, most started questioning the wisdom of "Go for Growth."

The chief executive began to talk about the need for a "period of consolidation." A companywide cost-reduction target was allocated across all businesses and functions on the basis of share of head count, share of sales, and "share of pain." Managers concentrated their resources behind the company's most profitable lines and customers. They put limits on promotional activity and reversed some price cuts. The corporate center rebranded its efforts as the "Go for Profit Growth" program.

Profit margins shot up, but they came at a price. The layoffs were necessary, but they were painful, time-consuming, and distracting. Some of the cost cuts seemed to put achieving "a fair share of the pain" across businesses above customer considerations. Customers resisted the price increases far more passionately than they had celebrated the previous price reductions. The moratorium on new acquisitions made sense, but it cut off a source of new revenue. The recent experience had raised the emotional hurdles for investment in growth projects as well as the financial ones. All of a sudden, competitors seemed to have lots of new investment ideas and seemingly much lower internal standards for justifying them. The company's revenue growth stalled. The board appointed a new chief executive. Shortly after her arrival, she told her new team that never in her life had she come across such an inward-looking company. . . .

TENSION 1: PROFITABILITY VS. GROWTH

The first tension that pulls companies into the corporate cycle is that between profitability and growth (Figure 2.1). In Chapter One, we explained that batting average on profitability vs. revenue growth—the proportion of years companies achieve both objectives—is correlated to total shareholder returns. As you move up the quartiles on batting average, TSR increases (Figure 2.2). In general, a 10 percent increase in batting average—hitting both objectives one more year every ten years—equals about two percentage points more in annual TSR. This is a big amount lost in a small number: an investment of $1,000 made in 1983 in the average S&P 500 company was worth around $5,600 twenty years later;

FIGURE 2.1. THE PROFITABILITY VS. GROWTH TENSION.

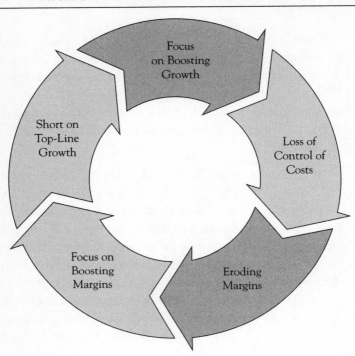

at a 2 percent higher return each year, that investment would have been worth more than $8,000.

But as we have seen, only 32 percent of companies bat over 50 percent, achieving both profitability and revenue growth more often than not. What makes producing positive economic profitability and positive real revenue growth at the same time so hard that close to three-quarters of all companies fail more often than they succeed?

THREE CONUNDRUMS

Three well-known management conundrums might make for a good explanation: focus vs. diversification, organic growth[1] vs. growth by merger and acquisition (M&A), and the needs of "profitability businesses" vs. those of "growth businesses."

FIGURE 2.2. THE VALUE OF HITTING A HIGH BATTING AVERAGE
ON PROFITABILITY VS. GROWTH.

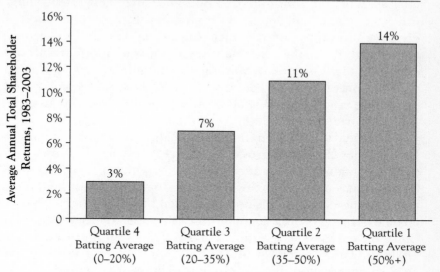

Batting Average on Profitability vs. Growth by Quartile

Although it can be hard to keep revenue growing with a narrow business portfolio, diversifying into other markets often ends up reducing profitability. Most research confirms that growth through diversification dilutes profitability, erodes shareowner capital, and leads to disposal down the line. The experience of Blue Circle Industries, a U.K. cement company, in the 1980s illustrates the point, perhaps to an extreme. Trapped in what executives considered to be a mature, low-growth market, the company responded with a series of moves into adjacent sectors: bricks, home heating, bathroom equipment, and lawn and garden machinery, to name a few. Although revenues doubled from £637 million in 1980 to £1.2 billion in 1990, Blue Circle had real revenue growth and a positive economic profit margin in only one year—a batting average of just 10 percent.

In the 1990s, Blue Circle managers reversed the moves. Their original rationale for diversification may have been suspect. (One retired executive said, "Our move into lawn mowers was based on the logic that you need a lawn mower for your garden—which, after all, is next to your house."[2]) But Blue Circle's experience illustrates the general challenge. It isn't hard to think of other cases of diversification that came unstuck: Coca-Cola's attempt to become a wine and film maker, Eastman Kodak's move into pharmaceuticals with the acquisition of Sterling Drug, Philip Morris's purchase of Miller Brewing, and so on. If it isn't easy to stick to a narrow but profitable portfolio and keep growing, neither is it easy to grow through diversification and stay profitable.

Whether straying from home or sticking close to it, companies face another challenge: growth via mergers and acquisitions is usually unprofitable. In study after study, the majority of acquisitions are found to have resulted in fewer benefits than costs. Although most research shows that acquisitions of related businesses stand a better chance of being profitable than those of unrelated businesses, even those have a low success rate. Time Warner's merger with AOL, Quaker Oats's purchase of Snapple, and AT&T's takeover of TeleCommunications Inc. were all moves into adjacent markets, and all are high-profile examples of growth by acquisition where profitability suffered. Generating high levels of organic growth may be challenging, but so too is making acquisitive growth profitable.

If these two challenges were not enough, leaders must also contend with the differing demands of managing growth vs. managing profitability. A manager suited to the task of growth is surely different from another suited to managing profitability. The latter will be more comfortable in a corporate environment that values consistent improvement, discipline, and enforcing the right ways of doing things. The growth manager will be better suited to more autonomy, greater risk taking, and less standardization. Companies designed to attract one type will repel the other.

The challenges of focus vs. diversification, organic growth vs. M&A growth, and the needs of profitable businesses vs. those of growth businesses present three dilemmas for the leader who wants profitability and growth at the same time: diversify the portfolio and risk reducing profitability, or keep the portfolio narrow and risk limiting your headroom for growth; limit yourself to organic growth and find it difficult to achieve enough growth, or grow by acquisition and find it difficult to maintain economic profitability;

meet the needs of "growth businesses" and fail to meet the needs of "profitability businesses," or vice versa.

So what are leaders to do? The conventional answer is to "balance": between a narrow portfolio and a diversified portfolio; between organic growth and growth through M&A; and between "profitability businesses" and "growth businesses" (with some organizational segregation between them in order to meet their different needs).

But as intuitively appealing as "balance" may be, it does not fit the facts of how batting averages behave. . . .

Portfolio Diversity and Batting Average

One of the most successful episodes of reducing portfolio diversity must surely be that of Nokia. In the last years of the twentieth century, the Finnish conglomerate transformed itself into a leading player in mobile telephones. In 1988, mobile telephones and telecommunications made up 10 percent of revenues, with the rest coming from floorings, chemicals, machinery, electrical wholesale, rubber, information systems, cables, paper, and consumer electronics. Four years later, management decided to narrow its portfolio. By 1999, mobile phones and telecommunications made up more than 90 percent of revenues. Nokia achieved both real revenue growth and a positive economic profitability only once in the seven years to 1992—a batting average of just 14 percent. In the seven years afterwards, it achieved both in six years, for a batting average of almost 90 percent. Surely such performance confirms that portfolio focus is the key to a higher batting average, right?

Well, no. Equally, you can point to the opposite. As Nokia made a fortune by concentrating on mobile phones, IBM reversed its waning fortunes by *diversifying* away from its core business of computer hardware. In 1992, hardware (principally mainframes) accounted for almost two-thirds of IBM's revenues and a similar amount of its gross profits. Faced with a commoditizing market for personal computers, servers, and semiconductors, the company moved into a host of information technology services, including outsourcing, financing, consulting, and software. By 2002, hardware accounted for only 34 percent of revenues and 25 percent of gross profits. From 1985 to 1994, IBM's batting average was 20 percent, placing it in the bottom quartile of our thousand-company data set. From 1995 to 2004, its batting average rose to 50 percent, placing it in the top quartile.

To find a more general relationship than two companies allow, we looked at eight hundred companies. We measured diversity of their portfolios by using the number of Standard Industry Classification (SIC) codes they reported: the more SIC codes, the more diversified the portfolio. The average company operates in two or three market categories defined by SIC codes.

We found that the degree of portfolio diversity has very limited impact on batting average. Companies in more than three market sectors have slightly lower batting averages than those in only one sector (Figure 2.3). But this relationship is nothing to write home about: the correlation is −0.21—weak at best. The visual relationship in the graph flatters the statistical one. The fact is that there are high- and low-batting-average companies with all degrees of portfolio diversity.

And we found no discernible change in batting average for companies that *changed* their level of portfolio diversity. Compa-

FIGURE 2.3. BATTING AVERAGE IN RELATION TO PORTFOLIO SCOPE.

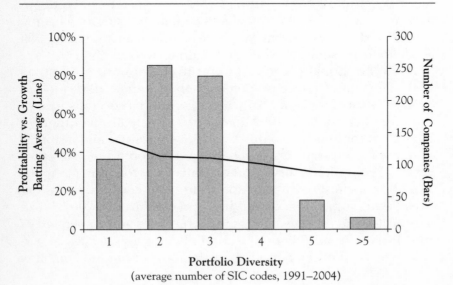

Portfolio Diversity
(average number of SIC codes, 1991–2004)

nies that increased their diversity—that added market categories—had a mean batting average of 37 percent. Companies
that went in the other direction—that became more "focused"—
had a mean batting average of 38 percent, hardly a meaningful
difference.

Acquisitiveness and Batting Average

Likewise, we found no relation between batting average and how
acquisitive companies have been. We defined a company's acquisitiveness as the purchase value of the acquisitions it made in a year
as a percentage of its start-of-year market value. We looked at the
acquisitiveness of a sample of 445 companies in our database
between 1995 and 2004. The average acquisitiveness was around 3
percent, meaning that during an average year, the value of acquisitions represented 3 percent of the company's market value at the
start of the year. We then looked at how that related to batting average. We found that as acquisitiveness rises, batting average stays the
same (Figure 2.4).

FIGURE 2.4. BATTING AVERAGE IN RELATION TO ACQUISITIVENESS.

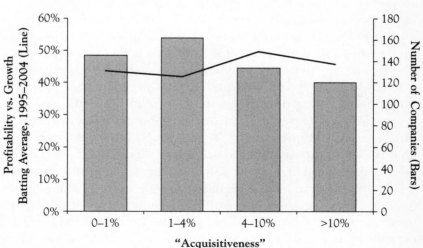

"Acquisitiveness"
(deal value as a percentage of starting value)
Annual average, 1995–2004

You don't have to look very far for companies that have been both highly acquisitive and also highly successful at achieving revenue growth and profitability at the same time. For example, in the decade between 1994 and 2004, Danaher, a U.S. instrumentation and tools manufacturer, made sixty acquisitions with a total value of more than $13 billion. This gave it an acquisitiveness score of 18 percent, which puts it in the top 11 percent of our sample. Danaher also had a batting average of 91 percent in that period, achieving real growth and profitability at the same time in ten of the eleven years. Far from diluting profitability, its growth by acquisition has come alongside a doubling of economic profit margins, to nearly 7 percent in 2004.

Market Exposure and Batting Average

Figure 2.5 shows how batting average varies by industry, from the most profitable and fastest growing to the least profitable and slowest growing.[3] For example, between 1983 and 2003, the health care sector had annual revenue growth rates of 9 percent and an average economic profit of 3 percent, placing it at the top of the rank ordering by attractiveness. The oil and gas sector came in last with 6 percent revenue growth and a −2 percent economic profit margin. Batting averages do indeed vary according to industry attractiveness. A company might expect, all things being equal, to score a somewhat higher batting average by increasing the exposure of its portfolio to more attractive industries. But the variance is nothing to get too excited about. There are only three industries out of the twenty-two where the average player scores a batting average of (just) above 50 percent: health care, retail, and pharmaceuticals. And all things are not equal. As we saw in Chapter One, batting average varies more *within* industry than *across* industry. The average difference across industries is 28 percent, but the average difference within industries is 76 percent. This means that portfolio mix—exposure to attractive markets—is less important in determining batting average than relative performance within a market.

Companies can have high batting averages on profitability vs. growth with all degrees of portfolio diversity, all levels of acquisitiveness, and all types of industry exposure. Leaders should be wary of seeking "balance." In the search for a higher batting average, a

FIGURE 2.5. PROFITABILITY VS. GROWTH BATTING AVERAGE BY INDUSTRY.

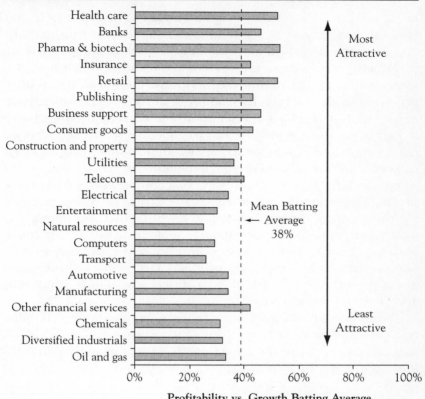

Profitability vs. Growth Batting Average
1983–2003

balanced portfolio scope, a balanced mix of organic and M&A growth, and a portfolio exposed to a balance of growth and profitability markets all turn out to be dead ends.

Batting average doesn't behave as you might imagine: companies with high batting averages have all degrees of portfolio diversity, all degrees of acquisitiveness, and all types of portfolio exposure. "Balance" is not the answer to scoring a high batting average.

COMMON BOND 1: CUSTOMER BENEFIT

If balance is not the answer, what is? The key to unlocking a higher batting average must be found in understanding how profitability and growth relate to each other. There are many ways to increase revenue: improve service; widen distribution to reach new customers; increase prices to increase revenue per customer; reduce prices to increase market share; improve the offer to customers; add new variants to products and services; link offers by adding services to goods, goods to services, goods to goods, or services to services; enter new market segments; acquire another company; create a new market by inventing something completely new for customers; and so on. Equally, there are many ways that companies try to increase profitability: increase the efficiency of current activities; increase the utilization of capacity; eliminate activities; increase prices; outsource to a lower-cost supplier; merge separate activities to increase scale per activity and reap economies of scale; change the mix of business with higher-margin products, customers, channels, and geographies; exit unprofitable products, customers, channels, and geographies; and so on.

What determines whether managers can achieve profitability and growth simultaneously is not which of these sets of activities they can undertake at the same time. It is the impact of such activities on *customer benefit*.

CUSTOMER BENEFIT

The customer benefit of a product or service is not what the product or service is or can do. It is *the reward that customers receive through their experience of choosing and using that product or service.* As such, customer benefit may well vary substantially by customer: the end user or consumer, the retailer, the wholesaler, and so on. It also often varies by individual. A benefit to one customer may not be a benefit to another. The reward one person gets from chocolate might be the pleasure of eating it; the reward another gets may be the pleasure of giving it to someone else. Context matters too. For example, a product that creates a benefit now may create much less benefit at a different time of the day or the year. A cold drink

---

Customer Benefit

Customer benefit is the reward—tangible or intangible, real or perceived—that customers receive through their experience of choosing and using a product or service.

The measure of customer benefit is willingness to pay. Thus an increase in customer benefit manifests itself in a higher price, a higher market share, or both, relative to products and services with comparable benefit.

The "customer" is any purchaser of the company's products and services, including the end user and intermediaries. The same product or service can have different benefits for different customers and in different purchasing contexts.

---

doesn't quite have the same benefit in winter as it does after a long run on a hot summer's day.

Customer benefit is very hard to measure directly because it varies by type of customer, individual, and context. But measuring its consequences is easier: if your product or service produces higher customer benefit than do comparable products and services, it should also produce either higher market share or higher price or both; if it doesn't, it's probably not producing higher customer benefit.

But here's the rub. It is possible for companies to grow revenue in ways that do not grow customer benefit. As a company's revenue grows, its customer benefit may not change at all. For example, companies can add new revenue by using advertising to raise awareness of what they have to offer, by making their product more available in trade channels, by increasing prices, or by acquiring a competitor. All these actions may increase revenue. None need necessarily change the fundamental benefit to customers of the company's products.

Increases in revenue achieved without growing customer benefit may turn out to be compatible with profitability, particularly if the company's product or service already creates a lot of customer benefit in the first place. But revenue growth that is not based on high or increasing customer benefit is much less likely to be profitable than revenue growth that is.

Why? First, without high or increasing customer benefit, a company constrains its ability to achieve higher prices: if they have other choices, customers are unlikely to consent to a high price for a low customer benefit. Furthermore, someone has to pay the costs of providing a product to customers. If that product has high customer benefit, the customer will be willing to share or offset or forgo those costs; for example, through word of mouth, they may do some or even all of the marketing and advertising to new customers for you. They will not need to be promoted to so aggressively to persuade them to keep on buying. Without high or increasing customer benefit, the only way of acquiring and keeping new revenue is for the company to keep paying all such costs itself. And high customer benefit means higher share, which in turn brings greater opportunities for capturing economies of scale. For all these reasons, revenue growth that is underpinned by high or increasing customer benefit has much higher odds of being profitable than revenue growth that is not.

Good Costs vs. Bad Costs

But it is not just that growth based on customer benefit is more likely to be compatible with profitability; the reverse is also true. Profitability that is based on customer benefit is more likely to be compatible with growth. At one level, all profitability helps growth. All things being equal, an increase in profitability increases the funds available to reinvest in growth. But all things are most decidedly not equal. Some actions to increase profitability are far less likely to support growth than others. When a company raises prices without a customer benefit justification or cuts high-potential R&D spending, it may increase its profitability, but most likely it will damage its growth prospects too. In contrast, when a company removes activities (and therefore costs) that customers don't care about or find positively irritating, it is likely to generate profitability that is entirely consistent with achieving growth. What matters is to distinguish between those costs that are integral to creating customer benefit and those that are not: to distinguish between *good costs and bad costs.*

A good cost is necessary to produce customer benefit; a bad cost is not. Much as customer benefit is specific to a company, customer, and context, so is what constitutes a good or bad cost. A fancy head office in a prime location may well be a bad cost for many companies, but it could be a good cost for an advertising agency trying to attract the best creative staff. Because customer benefit often differs by individual, to some customers one cost is good while to others it is bad. An in-store refrigerator is a good cost for someone looking for a cold drink but a bad cost for someone who is buying to stock up for later in the week. Furthermore, a good cost is always at risk of becoming a bad cost when a company finds a new and cheaper way of doing something or if what customers find beneficial changes. For example, photographic film makers have seen almost all the costs they have poured into chemical-based film—from R&D to manufacturing capacity to sales capabilities—turn from good to bad as digital film has become the preferred form of photography. On a much smaller scale, discovering that the work of three people can be accomplished with two is to discover that one-third of your operating costs are bad costs.

The distinction between good and bad costs is difficult to make and is constantly changing. But the distinction lies at the heart of whether actions to improve profitability will support or damage growth. Reducing the costs that are unnecessary for customer benefit is what makes possible higher profitability without damaging growth. If companies manage profitability without clearly distinguishing between good and bad costs—treating all costs equally and as equally bad—they will likely undermine customer benefit and therefore growth.

Even with high customer benefits and low bad costs, companies can still grow slowly and be unprofitable. This is particularly true if they make pricing mistakes (charging either far too little or too much for the benefit than customers are willing to pay) or if customer awareness of their products and services and the benefit they bring is low.[4] But companies with low customer benefit and high bad costs will find it difficult, if not impossible, to maintain profitability with growth at the same time no matter how well they

Bad Costs: Three Types

Bad costs are costs that are not necessary to produce the company's customer benefit, either now or in the future. They come in three types, some easier to identify than others:

1. *Costs that are not necessary to accomplish a given activity.* For example, if a business could accomplish Step 5 of its process for shrink wrapping its product with 10 percent fewer costs, then at least 10 percent of the costs for Step 5 are bad costs.

2. *Activities that are not necessary to produce the customer experience.* A business might have the most efficient process for conducting Step 5 of its shrink-wrap packaging process, but that entire step might be unnecessary to produce the final package (relative, perhaps, to an alternative packaging technology or way of doing things). In that case, all of the costs associated with Step 5 would be bad costs.

3. *Elements of the customer experience that produce no or even negative customer benefit.* A company might have the lowest-cost shrink-wrap packaging process possible. But if customers find no benefit from that form of packaging or find the packages difficult to open, the entire cost associated with packaging (at least in this form) are bad costs.

Day to day, companies naturally tend to fixate more on the first type of bad cost than on the other two.

price or create awareness. They will soon find themselves having to choose profitability or growth.

When companies uncouple revenue growth from customer benefit, sooner or later such growth becomes unprofitable. When they uncouple profitability from customer benefit, sooner or later they will undermine growth. When customer benefit is high or rising or both, growth in revenue and profitability can be achieved at the same time more of the time. Customer benefit is the common bond between profitability and growth.

> *To maximize its chances of scoring a high batting average,*
> *a business must grow customer benefit and shrink bad costs*
> *at the same time.*

THREE ROUTES TO A HIGH BATTING AVERAGE ON PROFITABILITY VS. GROWTH

Three of the companies we met before, Nokia, Nucor, and BMW, illustrate three different routes that companies can take to grow customer benefit and reduce bad costs.

NOKIA

Nokia helped create the mass mobile phone market that brought customers a previously unavailable benefit: the ability to make calls anywhere. To be sure, Nokia did not invent this customer benefit. Other cellular phone manufacturers and service providers played important parts. Yet whereas Nokia scored a batting average of 88 percent between 1992 and 2000, its main rival, Motorola, scored 33 percent. So Nokia's performance was not simply due to entering a vast new market that brought a substantial new customer benefit. The company raced ahead in the exploding market by being the first to recognize that mobile phones also produced customer benefits similar to fashion accessories. For many customers, they were fashion items, not just communication devices. Consequently, Nokia worried more about design, branding, and ease of use than its competitors did. Its phones were simpler to use, better designed, and more able to be personalized—all factors that cell phone rivals had not expected to be so important. Nokia's revenue growth came hand in hand with growth in customer benefit—both from the new market and how the company tackled it.

Furthermore, Nokia produced new customer benefit while adding few bad costs—that is, costs that were not necessary for the customer benefit of its products. The company contained costs by standardizing handsets (many phones shared the same innards), making few acquisitions (so its costs to generate new volume were lower than those of competitors growing by acquisition), and paying famously low salaries and low bonuses, typically 20 percent of base or lower.[5] The costs Nokia did incur—for example, R&D, design, and branding—were central to the customer benefit it created. As a result, the company's operating margins were about twice that of Motorola. This chapter in Nokia's history is a good example of creating new customer benefit while not adding bad costs.

NUCOR STEEL

By now, the story of Nucor is well known.[6] The company's success shows what can happen when bad costs are eliminated to better match overall costs to customer benefit. Once a maker of nuclear testing equipment (the Nuclear Corporation of America), Nucor stumbled by acquisition into the bottom end of the steel market in the 1960s. Throughout the twentieth century, the standard technology for producing steel had been the "integrated" mill, which transformed iron ore, coal, and limestone into steel. In the 1960s, a newer technology became viable: the mini-mill. This used scrap metal as feedstock and melted it in electric arc furnaces rather than blast furnaces.

Nucor built the first mini-mill in 1969 in Darlington, South Carolina. The mill produced low-quality steel. But quality was not an issue in the least attractive segment of the steel market: the market for reinforcing bars, or rebars. For rebar customers, the capital and operating costs of large, integrated mills churning out high-quality sheet steel contribute nothing of benefit. Whereas the extensive R&D spending, selling expenses, and overhead of the integrated mills were good costs for customers of sheet steel, they were, in effect, bad costs for rebar buyers, to whom high-quality, blemish-free steel did not bring a benefit.

By improving quality and consistency, Nucor moved into other steel market segments that demanded higher quality than the rebar segment: first, other bars and rods, then structural steel.

Nucor's next big step was adopting a new process invented in Germany called continuous thin-slab casting. The process eliminated the need for reheating and reduced the effort required in rolling sheet from thick slabs. Mills using this new technology could also be built for a fraction of the capital cost of a traditional sheet mill. Again, the technology couldn't match the defect-free quality that top-end customers required for the highest-premium uses, such as in cars and cans. But it allowed Nucor to break into those parts of the sheet steel market where "defect-free" was not a benefit—for example, corrugated steel and construction decking.

Nucor squeezed costs in other ways. It used a hard-nosed pay-for-performance scheme to get another cost edge over integrated mills saddled with more expensive and less flexible labor contracts. It banned management dining rooms, company planes, and first-class travel for executives.

As a result, Nucor built mills in one-fifth the time and at one-quarter the capital cost of traditional mills. It ran them with one-tenth of the workers, at one-third the operating costs. By 2000, Nucor could produce nearly all qualities of steel at dramatically lower costs than its rivals with integrated mills. Throughout this time, Nucor shared the gains from its lower costs with customers in the form of lower prices. In commodity markets such as steel where the customer is not the end user, low price can be thought of as part of the benefit to customers. So you could say that Nucor increased customer benefit at the same time that it reduced bad costs. Any way you look at it, the ability to redefine which costs are really needed to produce customer benefit allowed Nucor to achieve a batting average of roughly twice its rivals *and* higher than many companies in much more attractive industries.

Nokia grew customer benefit without growing bad costs; Nucor reduced bad costs and offered comparable customer benefit. Their experiences are perhaps extreme, as they involved tumultuous technological change in their industries. In most cases, the ability to achieve profitability and growth at the same time depends on simultaneously increasing customer benefit and reducing bad costs. This is what explains BMW's high batting average.

BMW

Over the last decade, the German carmaker has been seeking to supply one model for each major segment of the car market, each occupying the position of highest benefit to customers—in this case drivers. To the 3, 5, 6, and 7 Series, BMW has added the entry-level 1 Series; the X Series sports utility vehicle; and a reengineered Mini Cooper. BMW has carefully nurtured a reputation for engineering cars for performance, handling, and quality. This is reflected in the fact that their cars retain more of their value than any other major make. BMW's bet is that drivers look for performance, handling, and a premium quality image in roughly equal measure. As it has added new models and different price points, the company has constantly upgraded existing models along these dimensions.

The other part of BMW's strategy has been to reduce costs that don't contribute specifically to their customers' benefit. It created a flexible manufacturing system that can switch easily between models. BMW makes this possible by keeping unnecessary specialization of components across models to a minimum. The company even committed heresy in the eyes of many carmakers by outsourcing engineering and production of the X Series SUV.

No doubt there is great tension between these two parts of BMW's strategy: bringing new customer benefit in each segment and reducing costs that don't contribute to it. For example, it is extremely hard to share components across models to keep costs down *and* ensure that the models—and their benefits— are distinct in the eyes of customers. This tension is only likely to increase as BMW enters new segments of the market. But BMW's success to date in walking this tightrope has enabled it to earn a batting average of nearly twice the sector average (despite a disastrous purchase and then sale of Britain's Rover Group). With only a quarter of GM's revenues, BMW commands a higher total market value.

For all three cases, the common bond between profitability and growth has been customer benefit (see Table 2.1).

How Companies Lose Sight of Customer Benefit

It is clear from our research that Nokia, Nucor, and BMW are the exceptions rather than the rule. As we have seen, only one-third of companies achieve profitability and growth at the same time more often than not. Many companies get trapped with low batting averages: with growth that is unprofitable and with profitability that undermines growth. Why? They lose sight of customer benefit.

No doubt some companies lose sight of customer benefit because they approach the tasks of managing profitability and managing revenue growth without starting from the customer. This is a mistake crystallized by Theodore Levitt in his classic 1960 *Harvard Business Review* article, "Marketing Myopia." He argued that a preoccupation with manufacturing and selling products can blind companies to the importance of identifying and meeting customer needs: "The organization tends to view itself as making things rather than as satisfying customer needs."[7] Thus efforts to increase the throughput of the factory or the sales force can lead to revenue growth that has nothing to do with better meeting customer needs.

Marketing myopia is alive and well in many companies in the twenty-first century. Efforts to improve performance by "increasing product performance," "improving capacity utilization," or "leveraging our assets and capabilities" continue to tempt companies into basing their profitability and growth plans on something other than customer benefit.

TABLE 2.1. THREE ROUTES TO A HIGH BATTING AVERAGE
ON GROWTH VS. PROFITABILITY.

Grow Customer Benefit	Shrink Bad Costs	Grow Customer Benefit and Shrink Bad Costs
Grow customer benefit relative to competitors without growing bad costs	Reduce bad costs relative to competitors while offering at least comparable customer benefit	Grow customer benefit faster and reduce bad costs more than competitors
Example: Nokia	Example: Nucor	Example: BMW

THE CUSTOMER FOCUS TRAP

But it cannot simply be lack of customer focus that explains why companies lose sight of customer benefit. If innovation in the discipline of management in the first half of the twentieth century was dominated by advances in manufacturing and finance, the second half saw sales and marketing catching up fast. Concepts of differentiation, unique selling proposition, brand positioning, customer satisfaction and loyalty, and customer relationship management are now all widespread. Today companies want to know who their customers are, what their behavior and attitudes are, and how satisfied they are. They constantly examine ways of increasing their share of customer spending and of reaching new customers. They debate the "saliency," "health," and "equity" of their brands. They think of revenue creation as essentially an activity that relies on increasing customer focus: continuously improving the customer offer, modifying it for differences across customers, working on providing better "value for money," innovating in sales and marketing approaches, and constantly targeting fast-growing customer segments.

But much as a producer focus—starting from production rather than the customer—can result in unprofitable growth, *so too can customer focus.* Companies don't get trapped in unprofitable growth because they take their eye off the customer. Rather, they confuse "customer focus" for "a focus on customer benefit." The trap is often well disguised.

The first port of call for increasing customer focus is to improve what you offer customers to distinguish it from competing offers. But in improving a customer offer, it is extremely easy to confuse its features with its benefits and thus add to or improve features without really improving benefits. It is this confusion that leads companies to equate new technology too quickly with new customer benefit. New technology can bring new possibilities for customer benefit, but it is not always a new function that brings the most customer benefit from a new technology. This seems to have been the fate of Nokia's mobile phone competitors in the 1990s. As they focused on making cell phones smaller, Nokia was content to build handsets that looked better.

Greater customer focus would seem to many managers to mean modifying their products and services to reflect differences across customers, and often it is. Many companies try to capture new revenue by adding new variants of existing products to their lines. But unless doing this materially adds to customer benefit, it will likely lead to a proliferation of low-volume lines. Manufacturers know only too well the profitability problems of low-volume lines: shorter production runs and more changeovers, lower scale and therefore higher costs for procurement, increased complexity and therefore more overhead, and so on. Equally, marketers will attest to the disadvantages of low-volume lines in competing for growth with higher-volume competitors that can carry greater investment in, for example, advertising, product design, or packaging innovation. Companies that focus on tailoring to the differences among their customers by adding variants to their products and services can all too easily obscure important similarities in customer benefit across customers.

If "customer focus" leads managers to improve features and add new lines, it also leads them to think about value for money. But such a connection can tempt companies to use a discount in price rather than a premium in customer benefit to push up market share. There are many ways to discount prices: promotions, coupons, new trade terms, larger pack sizes, or straightforward price cuts themselves. Growing share through such discounting is generally considered a dubious route to improved profitability. But it is not discounting in itself that is the trap; it is discounting when the benefit of your offer isn't any higher than anyone else's. The gains from such approaches are usually transitory at best.

Companies use many different marketing and sales approaches to try to increase the appeal of their customer offer. If these are not underpinned by a high or increasing customer benefit, success ultimately may be sustained only through higher spending on such approaches. Marketing communication based on increasing awareness of products and services with high or recently increased customer benefit is more likely to be profitable than communication treated as a benefit in itself. It is easy to confuse the message and the benefit. "Cross-selling," whereby companies try to sell one of their products off the back of another, has become a stock favorite way to generate higher revenue without incurring all the costs of stand-alone customer acquisition. But where the cross-sold product doesn't have the same or higher customer benefit than products available elsewhere, the only benefit left is the convenience of a single transaction. This may not be enough. Many customers will suffer great inconvenience for high customer benefit or a lower price. In the name of sharper customer focus, businesses can be lured into using sales and marketing "push" when there is not enough customer "pull."

The final risk that "customer focus" runs is to tempt managers to base their search for new revenue on the size and growth of new customer markets rather than on the strength of the new benefits they have to offer to customers in those markets. They then usually find, to their regret, that a weak position in a fast-growing market is less rewarding than a strong position in a slower-growing one. Microsoft's move into the web portals markets is a good example. The portals market has been growing at extraordinary rates since the late 1990s; from 2003 to 2005, the combined revenue of the top three portals, AOL, Google, and Yahoo!, grew at more than 30 percent per year. Faced with less exciting growth rates in its original markets, Microsoft entered the portal business with its Microsoft Network (MSN). But rather than enjoying the benefits of a fast-growing and by now profitable market, the company has found itself without obvious advantages over the top three players. MSN lost share, and by 2005 was earning only around half the operating margins of rivals like Google, probably meaning that MSN was still losing money on an economic profit basis. In all three years since 2002, MSN revenues grew at slower rates than Microsoft's overall business. Customer focus can create the impetus to enter new markets because they look attractive to you rather than because you look attractive to them.

So we see that attempts to sharpen customer focus can very easily become divorced from increasing customer benefit. Customer focus creates a frame of reference and lines of exploration that risk placing attention on the features of the customer offer rather than its benefits; on how customers differ rather than how, or whether, benefit differs; on the prices customers pay rather than the benefit they are willing to pay for; on the opportunities to grab customer attention rather than the reasons it should be grabbed; and on attractive customers rather than the attractions of the new benefits that can be brought to customers.

Companies run the risk of distracting themselves from customer benefit by asking themselves the apparently innocuous questions that "customer focus" inevitably prompts such as: How can we improve the customer offer? How should we tailor the offer to different customers? Where can we use price reductions to increase market share? How can we use sales and marketing communications to increase the appeal of our products? Which of our adjacent markets look the most attractive? All these questions are valid. Yet, although they won't produce "marketing myopia," they might lead companies into a more profound type of myopia: "benefit blindness." Customer focus itself can blind companies to customer benefit.

THE TYING-COSTS-TO-EARNINGS TRAP

Much as increasing customer focus has become a sign of good management, so too has the discipline of tying costs to earnings. The logic is clear. If managers link costs to earnings at all times, they will never let costs grow out of control and therefore undermine profitability. Central to this discipline is creating budgets that tie costs to target earnings and prices. Then, if costs look like they will rise too fast or revenues too slow and erode earnings, managers take corrective action. In particular, they reduce variable costs and expenses for activities that are far from customers. They seek scale economies wherever possible. If earnings growth exceeds the target they set, then managers can reinvest some of the difference, in part as a reward for good cost discipline.

Tying costs to earnings can be just as sensible as increasing customer focus. The trouble is that it too can lead companies to lose sight of customer benefit because it blurs the distinction between good costs and bad.

First of all, it is easier to turn a blind eye to cost increases when revenue is growing enough to mean overall earnings targets are met. Removing costs is never a pleasant activity; doing so is easier when you have a "burning platform" of bad performance underneath you. If times are good and earnings are high, the pressure will be not to act. But this only allows bad costs to grow unchecked and get locked in. Plus, bad costs reduce the scope for growth by keeping profitability lower than it should be. Bad costs are always an anchor on growth too—not just on profitability. When the bad times come, as they inevitably will, the imperative will be to cut costs across the board—including the good costs needed for growth.

In tying costs to earnings, it seems sensible to tie prices to costs. If prices can be increased to maintain acceptable earnings, they should be increased; if not, then costs should be reduced. But this is a trap. Increasing prices to meet an earnings target may encourage managers to tolerate bad costs when they should not. Cutting costs to preserve margins may indeed preserve margins, but will likely result in static customer benefit, at best. Worse, if managers cut good costs, they will undermine benefit and therefore growth.

To ensure that a close link can be achieved between costs and earnings, it seems equally sensible to distinguish between fixed and variable costs. But here too, the risk of eventually undermining growth is high. All efforts center on getting volume, profitable or not, to cover fixed costs, good or bad. The company is in effect treating fixed costs as if they were good costs, not as costs that are just difficult to reduce quickly. Very soon the company will generate a lot of unprofitable volume and bad costs protected by the label "fixed." Once again, such bad costs hold back growth because they divert resources away from investments that increase customer benefit. Nucor's integrated mill competitors were trapped between achieving higher volume at poor profitability to cover their high fixed costs or making massive investments to shed those fixed costs. They chose the former path and have remained unable to compete effectively for growth.

If the fixed-variable definition of costs blurs the distinction between good and bad costs, so too does the treatment of "owned" versus third-party costs. Cost reduction is never pleasant, so it is often natural to turn attention to getting other people to reduce theirs. This, in part, is why procurement is often a top priority for finding cost savings. But unless owned costs are more often good and third-party costs more often bad, this approach puts insufficient pressure on owned costs. Similarly, if there were always a perfect match between costs that support customer benefit and costs that the customer sees, it would make perfect sense for managers to aim their cost reduction efforts disproportionately on the back office. But there isn't. Unfortunately, in tying costs to earnings, it is too temping to exempt "customer-facing" costs from the same discipline as "back office" costs.

In the search for the right level of earnings, another temptation is to combine operations or push for greater volumes in order to achieve scale economies. All too often, more volume means greater scale and greater scope at the same time, especially if achieved through proliferating product lines. With scope comes complexity. That, in turn, brings all kinds of bad costs, many difficult to see unless and until the complexity is removed. This trap lies behind the observation that as revenue grows, unit costs often do not fall as theory might predict. Tom Glocer, CEO of Reuters, the information services company, puts it this way:

> If you have a lot of complexity, it can become almost impossible to tell what is a good cost and what is a bad cost. There's just too much clutter. When I started, people used to tell me that we had a scale advantage. If we had had 360,000 users all on the same technology platform, that would have been huge scale: you would expect that the marginal cost of adding another user would be much less than the marginal revenue. Instead, we had many different IT platforms. We had size—not scale. With complexity, size is more likely to be a disadvantage than an advantage.

In a typical case of seeking economies of scale, one of our clients, a distributor of newspapers and magazines to retailers, had logically sought to save money by putting the magazines on its newspaper delivery trucks rather than adding a separate fleet. The benefit to retailers of daily delivery for newspapers is obvious, but not so for magazines, which are distributed generally weekly or monthly. In effect, what are good costs for newspapers—the logistic activities necessary to support daily delivery—are bad costs for magazines. This difference in customer benefit was large enough to require separating the delivery operations of newspapers and magazines. Creating two distribution systems—each at lower volume—ended up being the lower-cost solution.

Even the seemingly harmless reward of reinvesting "surplus" cost savings—those beyond what is needed to hit an earnings target—can be a license to build up bad costs. At the end of many cost-reduction efforts, executives often lament that all the notional savings seem to reappear somewhere else in the system in the form of higher pay, more people, or price discounting. These may very well be good investments in growing customer benefits; but if not, "surplus" cost savings have simply been translated into new forms of bad costs, obviously undermining the intended effect.

Budgeting costs to hit an earnings target; tying pricing decisions to margin "requirements"; giving priority to reducing costs in difficult times and to boosting revenue growth in boom times; managing "fixed" vs. "variable" costs and "owned" vs. "contracted-out" costs; combining operations or pushing for volume in order to get scale economies; and rewarding "surplus" cost savings with a promise of reinvesting them—these are widely used techniques for managing costs to engineer a certain earning outcome. The common denominator behind all of them, however, is that they are blind to customer benefit and do not distinguish between good and bad costs. Thus they stand more chance of keeping companies trapped in a vicious cycle of trading off profitability and revenue growth than they do of helping companies achieve both at the same time most of the time.

BENEFIT BLINDNESS

These two axioms of good management—focus on the customer and tie costs to acceptable earnings—are so widespread that managers apply them almost unconsciously. But they are direct causes of benefit blindness (see Figure 2.6). Rather than marketing myopia, benefit blindness is what causes so many companies to fail to achieve profitability and growth at the same time.

We are not arguing that any approaches to improving performance that arise from these two axioms—segmentation, discounting, cross-selling, combining operations to get scale economies, and so on—are automatically ill fated. In fact, they all may increase customer benefit and reduce bad costs. Our case is simply that they run a high risk of taking on a life of their own, one independent of—and blind to—customer benefit.

Back to GM

The practice of focusing on the customer and tying costs to acceptable earnings and their various manifestations help to explain why companies end up with low batting averages. As we saw in Chapter One, GM had a batting average of 30 percent on profitability vs. growth over the last two decades. With the wisdom of hindsight, it is clear that GM fell into both traps at various stages of its recent history.

GM has made constant improvements to its lineup of cars. But in the 1980s and 1990s, GM, along with other U.S. carmakers, confused features for benefits. It added lifestyle features to its cars while Japanese competitors improved reliability benefits. Also, over the years GM has added models to better target different customer segments. But because this didn't add much in the way of new customer benefit, such segmentation has simply constrained GM's ability to grow and be profitable at the same time. For example, in 2005, GM's capital expenditures were $7.5 billion across its eight brands and the seventy-six different models within them. Toyota spent twice as much (around $15 billion) across three brands with a total of twenty-nine models. On a per-model basis, Toyota's capital expenditure advantage is not two times that of GM but more than five times. It is hard to imagine that this lower spend per model does not constrain GM's ability to grow profitably. Furthermore, to increase market share, the company on several occasions has been tempted into price cuts. But the gains have been transitory at best. When it offered "employee prices to everyone" in June 2005, GM's North American market share shot up to 32.8 percent from 25.5 percent the previous month; by October, when the discount ended, share fell below the prediscount level, to 22.1 percent. All this activity—new features, new models, promotional campaigns—amounted to a lot of customer focus without much customer benefit.

Nor did GM avoid the trap of linking costs to earnings rather than to customer benefit. When times were good, such as in the late 1980s and late 1990s,

FIGURE 2.6. THE TWO PROFITABILITY VS. GROWTH TRAPS AND THEIR SYMPTOMS.

Customer Focus Trap	Tying-Costs-to-Earnings Trap
Confusing features for benefits	Managing costs more closely in the bad times than in the good times
Proliferating the offer rather than increasing the benefit from the offer	Basing prices on costs or costs on prices
Assuming that lower prices mean higher customer benefit	Treating costs differently according to who owns them, who sees them, or whether they are fixed or variable, as opposed to whether they are good or bad
Leaning on sales and marketing "push" when there is not enough customer benefit "pull"	
Entering new customer segments because they look attractive to you rather than because you look attractive to them	Overestimating economies from scale; underestimating complexity from scope
	Reinvesting cost savings into bad costs

Growth without profitability

Profitability without growth

the company managed costs much less closely than it was forced to do in the bad times of the early 1990s and early 2000s. Seeking high volumes to cover fixed costs and reach lower unit costs has proven a very difficult habit to break. Because GM has increased its number of models much more than its volume per model, any scale economies due the company for its enormous size have been more than dissipated by the massive scope—and therefore complexity—of its model portfolio.

With its products offering a low relative customer benefit in relation to its Japanese competitors, the company has watched its market share decline. In turn, this has led to a huge buildup of bad costs and bouts of massive restructurings to deal with it. Such restructurings only converted "fixed costs" into "legacy costs," notably pension and health care liabilities. By 2006 these costs had grown to $1,500 per car, and that amount will only increase if GM sells fewer cars. Of course, this money would be much better spent on product innovation to develop better cars and build growth on the back of new customer benefit. With the wisdom of hindsight, we can see that if GM had consistently treated costs as good and bad instead of as fixed and variable, it might have escaped the trap of needing growth but being unable to get it because of its huge anchor of bad costs.

Again, this discussion is not intended to single out one company for criticism. GM's batting average is typical of the one thousand companies we studied, and even above average for its industry. In falling into these traps, GM is in good company.

Overcoming the Traps: The Example of Gillette

In February 2001, Jim Kilts took over as chairman and CEO of Gillette Co., the maker of Mach3 and Venus razors, Oral-B toothbrushes, and Duracell batteries. The company's market value was $34 billion. Four-and-a-half years later in October 2005, the company was bought by Procter & Gamble for $57 billion. What happened in the intervening time illustrates a systematic and explicit approach to growing customer benefit and shrinking bad costs at the same time.

Kilts's philosophy was simple and hadn't changed since his days as president of Kraft USA and then as CEO of Nabisco: "What you call customer benefit is what we call brand value. Growing brand value and productivity at the same time lets you have growth at a premium return. The way we operate is to drive functional excellence to drive productivity growth to pay for innovation to drive brand value."

According to Kilts, high brand value entails "delivering more relevant benefits to target customers than competitors in order to drive preference"— having a small number of "relevant and differentiated benefits" that in combination no other competitor can match.

The customer benefit of Gillette's products has been high for a long time, for the consumer who values the performance of its products and the retailer that values the margin it makes on them. The evidence is high market share and high relative price. For instance, 70 percent of American women use Gillette's Venus brand of razors. Its pricing has been high enough to also allow retailer profit margins of around 40 percent—higher than for alternative uses of store space. From the mid-1980s to the mid-1990s, Gillette produced a batting average of 67 percent, with double-digit annual revenue growth and economic profit margins averaging 6 percent.

But from the mid-1990s to Kilts's arrival in 2001, Gillette had fallen into the traps of customer focus and earnings-based cost management. It had allowed product lines to proliferate. By 2001, the company was managing more than twenty-five thousand lines, less than 10 percent of which accounted for over 90 percent of sales. It had resorted to extensive use of price promotions and coupons to try to keep share up. It paid $7.3 billion—a 20 percent premium— for battery manufacturer Duracell in 1996, assuming incorrectly that Gillette's model for high-performance, large-premium products would work for batteries.

Gillette had allowed its previous years of good earnings performance to obviate the need to push for best-in-class performance in each of its functions. As a result, the company had allowed bad costs to accumulate. Then when times got harder, it fell back on "trade loading"—pushing hundreds of millions of dollars of stock onto retailers at one point—to try to hit its earnings targets. In 2000, the company shipped around 45 percent of its annual volume in only four weeks of the year—the last week of each quarter. When Kilts arrived, the company's revenue had stalled, and its economic profitability was declining. Since 1996, Gillette hadn't had a single year of both real growth in revenue and a positive economic profit. Its batting average was 0 percent.

The new management team worked on Gillette's performance on two fronts simultaneously: they identified and removed bad costs and, at the same time, they identified and invested in opportunities to grow customer benefit.

Gillette's main way of identifying bad costs was by benchmarking functional performance: comparing the costs of each function against those of relevant peers, with the productivity difference being bad costs not needed for customer benefit. Through such exercises, Kilts's team discovered, for example, that its finance function cost 30–40 percent more than comparable functions elsewhere and that its human resources department cost 15–20 percent more. They also learned that Gillette was the fastest payer and the slowest collector of debts, which explained, in large part, why the company had a 36 percent ratio of working capital to sales at the end of the 1990s. (In comparison, P&G's equivalent ratio was 1 percent and Colgate-Palmolive's was 2.5 percent.)

Beyond the initial comparison, Kilts set the standard for continuous productivity improvement, again using benchmarking to inject a sense of possibility into the organization: "I demand continuous productivity growth from the functions. If they come in with 1 percent and I think it should be 3 to 4 percent, I bring in external resources to benchmark and show them that more is possible. It's amazing how fast they change their tune."

To avoid the trap of watching cost savings disappear into other bad costs, the company instituted two policies: "zero overhead growth" and "repatriating" savings to the corporate center. Overhead costs fell 4 percent within the first year. A purchasing initiative cut the pretax costs of procurement by $90 million in 2001, savings that rose to more than $200 million annually two years later. Further savings came from closing seven manufacturing facilities, reducing inventory, and cutting working capital over four years. Savings came across the board and from the outset. The company also reduced its earlier emphasis on "push" activities, such as price promotions, which according to Kilts "have a place but are grossly overused." Gillette lowered trade promotion spending as a proportion of total spending and in absolute terms. It stopped trade loading dead in its tracks on threat of immediate dismissal, and increasing product lines became a cardinal sin.

These actions substantially improved cash flow. Gillette retained some of its cost savings in the form of higher profitability and reinvested other savings in activities that would grow customer benefit. "As a rule, we reinvested 50–60 cents of every productivity dollar into growing brand value," said Peter Klein, former senior vice president of strategic planning and business development and a long-term associate of Kilts.

Kilts's team searched for new customer benefit at three levels: consumers of Gillette products, retailers, and what they thought of as *internal* customers. This approach served as a framework that encompassed everyone in the organization.

For consumers, Gillette's new investment priorities included getting new products quickly to market and outspending competitors on consumer brand marketing for core brands. The company brought its M3Power razor to market earlier than planned; it became the top-selling razor in the United States in its first three months. Gillette had had the technology for putting a battery in a razor for a decade. It had been saving it for fear of cannibalizing its current brands. When Kilts first saw the product demo, he immediately asked for the launch to be as fast as possible.

Kilts accelerated other major product launches as well: an upgrade of the women's shaving brand Venus Divine, a battery-operated toothbrush, and the Hummingbird battery-operated dental flossing tool. In another break with tradition, Gillette launched Sensor 3, the company's first premium disposable razor. New research on consumer switching behavior convinced the company that the disposable razor would not cannibalize its nondisposable razor products. Kilts also poured more money into advertising. For example, to reverse Duracell's market share losses, Gillette rolled out a $50 million ad campaign. To increase the chances that these investments would be well targeted, Kilts raised spending on market research and used a concept called Innovative Marketing Intelligence designed to help managers understand the facts about consumer benefit.

For its second set of customers—retailers—Gillette directed new investment more at what mattered to them, above and beyond products with high benefit to consumers: high service levels and "perfect orders"—complete, on time, and correctly invoiced.

The third consideration in growing customer benefit was those units that supplied services not to consumers or retailers but to other parts of Gillette. Here the company's main spending priority was a major upgrade of training to build understanding and skills in Gillette's philosophy of "total brand value." The goal: teach each part of the business how to increase benefits for its internal customers.

What Gillette did is easy to describe at this summary level, in retrospect and in terms of what the company achieved. *How* the company did it is a more complex question. Upgrading management discipline was central to the new regime's focus. It emphasized keeping things simple, going faster, and continuously getting better. That didn't create a comfortable environment. Between 2001 and 2004, sixty-five of the top eighty positions changed. And Kilts raised the bar on performance. In the two years prior to his arrival, 59 percent of the top three thousand managers had performance ratings of "highly effective," and 34 percent were rated "effective"—even though the company had no overall growth in sales and only 4 percent growth in earnings per share (EPS). Three years later, only 24 percent of the top twenty-five hundred managers "exceeded expectations," and 74 percent "met expectations," despite a markedly improved financial picture: sales growth was 13 percent and EPS growth was 25 percent.

From 2002 to 2005, Gillette scored a batting average of 75 percent. It missed revenue growth only in Kilts's first full year (2002), when the halt in trade loading hit sales. In the previous five years, Gillette hadn't had one in which it both increased revenue and had a positive economic profit margin. Since 2003, the company's revenue growth has picked up to double-digit levels and economic profit margins are nearly twice their long-term average. Shareholder returns, which had been falling far behind peers, went on to far outstrip them (see Figure 2.7).

It is arguably easier to raise your batting average with a legacy portfolio of products that have such high customer benefit and after a previous management regime that fell into a series of traps. That shouldn't lessen the achievement of Kilts and his management team. They made systematic efforts to shrink bad costs and grow customer benefit. They restored the company to superior performance on profitability and growth, and achieved commensurately high

FIGURE 2.7. GILLETTE'S PROFITABILITY VS. GROWTH BATTING AVERAGE, 1984–2005.

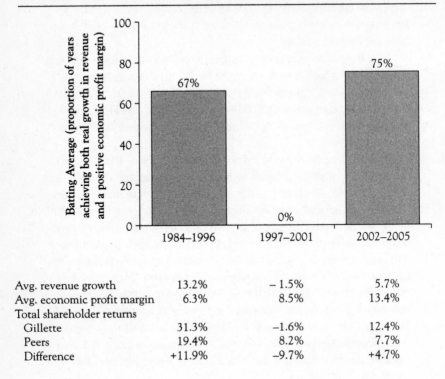

	1984–1996	1997–2001	2002–2005
Avg. revenue growth	13.2%	– 1.5%	5.7%
Avg. economic profit margin	6.3%	8.5%	13.4%
Total shareholder returns			
Gillette	31.3%	–1.6%	12.4%
Peers	19.4%	8.2%	7.7%
Difference	+11.9%	–9.7%	+4.7%

returns for shareholders. Under Gillette's new parent, the company's future profitability and growth will depend on its ability to keep growing customer benefit and finding new sources of bad costs to remove. "We're set for the next three years, but we need to keep working on the years after that," Kilts says.

WHAT THE LEADER CAN DO

As we've mentioned, companies fall into two main traps that create benefit blindness: confusing focus on customers for a focus on customer benefit, and tying costs to earnings. Whether your company has a high or low batting average is determined by your leadership team's effectiveness at avoiding these traps and replacing them with better practices. This will depend on how closely you keep the company's attention on customer benefit—both in the search for new revenue and in the management of costs. The subjective and elusive nature of customer benefit makes this very difficult. It is often hard to know in advance what will grow customer benefit or how to distinguish between good and bad costs.

So what can you as a leader do to keep customer benefit front and center in your organization's search for profitability and growth opportunities? How can you guide your company to achieve a high batting average on profitability vs. growth?

MAKE "GROW CUSTOMER BENEFIT" YOUR BROKEN RECORD

Sometimes the best thing you can do as the leader is to ask the right questions of the organization. The leader's "broken record" is the set of questions and comments everyone just knows you will ask and that therefore get ingrained in how they prepare for their interactions with you and in what they think about when you're not there. Chris Jones, former chairman and chief executive of advertising agency J Walter Thompson (now JWT), believes three questions matter most:

> The most important question: "Is this intended to increase customer benefit?" I can think of a number of initiatives where had such a question been asked—and considered important by everyone to answer—it seems unlikely that the answer would have been yes. Then there is the question of "*How* is this intended to increase customer benefit?" There has to be something detectably different about the customer's experience. If we can't convincingly describe that, it is probably not going to change the benefit they get from the product. The third question is "What is the evidence that we have in fact increased customer benefit?" This is in principle an easier question to answer in a business-to-business context, where perhaps you can directly measure how much money you are making or saving for your customer, than in a business-to-consumer context. But even there you can ask whether the consumer's experience really is better than it was before. Your answers should tally with the ultimate arbiter of whether you have, in fact, increased customer benefit: whether your price and/or volume vs. competitors is higher than it was before.[8]

An example of how this kind of broken record can have an unexpected benefit is in M&A growth. Asking the question of how a proposed acquisition is intended to grow customer benefit can be a very effective means of increasing the odds that M&A will be conducted by logic rather than emotion. Managers are more used to justifying acquisitions on the grounds of cost "synergies" than customer benefit. However, if an acquisition is unlikely to grow customer benefit then it is unlikely to contribute to a higher batting average on profitability vs. growth.

ASK HOW TO GROW YOUR MARKET, NOT JUST YOUR MARKET SHARE

Another question that can keep a company's attention fixed on customer benefit is "how can we grow our market?" Market share makes you look to your competitors; market growth makes you look to your customers and the fundamental benefit of your market. You can grow your share with or without growing customer benefit; it is harder to grow an entire market without also growing its benefit at the same time. And whereas attempts to take share often reduce profitability for everyone in the market because they demand a competitive response (perhaps through price discounting), efforts to grow the market can avoid such pressure.

In 2001, confectionery and beverages company Cadbury Schweppes had a 5.3 percent share of the global confectionery market. Five years later, and without compromise to profitability, it had 10 percent and was number one or two by share in 24 of the top 50 markets.

Many initiatives sit behind this performance, often designed directly for share growth. The company's biggest move was its $4.2 billion acquisition of Adams in 2003, bringing with it brands such as Trident, Dentyne, and Halls. And in its major markets, Cadbury Schweppes has grouped its R&D and marketing resources behind fewer, bigger brands to create stronger platforms for share growth.

However, part of the company's share gain has come from asking a different question: how can we grow our market? As CEO Todd Stitzer puts it, "One of our main goals is to profitably and substantially increase our global share of confectionery. That means finding the right acquisitions and massing our variety under fewer brands to resolve the classic marketing conundrum of too many (brand) mouths to feed. But we have also become more disciplined about using innovation to drive market growth—and our share along with it."

The company's approach to the U.S. chewing gum market is an example. With little development to its benefit and format— breath freshening conveyed in a mint flavor in the familiar stick pack—the market had started to stall, growing just 5 percent in the five years from 1998. Another benefit of gum has been known for some time—chewing generates saliva which cleans teeth. But this benefit is not real if it comes with sugar. Cadbury Schweppes noticed that the U.S. market had a much lower proportion of sugar-free gum than other similar markets, particularly in pellet form.

To grow the sugar-free segment, they increased advertising to raise awareness of their Trident and Dentyne gums (all sugar-free), reformulated packaging design, and launched new products in sugar-free pellet form to help whiten teeth, prevent stains, and even repair cavities. They also introduced new flavors that offered benefits more akin to other confectionery categories.

The headroom for the market had been tied to gum's original benefit. Thinking of gum as a delivery mechanism for many different benefits has stimulated the market, with competitors following suit in their new product development. Future innovation will no doubt include additional flavors and functional benefits, perhaps including treating upset stomachs and migraines and even helping combat obesity. Since 2003, the U.S. gum market has grown at 7–8 percent per year with consumption of gum increasing along with its average price—a combination indicating greater consumer benefit. Meanwhile, Cadbury Schweppes share has grown from 27 percent to 31 percent.

The company also developed new approaches by considering how to grow category benefits for its other customer group, retailers. Andrew Cosslett, currently chief executive of InterContinental Hotels Group, used the grow-your-market-to-grow-your-share approach when he ran Cadbury Schweppes' U.K. confectionery businesses. When he took over in 2000, the big retailers had started to consider the slow-growing confectionery category as unimportant to their own performance ambitions.

Cosslett's team reexamined the U.K. confectionery market from the perspective of its benefit to supermarket retailers. They discovered that two-thirds of shoppers deliberately avoid the confectionery aisle, but two-thirds of those who go down it purchase something. Consumers were being put off with confectionery grouped together as a single category. The company conducted joint experiments with retailers including placing confectionery in multiple in-store locations and alongside products whose purchase was based on similar consumer behavior (wine and flowers, for example). Category sales went up because a latent benefit of the category to retailers was more effectively tapped: its impulsive nature and therefore potential to boost revenue per customer visit. As a result of this and other Cadbury-led initiatives, growth returned to the category. The company gained share and profitability remained strong.

Cosslett is clear about the responsibility of being the market leader: "If a category shows no growth, it's the category leader's problem. You've got to commit to investing and innovating even though you know your competitors will benefit from market growth as well. This responsibility demands that you know more about the consumer, have better relationships with customers, and develop the best people in the market. If you get that right, then share will follow."

Whether you are the share leader or not, asking how you can grow your market forces you to look at what determines, and limits, consumption. It therefore leads you more directly to insights about customer benefit than does asking, "How can we grow share?"

ASK WHAT WOULD GROW BENEFIT FOR THE CUSTOMER'S CUSTOMER

Sometimes, changing the question by changing the customer you are considering can lead to new avenues for profitable growth. Alcan, the aluminum and packaging company, doesn't deal directly with the end consumer of its products. Nonetheless, the company's North American packaging business asked what would increase the benefits of its products for the consumer, rather than the intermediaries that were Alcan's direct customer. The company identified packaging innovations that consumers were willing to pay for.

These were also packaging innovations from which everyone in the system—retailers, manufacturers, and Alcan itself—could benefit.

Alcan supplies packaging for a wide range of uses, including pharmaceutical bottles, roll labels on beverages, gum wrappers, and pet food. In the pet-food segment, consumers (by which we mean the owners, not their pets) are slowly switching from using cans and paper bags to working with more flexible, plastic formats. Traditionally, Alcan asked manufacturers for their views on packaging changes. But to capitalize on consumer adoption of plastic pet-food packaging, the company took a different approach. It went directly to pet owners, giving them packaging format options, each with an associated cost. It turned out that pet owners were most willing to pay extra for convenience benefits such as those that come from the ability to stand a bag of pet food upright, open it, and reseal it again easily. Alcan took the results to its direct customers, the pet-food manufacturers, and proposed packaging changes from which everyone in the system could benefit.

There are no guarantees that any of these approaches to asking the right question will result in finding the right answers. But they do increase the chances that a company will have its sights firmly set on how to grow customer benefit.

DEFINE YOUR BUSINESS BOUNDARIES BY CUSTOMER BENEFITS, NOT JUST PRODUCTS

It is natural for managers to define their business by its products rather than by the customer benefits of those products. To get managers to concentrate on customer benefits, ask them to consider the business in both ways. One of the world's largest oil companies, BP, describes itself in terms of the benefits it provides as a company: "the freedom to move, to heat, to see." Its rivals usually describe themselves in terms of product—for example, on its company website, Exxon Mobil Corporation says it is "committed to being the world's premier petroleum and petrochemical company." Why did BP describe itself in terms of benefit for customers? Is this simply corporate window dressing?

Not so, according to BP's chief executive, John Browne. The company's self-description plays an important role in preventing

BP from losing sight of customer benefit, and it has real consequences. It arose from a senior executive discussion of the BP
brand. "Our discussion turned around a definition of our role in
life," says Browne. "A company needs an understanding of what
human needs it serves. Our subset of those human needs is light,
heat, and mobility. The institutional role for BP is to create shareholder value in serving those needs."

In part, BP's move to define itself in terms of benefit was a consequence of decisions it made in the mid-1990s to move heavily
into gas, a cleaner fuel than petroleum. BP moved earlier and has
invested more heavily in gas than the other "supermajor" oil companies. BP is now the largest non-government-owned gas business
in the world.

In addition, Browne is firmly fixed on where the market for
serving those customer benefits is heading. "We are at an inflec-
tion point of substitution between forms of energy," he told us.
"We're pretty convinced that the three drivers are going to be lots
of new technologies, anything that improves the localization of
energy—because people are always worried about security of supply—and reducing carbon emissions. We intend to be in a leadership position to benefit from this substitution rather than lose out."

As a result of this perspective, BP has been investing earlier and
more broadly in forms of energy that fall outside the scope of a
product-oriented definition of its principal businesses but still fall
squarely within the boundaries of their target customer benefits.
The company manufactures solar panels, operates wind farms, and
is researching alternative fuels, for example, spending £500M a
year (around $900M) on R&D in ethanol production from crops.

BP knows that defining itself by its three customer benefits
does not give it the license to enter into any business that generates those benefits. For example, the company does not manufac-
ture cars or home heating equipment. BP's customer benefit
description is not a precise statement of its business boundaries. It
is more a reference point for thinking about its domain. As such,
heat, light, and mobility does provide some guidance as to what
should be in and out of scope. For example, even though BP has
built a strong convenience store business and brand (BP Connect)
at its gasoline stations, it has decided not to have stand-alone con-

venience stores. If it isn't about heat, light, or mobility, then it's not in scope.

The threat of product substitution hangs over all companies and all industries at all times. Defining a business by its benefits and not just its products is one technique for increasing its adaptability to such substitution. It is no panacea, of course, nor does Browne claim it as such. Whether BP gains disproportionately by focusing on customer benefits rather than just product lines will depend on many factors. One is the extent, timing, and effectiveness of investments in new forms of energy. Another is whether players like ExxonMobil, with more tightly knit product perspectives on their businesses, can achieve greater benefits through focus.

That said, however, it is hard to believe that BP will wander unaware into the trap of clinging too hard to one set of products whose customer benefits are all of a sudden better provided by substitutes.

PREFER MARKET STRENGTH TO MARKET ATTRACTIVENESS

As we have seen, a company's relative position within its markets matters more to a high batting average than being in an attractive market. To continue to tie growth to customer benefit, managers must not be lured into following "growth" markets where their products convey no more benefits than anyone else's or where their bad costs are no smaller than those of others.

We all talk about the need for "competitive advantage." However, few actually make this a real company discipline. Barclays, the financial services group, has been an exception. As Matthew Barrett, former chief executive and current chairman, puts it: "The first job is to understand where you have competitive advantage in what you do for your customers, and where you don't. We said we will go to market where we have such a competitive advantage."

This simple dictum has had a profound effect at Barclays. Two of the company's largest investments in recent years have been for accelerating growth in Barclays Global Investors (BGI), an investment management business, and in Barclays Capital (Barcap), an investment banking business. In both cases, Barclays based its investments on the philosophy of preferring customer-centric market strength to company-centric market attractiveness.

BGI was a pioneer in the 1970s of indexed mutual funds in which investments track stock market indexes. With lower administration costs, indexed funds had after-fees returns that were usually higher than those of the average actively managed fund. BGI grew on the back of huge market growth it had helped create. But by 2000, the market and the business were starting to look less attractive. In 2000, BGI's funds under management were £435 billion, but its operating profit was a slim £65 million. Barclays even reached the stage of considering spinning off the business in a management buyout. After ruling that option out, the company decided it had to do the best it could with the business. That required the management team to understand what was going on behind the numbers. They discovered two areas in which BGI had important advantages, one related to costs and the other related to customer benefit. They discovered that because of its scale—and this is a business in which there are very real scale economies—BGI had lower unit costs than competitors. In other words, it had fewer bad costs than competitors.

Plus, in one new and fast-growing area, BGI had a strong position in a product that produced more customer benefit than other indexed funds: exchange-traded funds. Exchange-traded funds are shares that are underpinned by index funds. Their advantage, and main benefit to investors, over traditional indexed funds is their lower costs and therefore higher returns. Barclays, though not the pioneer of the concept, had a strong leadership position with its range of exchange-traded funds. The funds operated under the brand of "i-shares" and were developed for many different indexes. Although i-shares were at that stage unprofitable for BGI, the customer benefit they produced was strong.

Armed with these two underlying advantages, BGI embarked on a new strategy to focus on i-shares. Originally, exchange-traded funds occupied a lower-return segment of the market. But Barclays was able to look behind the unattractive numbers to its advantages and how to play to them. BGI's performance has been stunning, thanks in part to i-shares. Profits have grown tenfold in five years.

The company applied the same approach to a very different business, Barcap. For nearly every investment bank, the most sought-after markets have been equity issuance and mergers and acquisitions. Barclays accepted that it had significant disadvantages in both markets. Its strengths were in what was then the less sought-after market: debt. The company determined that it had better product innovation and lower costs than its competitors. But in this instance, Barcap's cost advantage was not through greater scale, but rather through greater focus: it tailored its back office to the debt market.

As a result of this assessment, Barcap pulled out of M&A business and all primary equity issuance. It focused instead on the debt market. From 1999 to 2005, Barcap has achieved revenues and operating profits growth of 24 percent per year. The results from BGI and Barcap have been crucial to Barclays' overall performance, making up 34 percent of 2005 pretax profits, compared to only 14 percent in 2000. Between 1999 (when Barrett took over as CEO) and 2005, the company as a whole has scored a batting average of 86 percent. (Barrett handed over the CEO role to John Varley in 2004.) This compares to Barclays' batting average in the previous decade of 0 percent. Its TSR since 1999 has been in the top quartile of the world banking industry.

Barrett is clear that in the effort to locate competitive advantages, managers must avoid the temptation to imagine advantages that aren't real: "We are careful to insist that the standard is no self-delusion. Do we have measurable competitive advantage in our product or service? Are we at par or below or superior vs. others in what we do with clients? When we studied BGI and Barcap, our advantages were clear. You have to be fact based about it and not delude yourself."

The danger of self-delusion is ever present. A recent survey[9] found that 80 percent of companies thought their offer was superior to that of competitors, yet only 8 percent of their customers agreed with them.

Make "grow customer benefit" your broken record; ask how to grow your market, not just your company's market share; ask what would grow benefit for your customer's customer; define your business boundaries by customer benefits, not just products; and prefer market strength to market attractiveness—all these are ways to ensure that revenue growth is tied to growth in customer benefit.

We offer them as examples rather than as an exhaustive list. But even with revenue growth running in lockstep with growth in customer benefit, companies have no guarantee of hitting a high batting average. They need to be managing the other side of the equation as well: bad costs.

In concept, the distinction between good and bad costs has intuitive appeal. But how can you make it a practical reality? How do you distinguish good costs from bad? How can you forge a link between costs and customer benefit?

Grow Productivity in Good Times and Bad

Uncoupling the link between costs and earnings is critical to avoiding the buildup of bad costs. As Gillette did, companies can set targets for continuous improvement in cost efficiency—and therefore reduction in bad operating costs—in both prosperous and challenging times. Those that are toughest on costs year after year don't have to be the biggest cost-cutters in times of crisis. Between 1993 and 2000, American Airlines' unit costs grew by 2.8 percent a year. With the passing of time, small numbers became large ones: after the 9/11 attacks, the airline had to launch a $4 billion-a-year cost-reduction program and fire seventeen thousand staff. It is hard to believe that such a major cost reduction effort didn't also damage American's ability to grow revenues at the same time. Southwest Airlines, in contrast, managed to maintain a smaller annual growth in unit costs of 0.6 percent over the same period. It rode out the 2001 crisis with relatively few cost reductions.

Companies use many different approaches for continuously unearthing costs that are not necessary to produce customer benefit. Some concentrate on "ring-fenced" blocks of costs judged to be less important to customers, such as indirect costs or those that customers don't see. In such efforts, it is important to have an external market benchmark by which to judge whether the indirect costs are good or bad. Although, as noted, the risk of such approaches is to hold direct or customer-facing costs to lower standards, companies that have not historically applied such discipline to reducing indirect costs are likely to remove bad costs from the system without touching good ones.

Many companies also apply the techniques of Six Sigma, looking for variation in quality, or Lean Manufacturing, looking for wasted time and effort, or both ("Lean Six Sigma").[10] Xerox's chief executive, Anne Mulcahy, says that for her company "we have an army of problem finders through our Six Sigma efforts. These people get their kicks out of finding costs we don't need, finding ways to make things lower cost. They are our way of preparing for the worst of times even during the best of times."

Other techniques look for opportunities to pool scale in order to reduce unit costs and for opportunities to reduce layers of management in the organization. (As Peter Drucker once noted, just as trees add rings with age, so companies add layers.) Every large company needs to do these things on a continuous basis. But all such techniques have blind spots. Ring-fencing indirect costs, or those not directly visible to the customer, can blind managers to all the bad costs that are direct or visible to the customer. Six Sigma can't see wasted time as closely as Lean Manufacturing can. Lean Manufacturing cannot see process variation as well as Six Sigma. Looking from multiple angles will increase the odds that bad costs are continuously being unearthed and removed.

But such approaches won't fully reveal the full extent of bad costs. Although they all take a different angle on costs—defects, waste, scale, layers, and so on—they all start by considering the activity or process as given. These techniques focus on the bad costs to be found in *how* the company does things. But there are also bad costs to be found in *what* the company does in the first place. In other words, there are bad "structural" costs as well as bad "operating" costs.

A different perspective is needed to get at bad structural costs, one that starts with customer benefit and moves on to good costs—the minimum needed to produce the target customer benefit. In a reversal of the operating perspective, you first decide what your customer benefit is, then look at how your costs map to it. Just as there are many different techniques for identifying bad operating costs, there are many ways of unearthing bad structural costs.

MAP COSTS TO CUSTOMER WILLINGNESS TO PAY

One way of locating bad structural costs is by understanding customers' willingness to pay for benefits—a reasonable proxy for level of customer benefit—and using it to evaluate how well costs are aligned with customer benefit. BP used this technique in its German lubricants business. The company's Castrol, Aral, and BP-branded lubricants make it the dominant player in the market. The main distribution channel for lubricants is the workshop (repair shop) channel. BP went to workshop owners, and asked them to rate different bundles of price points and features, such as brand, product performance, channel exclusivity, sales force advice, and finance support. They could indicate their willingness to pay for each feature.

The survey increased BP's understanding of customer bene-fit and, in turn, where there were bad costs in what the company was doing. For instance, the company's preferred form of cus-tomer promotion—sponsorship of motor racing events—wasn't a part of any offers that were highly valued by the workshop own-ers. What's more, the survey results indicated that workshop own-ers were prepared to pay more than expected for lubricants that would be exclusive to their channel. That told BP management that their existing plans to reduce the number of brands and streamline the product portfolio might cut into good costs rather than bad.

One of the most successful retailers in the United Kingdom in recent years, clothing company Next plc, applied the same principle of mapping costs to customer benefit in a different way. For example, it asked itself how it could make and sell a higher-quality product for a lower price point. Managers concluded that they could hit such a price point only if they made changes to how the products were designed, sourced, supplied to stores, and sold. The learning from this exercise of engineering costs to a lower price point helped Next identify wider opportunities to cut costs across other lines without damaging their customer benefit.

According to Sir Brian Pitman, former chairman of Next, the exercise forced the company to think about costs in radical ways: "The assumption was always that a shirt made of Egyptian cotton would be impossible to retail profitably at a low price. But man-agement's task was how to increase quality for customers and reduce costs at the same time. There is no doubt that this disci-pline has helped to get much more profitability and growth."

SEGMENT ONE LEVEL LOWER THAN THE COMPETITION

When he was chief executive of Barclays, Matt Barrett (now chairman) had a simple technique for unearthing bad structural costs. He would ask for a business to disaggregate its economic profits by product line, customer group, channel, and geography and to keep getting more detailed within each of those dimensions until managers found areas where the company was losing money. "The problem was, when I first saw the numbers, everything was profitable. The charts came back with everything over the line. So I told them to keep going until they found something negative. We found some real opportunities that way." Not all subsegments were losing money because of bad costs. But on further investigation, many were. And in some cases the exercise revealed areas of low customer benefit as well.

APPLY BOTH AN OPERATING PERSPECTIVE AND A STRUCTURAL PERSPECTIVE TO COSTS

The operating and structural perspectives on cost management both have blind spots. The structural perspective has the potential to find costs in places you didn't expect and might miss with a conventional cost-reduction effort. It lends itself to a more root-and-branch connection of costs to customer benefit. But it risks overlooking how well things are being done. The operating perspective lends itself to being a continuous process, but risks perfecting activities and processes that have limited customer benefit.

The answer is to continuously apply both perspectives. This is what Travis Engen did as chief executive of ITT Industries and then at Alcan. He used continuous improvement techniques of Lean Management and Six Sigma alongside a process for taking a more structural perspective on the business, which Alcan called "value-based management"—its process for determining which market segments to participate in and how to compete within them. "Value-based management tells us where to focus in growing the value of the company," says Engen. "We use the principles and practices of Lean Six Sigma to improve quality and speed, and minimize waste in everything the company does, from manufacturing to HR processes, year in and year out. It's the two together—Lean Six Sigma and value-based management—that make the difference."

In any company, there are always "bad" costs, in part because no organization, process, or team is ever perfectly efficient and in part because customer benefit is always changing, and such change turns what were previously good costs into bad costs. Managers must search for bad costs continuously and relentlessly, in good years and in bad, irrespective of company performance. Taking both perspectives—operating and structural—and using multiple lenses on each are the best ways to increase the odds that company costs are cut ever closer to what is absolutely necessary to produce high and growing customer benefit.

PROFITABILITY *AND* GROWTH

The conventional wisdom holds that the answer to how to master the tension between profitability and growth is balance—of portfolio focus and diversification, of organic and M&A growth, and of growth and profitability markets. But the evidence suggests that the "balance" approach is a dead end.

What really connects profitability and growth is customer benefit: the reward customers receive from choosing and using the company's products and services. Profitability and revenue growth become uncoupled when either or both become uncoupled from customer benefit.

But customer benefit and its sister concept of bad costs are elusive. Neither is easy to measure directly, both vary by customer and context, and both can be managed only indirectly. As a result, any company can very easily lose sight of them. Two axioms of good management—customer focus and tying costs to earnings—can lead companies into benefit blindness.

Instead, to hit for a high batting average on profitability vs. growth, companies should grow customer benefit and shrink bad costs. This involves both art and science: the questions you ask, the way you think about the boundaries of your business, where you choose to focus resources, how strict you are about managing costs tightly in the good times, the structural vs. operational perspectives through which you look at costs. There are no doubt many other

ideas with similar potential. Our message is this: the first imperative in breaking the corporate cycle is to do everything you can
to prevent customer benefit from falling into your company's
blind spot.

QUESTIONS TO CONSIDER FOR YOUR COMPANY

1. What is our batting average for profitability vs. growth? How
   does it differ across our businesses, regions, channels, and customers? How does it compare with competitors and companies
   we admire?
2. What benefit do we provide to our customers? How does it differ by customer and context? How does it compare to the benefit customers can get elsewhere?
3. How well are our efforts to grow revenue directed at growing
   customer benefit? Are we avoiding the trap of confusing "customer focus" for focus on customer benefit?
4. How well are our efforts to improve profitability directed at
   shrinking bad costs? Are we avoiding the trap of managing
   costs to produce earnings?
5. Which ideas for what the leader can do might be most useful
   for us?

Ideas for What the Leader Can Do to Grow Customer Benefit and Shrink Bad Costs

- Make "grow customer benefit" your broken record.
- Ask how to grow your market, not just your market share.
- Ask what would grow benefit for your customer's customer.
- Define your business boundaries by customer benefits, not just
  products.
- Prefer market strength to market attractiveness.
- Grow productivity in good times and bad.
- Map costs to customer willingness to pay.
- Segment one level lower than the competition.
- Apply both an operating perspective and a structural perspective
  to costs.

CHAPTER THREE

TODAY VS. TOMORROW

*[The] task of the manager is to harmonize in every
decision and action the requirements of immediate
and long-range future. . . . He must, so to speak,
keep his nose to the grindstone while lifting his eyes
to the hills—which is quite an acrobatic feat*
PETER DRUCKER, *MANAGEMENT: TASKS, REQUIREMENTS,
PRACTICES,* 1973

Shortly after the new chief executive arrived, a corporate staff member passed him a presentation titled "Our Long-Term Strategy." He handed it back without even opening it and said, "We don't have time for long-term strategy; in the long term we're all dead. My strategy is simple: results."

He defined "results" as 12 percent growth in earnings per share—year in and year out. This target was broadcast externally, to investors and beyond. Internally, it created absolute clarity of purpose. The word around the water cooler was, "About time. We need less talking and more walking, less strategy and more execution." "Strategy off-sites" disappeared from calendars overnight, working capital shrunk, "fat" in budgets was trimmed, and speculative investment evaporated. A sharper focus on performance emerged across the company, from sales to distribution to order administration.

Soon the "low-hanging fruit" disappeared. But the pressure to hit the numbers did not. So the CEO and his executive team went after the usual suspects:

cutting back the advertising, marketing, and R&D budgets; delaying investment in worthy projects with long paybacks; putting a hold on all nonessential maintenance; and holding the procurement director out the window and shaking him one more time to see if any more cash fell out of suppliers' pockets. The timing of changes to accounting conventions, previously considered too arcane for scrutiny, became important items on the senior executive agenda. Privately, the chief executive admitted that a big acquisition—and the restructuring charge it allowed—would be quite timely.

But soon competitors were outgunning them on advertising, marketing, and innovation, putting more pressure on market share. The faster-payback projects had dried up, and managers were left with the tougher, longer-term projects that everyone knew were necessary but that just wouldn't bring rewards any time soon. Now all that zero-return maintenance had become urgent and even more expensive than ever. The procurement director didn't have anything else in his or his suppliers' pockets, no matter how hard he was shaken. There was no acquisition opportunity anywhere on the horizon to save the day. The pressure mounted to come clean to the analysts. After one point-blank denial, the chief executive was finally forced to announce a cut in the dividend, new and lower earnings targets, and his decision to move on to "new challenges."

A new CEO entered the scene. He missed no opportunity to get into the open every piece of bad news that he could credibly associate with his predecessor. The company took a large restructuring charge. He declared to his team that "From now on we will do what is in the interest of the long-term health of the company, irrespective of the effect on short-term earnings. Investment is not the constraint—the best ideas for investment are."

Employees knew things had changed when the word strategy returned to the approved lexicon. The business units needed no further encouragement. A whole host of new ideas for investment duly emerged. Unfortunately, almost all of them had the same "hockey stick" financial profile: large up-front investment but long-term paybacks that, if achieved, would be well worth the climb. The chief executive balked somewhat on the investment requests but erred toward giving managers the benefit of the doubt.

Investors started asking why they should wait for earnings far in the future when the company's track record was less than inspiring. And so much time had been spent on planning that it seemed as though running the business had become an inconvenient distraction.

Then one of the main investments didn't work—in spectacular fashion. The projections had been as wrong as their proponents had been sincere. The analysts had a field day. The chief executive seemed to change personality overnight. When one of his team tried to suggest that things would turn out all right in the long term, he replied, "In the long term we're all dead; what we need right now are results."

TENSION 2: TODAY VS. TOMORROW

The second tension that pulls companies into the corporate cycle is that between producing results today and building for results tomorrow (Figure 3.1).[1] But isn't it the case that most managers feel one side of the tension more keenly than the other?

THE PRESSURE FOR SHORT-TERM EARNINGS

Hitting short-term earnings targets is critical to most companies. Managers will sacrifice a lot to make sure they do. We asked the executives in our survey what steps their company would be prepared to take to safeguard short-term earnings. On all but one action—changing accounting assumptions—the majority said they would consider taking actions that either had no economic benefit or could be positively damaging to the company's future health (Table 3.1). Some 81 percent said they would often or sometimes be prepared to cut spending on R&D, marketing, or IT; 77 percent said they would often or sometimes delay a project to meet a short-term earnings goal, even if the project would be profitable.

These actions have a price. Relying on such means to meet short-term earnings targets can gradually undermine long-term investment and eventually make it impossible to keep meeting short-term earnings targets. Why then are so many managers willing to risk tomorrow's performance for performance today?

FIGURE 3.1. THE TODAY VS. TOMORROW TENSION.

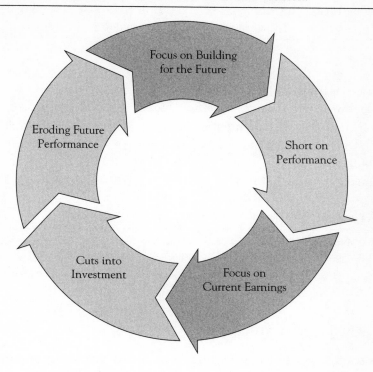

The answer is this: nearly two-thirds (63 percent) of the managers in our survey said that the capital markets are biased toward short-term earnings. Managers risk a lot to hit ambitious short-term earnings targets because they are convinced that the market cares disproportionately about the next set of earnings. Further, they are confident that the stock market rewards companies that are able to produce an uninterrupted run of consecutive increases in earnings. They think that the stock market's short-term pressure forces them to choose between short-term earnings and long-term health.

But our research found that conventional wisdom is simply wrong. Both beliefs—that stock markets have a short-term bias and that they value consecutive increases in annual earnings—are in fact myths.

TABLE 3.1. RESPONSES TO THE QUESTION, "HOW OFTEN WOULD
YOUR COMPANY BE PREPARED TO TAKE THE FOLLOWING ACTIONS
TO SAFEGUARD SHORT-TERM EARNINGS?"

	Often (%)	Sometimes (%)	Never (%)
Change the timing of a disposal or sale of an investment stake	13	72	15
Cut spending on R&D, marketing, or IT	27	54	19
Delay a project even if it would be profitable	13	64	22
Change the timing of introduction of accounting conventions	10	41	49
Change accounting assumptions	6	40	54

Source: Management survey by Marakon Associates and the Economist
Intelligence Unit, Mar. 2005. $n = 193$ responses.

THE MULTIPLES MYTH

Stock market analysts tell you that a company's earnings multiplied
by its price-to-earnings (P/E) ratio—its "multiple" for short—determines its share price. Many managers feel that they cannot hope
to have much influence on the multiple—it depends on their
industry's multiple, interest rates, and gyrations of the capital market and the general economy. In their minds, they are left with only
one means of affecting the share price of their company: the next
set of earnings results. They are led to believe that the short term
is what the market really cares about. The drumbeat of quarterly
earnings announcements, the incessant questions from analysts
about next quarter and next year, the great swings in share price
that accompany announcements of unexpected quarterly results—
all these act as confirmation.

This conventional wisdom, that all the stock market cares about
is the next quarter's earnings, implies that multiples don't change
much, particularly the average multiple of an industry. But multi-

ples do change—quite a lot, in fact. Across the one thousand large public companies we studied over twenty years, we found that for every company that increased its annual earnings, the odds were 60 percent that its P/E multiple fell and 40 percent that it rose. Faith in the idea that a company's multiple determines its share price is seriously misplaced.

Coca-Cola vs. PepsiCo

A good illustration of the multiples myth is the comparison of the performance of Coca-Cola and PepsiCo from the end of 2000 to the end of 2005. Over those five years, Coca-Cola's annual earnings grew 22 percent, whereas PepsiCo's increased 18 percent. If earnings are what matters most, you would expect similar increases in each company's share price. But Coke's shareholder returns *fell* by an average of 5 percent annually over the five years, while PepsiCo's *grew* 6 percent per year. Why the disparity? After all, they are in the same sector. The answer: Coke's P/E ratio dropped from 69 in 2000 to 21 in 2005, whereas PepsiCo's fell less severely, from 33 to 24. It was the change in each company's P/E ratio, not the difference in their earnings growth, that determined the relative performance of their shares. Thus, despite lower annual earnings growth, PepsiCo for the first time overtook Coca-Cola in market capitalization in December 2005, with a value of $98.4 billion vs. $97.9 billion.

Multiples are perhaps best thought of as the outcome of the capital market's attempt to assess the longer-term potential of a company's earnings. This longer-term potential is critical in determining a share price. Indeed, only around 10–30 percent of the average company's share price can be explained by the next three years of expected earnings. Clearly, in 2005 the market judged Coke's earnings to be considerably less likely to endure and grow in the longer term than it did in 2000.[2]

The formula *price = earnings × price/earnings* does not determine share prices. It simply disaggregates them into a tautology. It is true in the same way that the equations *price = age of chief executive × price/age of chief executive* or *price = number of potted plants at head office × price/number of potted plants at head office* are true. It would be wrong to draw the conclusion that waiting for the chief executive to grow older or putting more potted plants in reception will lead to a higher share price.

THE MYTH OF CONSECUTIVE EARNINGS GROWTH

If the market doesn't necessarily value just the next set of earnings, surely it does value a company's ability to keep increasing earnings year in and year out? Isn't this what lies behind the precipitous falls in the share price of companies that miss their targets for annual earnings growth? Coca-Cola, for example, ended a ten-year run of consecutive earnings growth in 1998.

The turn of the last century was marked by a plethora of companies that were roundly punished by the stock market when they missed their own heroic targets for earnings-per-share (EPS) growth.[3] Home Depot aimed for EPS growth of 23–25 percent; in October 2000, it said it would miss that target. Its stock fell 29 percent in one day, taking $32 billion off its market value. At Hewlett-Packard (H-P), CEO Carly Fiorina set goals for 12–15 percent revenue growth and "earnings faster than that." Later she set the bar even higher. In November 2000, she was forced to announce that the company couldn't achieve its targets, and in three days the company lost $23 billion in market value. As we saw in Chapter Two, Gillette in the late 1990s set EPS goals of 15 and 20 percent, missed them consistently, and saw its share price fall. Kilts jettisoned them in 2001.

It is very hard to achieve an extended run of consecutive earnings growth even at much lower levels than the targets of Home Depot, H-P, and Gillette. We found that between 1983 and 2003, only 40 percent of companies had five consecutive years of EPS growth of any level above 0 percent. Only 11 percent achieved five straight years of EPS growth of 15 percent or more at some time during the twenty years.

But are constantly increasing earnings really valuable? We looked at the relation between consecutive earnings growth and total shareholder return (TSR). To get a clear picture, we grouped companies together by how often in our twenty-year research period they increased their EPS. Not surprisingly, companies that frequently increased EPS had higher returns than companies that did so less often. For example, companies with growth in EPS in twelve out of the twenty years had higher returns than those with growth in EPS in eleven years out of the twenty.

But the stock market doesn't seem to value the ability to produce *consecutive uninterrupted runs* of positive earnings results. We found that within each band of frequency of achieving EPS growth, companies with high levels of consecutive EPS growth actually earned slightly *lower* TSR than did companies that grew EPS as often but more sporadically (Figure 3.2). Sustaining a consecutive streak of growth in EPS is both very hard to do and, it would appear, quite unrewarding.

Both conventional wisdoms—that the market is biased toward short-term earnings and that it prizes consecutive runs of earnings growth—are simply unsupported by the facts. To make the capital markets the culprit in forcing managers to sacrifice long-term performance for near-term results is perhaps satisfying, but it isn't correct.

FIGURE 3.2. NO VALUE IN CONSECUTIVENESS.

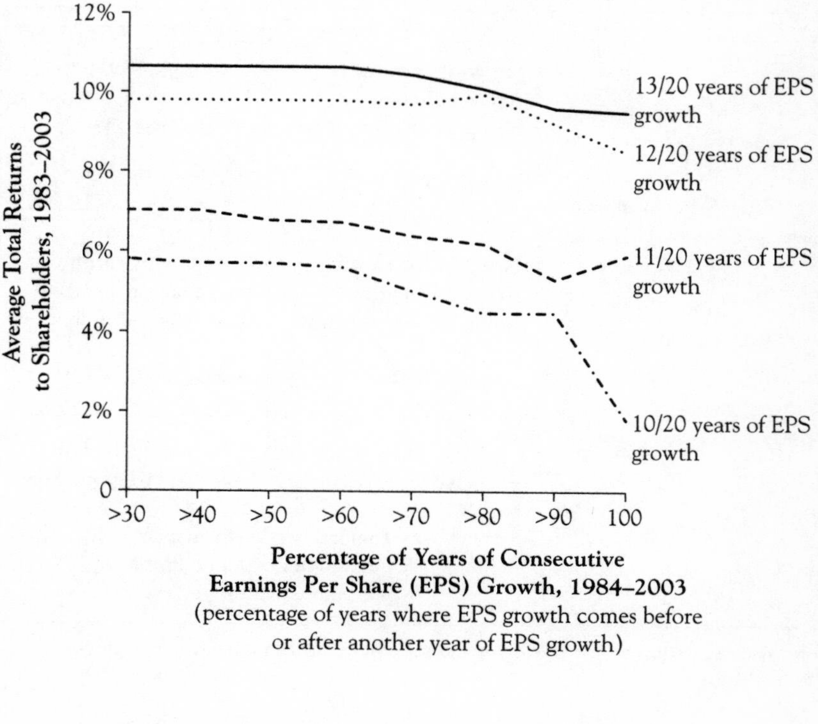
12%
10%
8%
6%
4%
2%
0
Average Total Returns to Shareholders, 1983–2003
13/20 years of EPS growth
12/20 years of EPS growth
11/20 years of EPS growth
10/20 years of EPS growth
>30
>40
>50
>60
>70
>80
>90
100
Percentage of Years of Consecutive Earnings Per Share (EPS) Growth, 1984–2003
(percentage of years where EPS growth comes before or after another year of EPS growth)

WHAT THE STOCK MARKET REALLY VALUES: TODAY *AND* TOMORROW

If the market isn't biased toward either short-term results or consecutive earnings growth, what does it prize the most? To find out, we looked at our one thousand companies for how good they were at increasing single-year earnings and how good they were at increasing multi-year economic profits and how performance on both these dimensions related to TSR. We organized the companies by whether they were more or less likely than expected to perform in a certain way relative to how the whole set of one thousand companies performed on average.[4] The results are shown in Figure 3.3. Unsurprisingly, companies that were poor on both dimensions earned the lowest TSR, at 1 percent. Companies good at increasing annual earnings but not good at achieving longer-term

FIGURE 3.3. WHAT THE CAPITAL MARKETS REALLY VALUE.

	Growing earnings today, but on a path to losing money tomorrow Average TSR = 6%	Growing earnings today *and* on a path to making money tomorrow Average TSR = 21%
More likely than expected to be positive **Today's Performance** Earnings Growth This Year		
More likely than expected to be negative	Not growing earnings today, on a path to losing money tomorrow Average TSR = 1%	Not growing earnings today, but on a path to making money tomorrow Average TSR = 12%
	More likely than expected to be negative	More likely than expected to be positive

Tomorrow's Performance
Cumulative Economic Profits
over Subsequent Five Years

Note: Average total shareholder returns (TSR) numbers are for the years 1983–1998.

economic profits growth earned the second-worst TSR, at 6 percent. This was half the returns of those whose performance was the reverse: companies whose long-term economic profits were more likely than average to be positive even if their short-term earnings were more likely to be negative in any given year. This provides more evidence that the market's supposed bias toward short-term earnings is more myth than reality.

The market rewarded companies that were better than average at achieving both short-term earnings *and* long-term economic profits. These companies' TSR was 21 percent per annum over the twenty years. These are the companies with higher than usual batting averages on today vs. tomorrow.

We repeated the same analysis of batting averages by quartile that we showed in the last chapter. As was the case with batting average on profitability vs. growth, the higher your batting average on today vs. tomorrow, the higher your TSR (Figure 3.4). Once

FIGURE 3.4. THE VALUE OF HITTING A HIGH BATTING AVERAGE ON TODAY VS. TOMORROW.

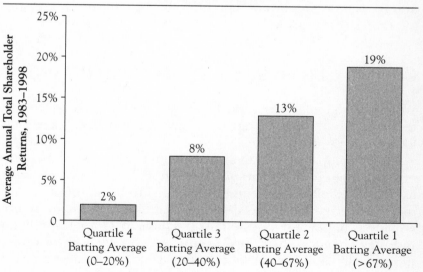

Batting Average on Today vs. Tomorrow by Quartile

again, the rewards go to those who achieve both objectives within a tension rather than just one or neither of them.

But if the market values both current and future performance, what explains the market's roller-coaster reactions to companies that miss their next earnings target? It is not just the short-term *result* itself. It is what that result says about the long term as well. Earnings announcements are the latest piece of information the capital markets have for judging long-term potential. The capital markets are always making a judgment on both the short term and the long term. They may not always get that judgment right on every occasion (although all the evidence is that they do, given enough time)—but that is not because they aren't constantly making one.

Those managers who believe that the stock market is biased toward short-term earnings are confusing a bias toward short-term performance with a tendency to (over)react to all new signals about short-term *and* long-term performance. So, far from just the next set of earnings, what matters to the capital markets is what should matter to all managers: improving today's performance and tomorrow's at the same time. A high today vs. tomorrow batting average is more important than high short-term earnings or consecutive earnings growth.

COMMON BOND 2: SUSTAINABLE EARNINGS

We shouldn't look to the capital markets for what makes it so hard to hit a high batting average on today vs. tomorrow. We should look to the product markets.

Every company needs to protect and renew the assets that generate earnings in its chosen product markets. Physical assets, such as buildings, plant, and computers, need to be maintained and upgraded. Intangible assets, such as brands and reputations, are equally as important to renew. As the basis of competition in an industry changes—with new products and new ways of doing things—companies must invest to protect and renew these assets to keep earning the right to generate profits. The scale and timing of such investments do not necessarily fit neatly with the organization's capacity to produce earnings today. When the needs for renewing and reconfiguring assets are great, it will be necessary to make trade-offs between earning and investing and, therefore, between performance today and performance tomorrow. When such needs are more modest, a company can avoid such choices more easily.

So what determines whether renewing and reconfiguring assets will force a trade-off between today's results and investing in tomorrow's performance? It is the proportion of company earnings that are *sustainable earnings*.

SUSTAINABLE EARNINGS

We define sustainable earnings as earnings that are not influenced by borrowing or lending between timeframes. Earnings can be borrowed from the future by cutting investment. Equally they can be borrowed from the past by "sweating" obsolete assets and capabilities. Unsustainable earnings of the first type are relatively easy to see if you know where to look. For those interested in perfectly legal ways to increase single-year earnings without the inconvenience of actually having to perform any better, the following is a checklist of things you can do: postpone projects that require up-front investment; cut marketing, R&D, and all other discretionary spending whose positive effect is beyond the current calendar year; sell assets for a capital gain that can be booked this year; reclaim investment funds; push stock on to customers; repurchase shares (to increase per-share earnings). The list is long.

All such actions can grow earnings. But they grow earnings by borrowing from the future—by not renewing assets necessary to keep on earning. Capitalizing as many costs as possible—recording them on the balance sheet—so that they don't touch the income statement (and therefore earnings) or changing accounting assumptions to pull earnings forward or push costs back can have a similar effect. They move earnings between timeframes without any economic reason.

Equally unsustainable are earnings increases from squeezing more performance out of a business model whose time has passed. This happens when the assets and capabilities that have generated earnings in the past have become obsolete and need to be replaced rather than renewed. It is a case not so much of borrowing from the future as of borrowing from the past. In some situations, the unsustainable earnings are readily apparent. Established telecommunications companies around the world have had to face waves of asset obsolescence with the introduction of new communication technologies—for example, 2G mobile phone technology becoming redundant with the advent of 3G and traditional fixed-line calls giving way to Voice over Internet Protocol (VoIP). The assets from which these companies used to generate earnings have become unable to compete with assets providing more customer benefit or lower costs and often both at the same time. Thus large swaths of their current earnings have become unsustainable. Much the same picture is true of makers of camera film with the rapid adoption of digital photography.

When such changes are slower, they can be more pernicious. The gradual shift of advertising revenue from offline channels (such as newspapers and TV) to online ones, the move of retail traffic out of town and then to the Internet, the shift between established airlines and low-cost carriers—all these have been taking place over many years. In these instances, companies can succumb to what has been called the "boiled frog syndrome." The water gets hotter so gradually that there is never a point at which the frog notices that it is being boiled—until it is too late. The rate at which previously sustainable earnings become unsustainable is so slow that by the time the situation is clear, it is too late to avoid a painful choice between results today and investing for the future. In such situations, deciding when to declare a previously successful business model obsolete is perhaps the hardest judgment a leader ever has to make.

Unsustainable earnings are those generated by borrowing between timeframes. Sustainable earnings are everything else. They are the earnings that are underpinned by assets and capabilities with a sustainable future life. Perhaps the purest example is a patent for a pharmaceutical company, whereby the earnings from a drug have a prescribed and protected future life. Nucor's thin-slab casting technology was protected by patent. Strong brands that stand for strong customer benefits are assets with a sustainable life. The capabilities underpinning sustainable earnings may not be "things" at all. For instance, the ability to consistently offer high levels of customer service has allowed Singapore Airlines to earn some of the highest returns in the airline industry. All these are

Sustainable Earnings

It is easiest to define *sustainable earnings* by what they are not: they are earnings that are *not* based on borrowing between timeframes. Borrowing can be from the future (by deferring investments that will need to be made) or from the past (by exploiting business assets or capabilities that are becoming obsolete). Thus sale of an asset contributes to earnings, but not of the sustainable variety. Thus cutting investments in brand building contributes to earnings, but not sustainable earnings—you can't keep on doing it. Thus raising prices for customers on your legacy telecommunications platform may grow earnings, but not sustainable earnings. Thus repurchasing shares may increase earnings per share, but you can only do that for so long.

Sustainable earnings are therefore earnings based on assets and capabilities that have a future life. To have a future life, such assets and capabilities are typically proprietary: they are owned by companies and cannot be copied by competitors easily, cheaply, or at all.

The leadership ideal is to be able to grow earnings by growing sustainable earnings rather than transitory earnings based on borrowed time.

"Growing sustainable earnings" is not the same as "sustainings earning growth." Although the former often results in the latter, the reverse is all too often not the case.

examples of assets or capabilities that competitors don't own or can't do as easily, as well, as cheaply, or at all.

The problem is that most companies are very unclear about how their earnings divide up between these three types: (1) sustainable because the earnings are based on assets and capabilities with a future life, (2) unsustainable because they borrow from the past, and (3) unsustainable because they borrow from the future. Assessing which earnings are sustainable requires insight into the longevity of the assets and capabilities—both tangible and otherwise—that underpin them.

In the search for better performance today *and* tomorrow, companies need to prioritize growing sustainable earnings over growing unsustainable earnings. This does not mean that they shouldn't work hard to protect earnings generated by old technologies or business models that will prove to be unsustainable, particularly if they are facing an industry transition between technologies or business models. But if companies want to hit for a high batting average, they should not focus on such earnings sources *instead* of on growing sustainable earnings. They should do both at the same time.

EXCESS INVESTMENT

We have been considering the challenge of ensuring that short-term performance is consistent with long-term potential. We also need to consider the challenge from the other direction: building long-term potential while producing the best short-term performance. In addition to borrowing between timeframes, there is also *lending to the future*—investing more than is needed for future profits. In mastering the tension of today vs. tomorrow, companies must meet another challenge: minimizing *excess investment*.

Excess investment is investment—in the broad sense of money, people, effort, and time—above the minimum level needed to achieve the future profits for which it is designed. All things being equal, the less investment a company needs to build tomorrow's business, the less often it will have to choose between long-term and short-term earnings. Cutting back excess investment is itself a way to increase sustainable earnings. It generates more earnings without damaging the future.

What are the sources of excess investment? For a start, managers often *ask* for more funds than they need, a deeply rooted and understandable behavior. They "game" the resource allocation system because whatever funds they ask for are always cut back anyway, so why not start with a higher number? They tend to play it safe in case they underestimate their investment needs. It is, after all, easier to report a positive variance from budget than to return cap in hand to ask for more.

Gaming can go the other way too: in some cases, we have seen managers ask for only enough to win approval of a project and

---

Excess Investment

Excess investment is investment—of money, time, people, and effort—above and beyond what is necessary to achieve the performance for which it is designed.

Note that under this definition it is still possible for a company to suffer from both "underinvestment" in an absolute sense (not investing enough for the long-term health of the company) *and* excess investment (investing more than necessary to achieve the target benefit of the investment).

The ideal is to minimize excess investment without causing underinvestment.

---

then return for more when the first slice of investment is "sunk" and the project cannot be abandoned. Most managers prefer options that call for more investment to build for the future over less investment-intensive ways of building for the future. We all prefer buying new things to making better use of what we already have. We hate to give up our own projects, even if they are not working. And leaders hate to say no. It has been said that the job of the chief executive is 80 percent saying no and 20 percent saying yes. The difference between saying no 80 percent of the time and 70 percent of the time is a major source of excess investment.

Another source of excess investment is poor project management: spending more time or more money than necessary in making a change, doing things that end up being unnecessary for the desired outcome, getting things wrong and having to redo them.

In most companies, the accumulated result of these behaviors is large amounts of excess investment—but of a type that is not always easy to see and touch. This hidden excess investment ultimately forces managers to choose between short-term and long-term performance when such a choice could have been avoided.

Our position is simple: companies should borrow and lend between timeframes only if it makes economic sense to do so. A company with a low percentage of its earnings that are sustainable and with a lot of excess investment will find that short-term performance conflicts sharply and routinely with long-term performance. A company with a high percentage of earnings that are sustainable and with low excess investment will find it much more possible to push on short-term and long-term performance at the same time with less conflict. Leaders intent on mastering this second tension should concentrate their efforts, and those of their managers, on growing sustainable earnings and minimizing excess investment. Sustainable earnings form the common bond between today and tomorrow.

> *To maximize its chances of having a high batting average on today vs. tomorrow, a business must grow sustainable earnings and minimize excess investment.*

How Companies Lose Sight of Sustainable Earnings

In Chapter Two, we saw how easy it is to neglect and weaken the common bond between profitability and growth—customer benefit. Here, too, the common bond between performance today and performance tomorrow is at risk from what at first seem perfectly reasonable management practices.

The Trap of Annual Earnings Growth

Adopting a target for annual earnings growth *can* be a very helpful way to encourage growth in sustainable earnings and minimize excess investment. It would be hard to think of a better example than Emerson Electric. According to Charles Knight, who ran the company for twenty-seven years, "If management concentrates on the fundamentals and constantly follows up, there is no reason why we can't achieve profits growth year after year. . . . The 'long term' consists of a sequence of 'short terms.'" Knight set targets for annual growth in Emerson's earnings, EPS, and dividends per share. He did it to pressure his managers to find new sources of profit while carefully managing investments in the future—and to keep on doing so year after year.

Emerson's record under Knight was impressive. Its batting average on today vs. tomorrow from 1983 to 1999 was 100 percent: in each year, the company increased annual earnings, and its cumulative economic profits over the next five years were positive. To do this for so long, Emerson managers had to think hard about what investment was essential and what was likely to be excess.[5]

The Risk of Growing Unsustainable Earnings

For less exceptional companies than Emerson (and even for the others), however, the target of sustaining growth in annual earnings or EPS risks constraining investments needed for the future. To keep hitting the numbers, a company risks curbing investments that in the worst cases bleed the business of its long-term performance potential—in other words, it risks growing earnings by growing unsustainable earnings.

This is where the conventional wisdom that the stock market is biased toward the short term and consecutive earnings growth comes in. This conventional wisdom may be wrong, but it cannot be discarded as unimportant. It is self-fulfilling: the more a company believes it to be true, the truer it becomes. The more leaders believe that the market cares only about the next set of earnings, the more they concentrate their investor relations (IR) story and internal management on meeting earnings guidance—the company's own forecasts announced to analysts. This forces the capital markets to base their predictions of long-term performance mostly—if not exclusively—on the latest short-term signal. This, in turn, will mean that the markets overreact to short-term results, thereby "confirming" the very suspicions about market "short-termism" that managers started with. If the only information that investors and analysts have to assess a company's long-term potential is management's confidence that the company will sustain annual growth in EPS, it should hardly be surprising that their faith in the long term is shaken when the company misses its earnings targets.

It is all too easy to find yourself a prisoner of your own model of how the capital markets work. In fact, one company we know went so far as to reorganize its entire budgeting, planning, and internal timetable around the quarterly calendar for external earnings announcements.

The dynamic goes something like this: you set your earnings growth standards high to create internal pressure to improve performance. You communicate your targets to the external world. This raises expectations, which you work very hard to meet. Sooner or later, meeting these expectations becomes an end in itself—a test of credibility. To hit the numbers, you do things that you wouldn't do if it was your own privately owned business: you start to rely on unsustainable earnings to hit the target. Eventually you can no longer produce those earnings. You fail to meet expectations, and you are punished by a reduced share price.

> It may sometimes be expedient for a man to heat the stove with his furniture . . . He should not delude himself by believing that he has discovered a wonderful new method of heating his premises.
>
> —Ludwig von Mises,
> Austrian economist

Gillette's Jim Kilts believes that many companies shoot themselves in the foot by communicating unrealistic earnings growth targets to the capital markets and then making all the wrong moves to try to meet them. He even has a name for it: "the circle of doom." "Even the best executives can get trapped in this circle of doom because they let their ambitions—and the short-term pressures of their product and capital markets—run ahead of a realistic view of what their business can achieve." Managers will be particularly tempted to resort to uneconomic or even unethical behavior when their short-term targets are significantly greater than their company's ability to meet them. Berkshire Hathaway's chairman, Warren Buffett, expresses his concern with annual growth targets for earnings this way:

> For a major corporation to predict that its per-share earnings will grow over the long term at, say, 15 percent annual is to court trouble. . . . Over the years, Charlie [Munger, his long-term associate at Berkshire Hathaway] and I have observed many instances in which CEOs engaged in uneconomic operating maneuvers so that they could meet earnings targets they had announced. Worse, still, after exhausting all that operating acrobatics would do, they sometimes played a wide variety of accounting games to "make the numbers."

These accounting shenanigans have a way of snowballing: Once a company moves earnings from one period into another, operating shortfalls that occur thereafter require it to engage in further accounting maneuvers that must be even more "heroic." These can turn fudging into fraud. (More money, it has been noted, has been stolen with the point of a pen than at the point of a gun.)[6]

There is nothing necessarily wrong with using an annual growth target for earnings as a tool for motivating performance, as long as it doesn't become an end in itself. The standard of consistently producing annual earnings growth doesn't in itself discriminate between how numbers are to be hit and how they are not to be hit—it is blind to the difference between sustainable earnings and unsustainable earnings. As a consequence, for example, a company may well find it impossible to perform to this standard and at the same time transition from one technology or business model to another. In the pursuit of a self-imposed earnings profile, companies can all too easily sleepwalk into a weak position relative to their competitors, hitting their numbers but missing the point. The trap is letting "sustain earnings growth" become more important than "grow sustainable earnings."

The Risk of Stop-Start Investment

In the desire to sustain annual earnings growth, companies change the timing of investments for reasons unrelated to the investment—for example, by cutting back "discretionary" investment in the second half of the year if earnings risk falling below target. Unfortunately, but unsurprisingly, managers often count as "discretionary" those costs that are easy to turn off during the course of the calendar year, often regardless of whether they are in fact important to long-term potential. Imagine building a house and stopping and starting the project several times. The work would probably be lower in quality, more expensive, and slower to completion than it would have been if the project had not been interrupted. In general, such projects work best if done once. The same is true of building a business. Managing to an annual earnings growth standard in order to squeeze out excess investment can be self-defeating: it can lead to stop-start investment and, therefore, excess investment. It is not at all clear that consistency of earnings growth is worth inconsistency of investment.

The Risk of Overinvesting During the Good Times

Determining how much to invest at any point can be approached in two ways: decide on the investment you want and let earnings drop out, or start with the earnings you want and let the investment drop out. The latter seems to be the preferred model for most companies. In Chapter Two, we discussed the trap of tying costs to earnings. An equally dangerous trap is to do the same with investment: raise investment levels when earnings are high and lower them when they are not. Linking investment and earnings in this way risks arriving at the next downturn with more capacity than you would have liked and at the next upturn with less capacity than you would have liked. The wisdom of the investment, not its mathematical relationship to earnings, is what matters to growing sustainable earnings.

The oil industry is an interesting example. Figure 3.5 shows the capital expenditure of the top ten global oil companies indexed against the price of oil. As the oil price increases, so do the funds available to invest. A study of investment patterns of oil companies with nonoil subsidiaries found that investment in those nonoil subsidiaries fell sharply after a drop in oil price.[7] Why should the price of oil change the economics of investment in nonoil subsidiaries so dramatically? It's difficult to conclude anything other than that companies judge how much to invest according to how full the coffers are.

There is a huge institutional bias toward overinvesting in the good times and underinvesting in the bad times. Furthermore, the good times and the bad times often come to whole sectors of companies at the same time. Therefore, companies are likely to be spending when purchase prices are high because everyone else is spending at the same time, and divesting when disposal prices are low because everyone else is divesting at the same time.

Obviously, this risk is immediately relevant to cyclical businesses. There are a surprising number of them, from oil to chemicals to property investment to media advertising. But because many companies base their investment levels on earnings, its relevance is much broader.

The discipline of achieving annual earnings growth *can* be highly effective for encouraging sustainable earnings and squeezing out

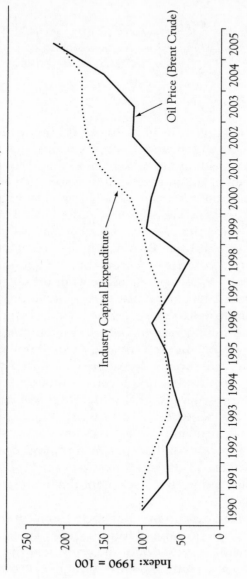

FIGURE 3.5. CAPITAL EXPENDITURE AND OIL PRICE (PART 1).

excess investment. But if it becomes an end in itself, it risks doing the opposite: squeezing out unsustainable earnings and encouraging excess investment.

> *The aim is not to sustain earnings growth*
> *but to grow sustainable earnings.*

The Present-Value Trap

Warren Buffett is known for applying the standard of "present value"—that is, following whatever path of earnings and investment is appropriate to providing a good return on that investment. Present value is the sum of all future cash flows discounted at the cost of capital.[8] In talking about Berkshire Hathaway's insurance business (GEICO), Buffet explained his standard in this way: "Because of the first-year costs, companies that are concerned about quarterly or annual earnings would shy away from similar investments, no matter how intelligent these may be for building long-term value. Our calculus is different: We simply measure whether we are creating more than a dollar of value per dollar spent—and if that calculation is favorable, the more dollars we spend the happier I am."[9] The present value of investment considers both short- and long-term cash flows. It ties the two together by reducing them to one number.

But this standard carries the opposing risk to the trap of annual earnings growth. If you ask your managers to give you a plan that "maximizes (net present) value," they will tend to come back with one that requires a lot of up-front investment and promises a lot of return later—a "j-curve" or "hockey stick" shape of performance forecast familiar to many business leaders. These plans may be sincere and sometimes warranted. But no CEO wants to have only options for investment that generate profits in the distant future.

Present value creates too much "wiggle room": it is always forward looking, always a promise of future performance. Because of that, with their managers no doubt sincerely believing that there will be "jam tomorrow," some executives will risk investing behind an ever-receding promise of future earnings. Their difficulty is compounded by the mismatch between the time horizon of company planning and the tenure in position for most managers: most will move on before their own long-range forecasts come home to roost. And just as suspicions are aroused by precise knowledge of future earnings, the present value of a business is an inherently difficult thing to judge given uncertainty about the future. In theory it is possible to address uncertainty by moving beyond simple forecasts—for example, by assigning probabilities or developing "option values." But in the end, this is to disguise ignorance with precision. You can know about today's performance, but tomorrow's performance is always uncertain. Into the void of knowledge created by this asymmetry come more basic behaviors, such as the desire for resources.

> "The rule is, jam to-morrow and jam yesterday, but never jam to-day."
>
> "It *must* come sometimes to 'jam to-day,'" Alice objected.
>
> "No, it can't," said the Queen. "It's jam every *other* day: to-day isn't any *other* day, you know."
>
> —Lewis Carroll, *Through the Looking Glass*

The present-value standard might encourage managers to think about sustainable earnings rather than unsustainable earnings. But in doing so, it risks inviting excess investment and allowing too little pressure on getting the most out of today's business.

And even if the capital markets value both the short term and the long term, this does not mean that there aren't a lot of short-term pressures on public companies. All the chief executives we interviewed felt strong investor pressure to meet short-term expectations for performance. As Xerox CEO Anne Mulcahy says, "You have to stay within a window of credibility every ninety days." Capital market pressure is very real. The world is impatient for near-term progress as well as long-term momentum. This is what Matt Barrett, chairman of Barclays, says is the real world that companies face. "When someone brings me a 'j-curve' forecast, I say, 'I'd like to be around when the top of the curve gets hit.' This is the real world. I'd like to make it through the night. In a world in which there are very short term metrics, some of this is a judgment. It's a bit like politicians saying that 'I can't do anything unless I get elected.' You need license. There's a bar to be cleared. You don't need to clear it by a foot, but you *do* need to clear it."

Furthermore, although we all feel intuitively that long-term returns demand more investment, the evidence on this point is ambiguous. A finding from our research that surprised us was that, on average, companies that reinvest more of their earnings than their industry peers are no more likely to earn higher shareholder returns over the long term than those that reinvest less. The chart in Figure 3.6 has the tell-tale signs of a complete lack of correlation: the look of something fragile that has been dropped from a great height. It suggests that big spenders are not always big earners.

There are two possible explanations for this:[10] companies invest in the wrong things or they invest too much to get the right things done. Most attention naturally gets placed on managing the first risk—allocating resources inappropriately. Most planning methods, and most scholars in the field of investment management, concentrate on the best methods for allocating investment. It is certainly the case that poor decisions on resource allocation can and do undermine long-term performance. But the other risk needs to be managed just as closely: *the risk of excess investment.*

We found in our discussions that all leaders struggle with the issue that the right amount to invest is essentially unknowable. The chief executive of Dow Jones, Richard Zannino spoke for many when he said: "You end up making these decisions on a somewhat arbitrary basis, often on a project-by-project basis. For example, we decide a level of CAPEX with a certain amount for maintenance and a certain amount for growth projects. We then ask our line managers for their wish lists. Then I try to watch out for good projects that might be turned down by these limits. Of course, you can never know if you would have been presented with more good projects if you had set a higher limit." Likewise, Roche's Franz Humer comments on the challenge of deciding the company's overall budget for research: "It is essentially an arbitrary judgment. You say we spend X; if you want to spend more, then show me the proposal; and, by the way, why not fund it yourself by saving money here? There is limited science behind this. It's a bit like the old advertising adage that 'half of our advertising spend is wasted but I don't know which half.' For the pharmaceutical industry it is even more extreme: 80 percent of our research investment is not leading us to new drugs but we don't know for sure which 80 percent; and the 20 percent that isn't wasted, *really* produces." Several of

FIGURE 3.6. BIG SPENDERS AREN'T NECESSARILY BIG EARNERS.

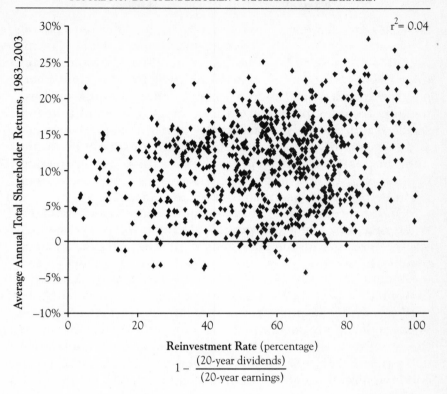

our interviewees noted that for them the real resource limit was capability, not money, and this helped them to decide the overall level of investment. For example, BP's John Browne said: "We have a list we call 'the list of usual suspects'—the finite set of people needed to really get things done. You have to be sure that they are deployed in the highest impact areas. There is a limit to the number of 'usual suspects' you have in any group. And this acts as the real constraint." In a similar vein, Barclays' John Varley notes: "The key consideration is not affordability but manageability. We've been very deliberate about building our business expansion by first making investments in risk and control. The other point is that you need to be really ruthless about short-term returns: the money stops flowing unless we can convince ourselves that we are controlling things enough to get the returns we expect."

THE WORST OF BOTH WORLDS

So here's the challenge: the standard of annual earnings growth can be very effective at addressing "undermanagement" of the present—not missing opportunities to get the most you can from the current business; the standard of present value can be very effective at addressing "underinvestment" in the future—not missing opportunities to invest for a stronger long term. But the first standard addresses undermanagement by risking underinvestment, and the second standard addresses underinvestment by risking undermanagement. Each approach raises the prospect of swinging the company from a focus on performance today to a focus on performance tomorrow, then back again, and so on.

On the face of it, the solution is simple: apply both standards at the same time as much as possible. That way you can create high levels of pressure on the management of today's business *and* on building for tomorrow's business. Indeed, most companies, including Knight's Emerson and Buffett's Berkshire Hathaway, attempt to combine aspects of both in some way. In particular, companies tend to use the earnings growth standard in short-term activities of budgeting, performance management, and IR. They usually use the present-value standard in longer-term activities of strategy development and capital planning. They then link their short term and long term through their annual planning cycle.

For most companies, the process on paper looks something like this: the corporate center issues guidance to the business units on the company's desired overall financial results and invites managers to develop multiyear plans. In some companies, managers are asked to present a set of options and bid for the resources they need to execute the plan with the highest present value. Each business unit gets the chance to discuss its strategies with the corporate center, which then adds up all the requests. Inevitably, there will be a gap: more resources requested and less performance promised in return for them than the top-down guidance requires. Managers are encouraged to revise their plans.

"Payback," the years it takes to pay back the investment, is used as a way of prioritizing resources, with faster-payback projects being favored. As much as possible, "discretionary" spending is isolated from essential spending so that contingencies can be made should performance fall short of plan. Pressure is put on long-term performance by developing multiyear plans and considering options. Pressure is put on short-term performance through up-front guidance, payback, and the isolation of discretionary spending. If performance seems likely to fall below short-term expectations, companies can then cut discretionary spending and postpone slower-payback investments. The result is an accommodation between short-term and long-term performance.

Well, that's how it's supposed to work. But for many companies, this hybrid model looks and feels a bit different. Perhaps the following will sound familiar to anyone who has ever participated in a typical planning cycle. The corporate center positions its up-front guidance as just that—guidance. But everyone knows that it is a top-down target that dare not speak its name. The business units know what plan they want to pursue from the outset and so spend their "strategy development" time in developing a case for their preferred plan. The business units also make sure to add in extra resources to their investment requests because they know they will be cut back anyway.

The "discussions" with the corporate center are presentations, not discussions. Adding up the proposals yields an attractive longer-term performance that is apparently achievable only by accepting an embarrassing near-term hit to earnings. The center then cuts back the resource requests automatically because it knows that the business units have padded those requests. A maneuver called "gap allocation" imposes targets on the business units that add up to the desired level of short-term performance *and* the desired level of long-term performance in ways that cannot clearly be reconciled to the preceding discussions, mostly in the form of plans for near-term actions and rough forecasts for future performance with no concrete plans for how they will be achieved. Everyone suspects that the most politically skillful get away with the lowest "stretch." The most honest business unit manager gets the toughest performance targets and resolves not to be so naïve in the future. As for the multiyear plans—they are never opened again.

Combining the two standards of annual earnings growth and present value can easily result not in the best of both worlds but in the worst: a lot of planning to maximize value, but an eventual default to an annual earnings growth target, all via a lot of gaming. This annual dance of sandbagging and gap allocation is a poor substitute for a genuine solution to the tension between today and tomorrow.

What the Leader Can Do

You are leading the business. You know that performance is about more than simply today's earnings—that's only half the equation. Great performance comes from producing the most from today's business *and* building a stronger future. You know that you should be able to do both, but you know it will mean doing things differently. You know the traps companies can fall into. But just because the challenge is clear does not mean that the solution is. It is very hard to judge which earnings will prove to be sustainable and which investments will be excess. It is easier to point to what may be unsustainable rather than what will prove to be sustainable. It is simpler to speculate about the hypothetical existence of excess investment than to tell the difference between an investment that is excess and one that is vital. You face two conundrums: how to encourage sustainable earnings without also creating unsustainable earnings, and how to discourage excess investment without also creating underinvestment. So what do you do?

Strive to Be Correctly Valued, Not Highly Valued

First, you have to set the right standards for company performance. And this starts with the company's attitude toward its valuation in the capital markets.

Companies fear being undervalued by the market—quite rightly. Undervaluation can severely constrain their ability to compete. It becomes harder for them to buy other companies at a good price because their main acquisition currency—their own shares—decreases. The morale of employees with stock or stock options weakens, making it harder to attract and keep good people, or at least to keep them motivated. The company may become vulnerable to bargain-hunting predators and external pressures to change the management team. Perhaps above all, leaders fear being constantly hounded by their investors and the press.

Although the fear of undervaluation is understandable, it shouldn't blind managers to the less obvious but equally serious dangers of being *overvalued* by the stock market. When a company's market value is significantly higher than its economic value, management will come under pressure to produce more results than the company is capable of producing—*by definition*. Succumbing to that pressure can lead to managing to unrealistic expectations— expectations embedded in the company's market value rather than what the firm can realistically achieve. It will then always be easier to hit the numbers by blurring the distinction between sustainable and unsustainable earnings. Sooner or later, the system breaks. Then management has to issue performance news that is below market expectations. The market's oft-noted tendency to overcorrect its mistakes means that overvaluation increases the risk of subsequent undervaluation, the very fear with which we started. Overvaluation is a curse masquerading as a blessing. It creates pressure for the wrong behavior. It will always be short lived. And any temporary benefits will be more than offset by the inevitable fall from grace.

As much as possible, you should seek for your company to be valued *correctly,* not highly. This means giving the IR department the charter of getting the company's market valuation close to its true economic value rather than drifting too far in either direction. In practice, this is a very different charter than the one the typical IR department feels it has. Until recently, the U.S.-based National Investor Relations Institute defined IR as "a strategic management responsibility using the disciplines of finance, communication and marketing to manage the content and flow of company information to financial and other constituencies to *maximize relative valuation*" (emphasis added).[11]

The alternative is to err on the side of the candid rather than the creative in investor communications, and provide a clearer line of sight into the company's true economic value. For example, oil giant BP plc holds separate discussions with investors: one on current results where no long-term development is discussed and one on long-term development where no results are discussed. Roche combines its annual report with a "sustainability" report: the first deals with how it is doing today, the second with what it is doing to make results last into the future.

The temptation to give earnings guidance is enormous. If possible, companies should resist it. Fortunately, the world seems to be moving away from this practice (at least for the moment). Kilts told analysts in June 2001 that Gillette would no longer provide quarterly earnings guidance. Four months later, Barry Diller at USA Networks announced the same thing. The trend hit mainstream when Coca-Cola said it would abandon quarterly and yearly earnings forecasts and instead provide more information on progress against longer-term growth goals.

The temptation to spend time on IR is also great. According to recent research[12] the average CEO spends up to 25 percent of his or her time on IR. CEOs would be better off spending most of this on directly managing the fundamentals of short- and long-term performance, rather than trying to manage expectations about them. CEOs can easily become much closer to the capital markets than to their product markets, but ultimately a company's performance is created in its product markets. The CEO who spends most of his time on the investor trail—rather than leading his managers in grappling with the company's product market issues and opportunities—may be helping his investors less than he thinks. Much as we saw with customer focus, "investor focus" is not necessarily the same as a focus on investor benefit. Xerox's Anne Mulcahy puts it this way: "You have to lead through stakeholders to create value for shareholders. Starting the other way around is very dangerous. And we have found that it makes sense to make a distinction between short-term and long-term shareholders. We are focused much more on communicating with those of our investors who are in it for the long haul."

We know that letting the performance dog wag the IR tail and not the reverse is tough advice to follow. The best position is to be performing well enough to have breathing space. Sometimes that's down to luck.

These points are relevant to you even if you are not the CEO, the CFO, or in the IR department. The parallel with IR for most managers is performance reporting to the boss. It is better for managers to let their performance speak for itself than to invest extensively in managing their bosses' expectations about performance. Cultures that don't reward the latter behavior are more conducive to solving the today vs. tomorrow tension—and the other two tensions as well.

SET GOALS FOR SUSTAINABLE EARNINGS

Gillette's Jim Kilts believes that setting goals for steady performance and growth each year, rather than being number one each year, is the best route to a high today vs. tomorrow batting average and superior results for everyone.

> The single most effective tool I have for managing the tension between the short term and long term is setting the right targets. If you achieve just above median performance year in and year out, you will be number one over five to ten years. If you seek to be number one year in and year out, you will do things that wreck the business. People get this wrong all the time. For example, when I was at Kraft, Altria [then Philip Morris, the parent company] wanted 10 percent earnings growth. I studied the food industry and came to the conclusion that revenue would only grow at 3 to 4 percent so that, given realistic productivity improvement, earnings could only be expected to grow at 6 to 8 percent. So I pointed out that if you averaged 6 to 8 percent year in and year out over a ten-year period, you would be the top performer.

Kilts believes that the sustainable industry revenue growth rate of Gillette's personal care business unit is 8 percent. He bases his operating targets on this assumption, along with his views on what Gillette can realistically sustain through productivity improvement. "The business units often come in too high," Kilts says. "The danger of high targets is inconsistent investment in the business, which leads to lower multiples. There's always a tension between what's a good aspiration for the longer term vs. what makes sense in any given year. The process of setting targets is about not only what will be achieved but how—both for a given year and over time. For me, this is the key to managing the tension between short term and long term."

Barclays took a different approach to setting targets, but paid equal attention to what mattered for performance over time rather than at any point in time. It started from an overall goal to be in the top quartile of TSR in its financial services peer group. As Matt Barrett explains, "We started with where we wanted to be in four or five years' time. In general, you need to be in the top quartile by economic profit growth over time to be in the top quartile by shareholder returns. Based on historical analysis, we decided that a compound annual rate of growth in economic profit of around 10 to 13 percent should get us to top-quartile returns. Actually, a lower level was all we needed as it turned out."

Analysis of our thousand-company database suggests that for the average industry, a long-term yearly growth rate in economic profit of 10 percent was usually consistent with top-quartile TSR. Second-quartile companies had annual economic profit growth rates of 5 percent. The position varies by industry. And history is not necessarily a perfect guide to the future. But, except in certain temporary situations such as early-stage business development or a business turnaround, profit growth targets much ahead of these levels will most likely tempt managers into damaging the future health of the company.

There's nothing necessarily wrong with adopting a standard of annual earnings growth. But it should be set at a level that is sustainable rather than heroic or even audacious. And you must see it as a means to an end rather than an end in itself: you should set the standard aside when it threatens the company's future prospects. As we have shown, you can be confident that the capital market will—with time—react more to the underlying wisdom of your investments than to the occasional pause in earnings growth.

MANAGE THE LONG TERM BY MANAGING *HOW* THE SHORT TERM IS PRODUCED

A conundrum facing managers is that what matters most to the value of their companies is sustaining earnings growth for the long term. But they can only ever manage in the short term. The way to manage long-term performance is to manage *how* short-term performance is produced. This requires an understanding of what lies behind the numbers.

Norm Bobins, chief executive of LaSalle Bank, the Chicago-based subsidiary of ABN AMRO, cites an example of a budget discussion that will sound familiar to many:

> One of my managers came forward and proposed a $180 million profit plan. I had in my head that $200 million should be possible. The manager's response when I challenged him was "Just tell me what you want and I'll deliver it." I said to him, "You don't get it. It's

not *what* I want; it's *how* I want it achieved." The quality of earnings is as important as how much earnings are produced. It would be easy to achieve $200 million just by lending more to customers with poor credit histories. That's why in the budgeting and negotiating process with my managers, understanding how earnings will be generated next year is as important as how much earnings will be generated.

What should you measure to understand the long-term picture behind the short-term numbers? As Robert Kaplan and David Norton have argued in their work on the balanced scorecard, traditional financial measures are *lagging* indicators of company performance.[13] What companies need to help them diagnose and guard against conflicts between short-term and long-term performance are *leading* indicators of future performance. In general, the balance between leading and lagging indicators a company uses to monitor performance will influence whether it will control its destiny or be a prisoner of current events.

One leading indicator of the sustainability of earnings is their source: margin or revenue growth. The more a company's earnings come from either margin improvement or revenue growth but not both, the more likely there is a long-term problem lurking behind the current earnings numbers. Coca-Cola's fall from grace over the last few years is a good example. The company had a batting average of 91 percent on profitability vs. growth between 1985 and 1995, achieving both objectives in all but only one year (1987). Between 1996 and 2004, Coke's batting average fell to just 11 percent. In 1996 and 1997, it had healthy earnings growth, but that earnings growth had become reliant on margin improvement, not revenue growth. It wasn't until 1998 that earnings started to fall. However, it was two years earlier that the company's batting average on profitability vs. growth started to fall. The recent TSR of some online giants such as Yahoo!, eBay, and Google illustrates the other warning signal: earnings growth coming overwhelmingly from revenue growth.

However, this may not be "leading" enough. By the time a CEO can conclude that his or her business will not be able to generate both profitability and revenue growth, it may be too late to build for long-term performance without achieving a compromise on short-term performance. Typically, when earnings growth masks a longer-term health problem, the chronology of indicators goes something like this: relative share of investment in the market falls; next relative share of market falls (a good indicator of declining customer benefit); then, as customer benefit falls, bad costs increase as a proportion of total costs; next the ability to grow and maintain or increase profitability falls. It is not until then that earnings growth is finally choked off. In monitoring how the company is producing its short-term numbers, you must pay close attention to measures of investment, market share, and pricing—all relative to both established and new competitors.

For example, when he was CEO, Bob Walter of Cardinal Health looked for indicators of the state of the customer pipeline: "I always said that you have to grow the quantity *and* quality of earnings. In every quarterly business review, I wanted to know the customer pipeline—sales prospects, contract renewals, new product development, whatever set of proxies for the customer pipeline that make sense for the particular business. And each quarter we can ask ourselves how the learning from the last quarter changes our view of the next three years."

HOLD A POST-EARNINGS REVIEW

The idea of post-investment reviews for new acquisitions and major projects is well known. It is a shame that the practice of "post-earnings reviews" is not commonplace. For most companies, performance "management" is performance monitoring: "How are we doing?" This is essential. But few leaders also ask, "What are we learning about the life span of our earnings?" In such a review, companies should disaggregate their earnings into categories: one-offs vs. repeatable, existing customers vs. new customers, market share vs. market growth, change in relative price vs. change in relative share, performance on core brands vs. on noncore brands, and so on. As a leader, you could use such information to debate three questions: Where did our earnings come from? What does that tell us about what proportion of them are sustainable? What can we do differently to grow sustainable earnings?

Pay for Tomorrow's Performance as Well as Today's

Blake Nordstrom, CEO of the $7 billion U.S. retailer Nordstrom, points to another issue for mastering the tension between today vs. tomorrow: "Many leaders are forced or feel compelled to focus on the short run due to the limited time they have as an executive or due to varying degrees of support. We're fortunate to have a strategy that is fully endorsed by our board and that allows us to invest the necessary capital and resources for both short-term and long-term results. In some instances, this is a real advantage for our organization compared with others that are dealt a different hand." Trying to overcome such short-term focus by increasing executive tenure in position may create big issues elsewhere—for example, by making it harder to develop managers by rotating assignments around the company. So how can you reward managers to ensure a focus on both short-term and long-term performance? How can you make pay reflect both time dimensions?

One approach is to use a reinvestment scheme for annual bonuses. Todd Stitzer, chief executive of Cadbury Schweppes, explains his company's approach: "For the top one hundred managers, we created a bonus reinvestment retention scheme that automatically matches 60 percent of the bonus with company shares. We created the opportunity to get a 100 percent match if you deliver 10 percent real growth in underlying economic profit over a three-year period. So in addition to short-term bonuses there is a medium term over which to build it up. We are serious about everybody investing annual bonuses in shares in the company. We track who is buying in to make sure it happens."

In some cases, we have seen incentives deliberately designed to be multiplicative—meaning that the overall payout is a function of a short-term performance score multiplied by a long-term score. Another approach is to pay solely on current performance and to promote solely on performance track record. There is no single route. But to manage the tension between short- and long-term performances, you must make sure that your rewards system defines "good performance this year" to mean performing well in both producing current results and building for a future with high levels of sustainable earnings.

INVEST AT YOUR LONG-TERM "OIL PRICE," NOT YOUR CURRENT ONE

We noted earlier the natural tendency to overinvest in the good times and underinvest in the bad times. The oil industry is as good an example as any. For most oil companies, capital expenditure has tracked current oil prices (as we saw in Figure 3.5).

BP's investment policy in oil exploration and production capacity is a counterexample. When the price of oil fell almost as low as $10 a barrel in the late-1990s and many expected it to fall further, the company massively increased capital expenditures on exploration and production (see Figure 3.7). Chief executive John Browne led a consolidation wave in the industry by buying Amoco in 1998 for $56 billion and Atlantic Richfield in 1999 for $32 billion. Now, at a time when the money from high oil prices is pouring in, Browne has maintained a steady pace of capital expenditure and is keeping up the pressure on the business to remove bad costs. "We have continued to divest. People are basing values on the current oil price."

A central aspect of BP's discipline has been to look at expected cash flow under a long-term assumption about oil prices. "We can't see in the very long run the price of oil staying at today's levels, because more substitution is induced," says Browne. "When the price of oil was nearly $10 a barrel, we were convinced the price would at least double, and we put our money on that price. Now it would be very risky to assume continuation of current (high) prices." Back in the mid-1990s, the company considered all of its then-current earnings to be sustainable. Events have proved BP's assumption on the oil price right, at least so far.

In a cyclical industry with a short- and long-term batting average of 28 percent, BP has scored 40 percent. Since 1995, BP's 13 percent average annual TSR has beaten the sector by 4 percentage points, a huge number when applied to the scale of its industry and the companies that compete in it.

How has BP approached investment management? According to Browne, "The first thing we think about is the overall value generation of all investments. Our objective is to maximize sustainable cash flow. Having considered that, we then move on to the timing

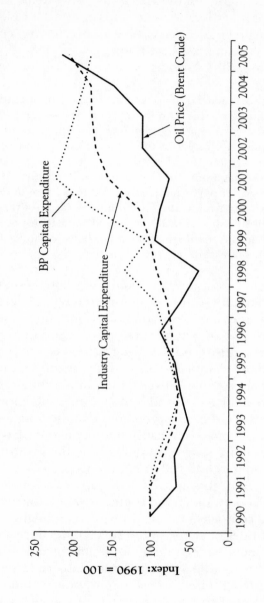

FIGURE 3.7. CAPITAL EXPENDITURE AND OIL PRICE (PART 2).

of investments. It would be value-destroying to start with the timing." BP uses a "control matrix" in its effort to avoid under- and overinvestment across the cycle. This considers a handful of factors, including oil price, to ensure that investment decisions at any point focus on sustainable cash flow.

Browne amplifies further:

> In our control matrix, we look at gross margin, operating expenditure, spending on safety and integrity, revenue expenditure, overhead, and capital expenditures down the side, and different control mechanisms across the top, including oil prices. Since we've been around for a long time—we're not a start-up—it is reasonable to expect our dividend should not diminish. This gives us the standard for performance we need to achieve under different oil prices. This gives us the set of oil prices and refining margins we should consider along with our overall capacity for investment. We use a financial framework of returns against volatility and see if investments fit within this control matrix.

No leader can know with certainty the "long-term oil price" for his or her company. And BP's judgment has not been perfect. For instance, outside of exploration and production, it assumed that refining would be an unattractive business and therefore invested less than competitors did. Refining turned out to be much more profitable than BP anticipated. With the wisdom of hindsight, we can say that the company invested less in building refining capacity than it should have. But BP's discipline is the impressive point, not its forecasts. Other oil companies also use long-term oil prices in their financial models. What is different about BP is that it seems to have been more successful in resisting the institutional bias to invest according to how full its coffers are.

By definition, this approach requires an "oil price" against which to judge how much the company should be investing. Every industry and company has one. In banking it might be the level of real interest rates or shape of the yield curve; in certain sectors of retailing, it might be the rate of disposable income growth relative to the general economy's growth rate; in certain sectors of high technology, it might be the level of corporate capital expenditure as a percentage of corporate earnings. If you gain an insight into the equivalent of the long-term oil price for your company's businesses, you will have an edge over competitors in fighting the tendency to overinvest in the good times and cut too far back in the bad times.

ALLOCATE MANAGEMENT TIME BASED ON SUSTAINABLE EARNINGS AT STAKE

How a company manages its investments greatly affects its short- and long-term performance. But so too, and less visibly, does its management of another scarce resource: collective management time. How managers allocate and spend their time is a hidden determinant of a company's ability to grow sustainable earnings.

In 2003, our firm conducted a survey with the Economist Intelligence Unit of top management from 187 companies worldwide with market capitalizations of at least $1 billion.[14] We found that top management teams spent an average of twenty-one hours together a month. Most executives based their meeting priorities on the crisis of the moment. Fewer than one in twenty said their company had a disciplined process for allocating management's time. As a result, managers did not spend appropriate time on items that matter most for growing sustainable earnings.

In fact, we found that companies earmarked as much as 80 percent of their time together for issues that affected less than 20 percent of their firm's long-term value. Matters relevant to long-term performance took up three hours a month on average. And what time that was spent together was not often productive in making decisions and generating action. Some 65 percent of meetings were not even called for the purpose of making a decision. Only 12 percent of the companies believed that their top management meetings consistently produced decisions on important issues.

As a result, many and perhaps most companies have a bias toward allowing the urgent to crowd out the important—reacting to events rather than shaping them. Often the effective result is that top management underdelegates the management of the short term and overdelegates, or abdicates, the management of the long term.

Few management teams think deeply about how they should allocate and manage their management's collective time. Cardinal Health is an exception. Chairman and founder Bob Walter and his team defined an "agenda" for the company to meet their long-term goals for company performance. Items for this agenda were screened on the basis of how much economic profit growth was at stake. They grouped topics on this agenda into short term and long term, splitting the latter between "strategy" and "capabilities." This produced a three-part agenda: operations, strategy, and capabilities (see Table 3.2).

In a reversal of the usual situation, the Cardinal Health executive team made sure the company's *business* agenda determined management's *meeting* agendas—not the other way around. They set a six-month-forward calendar for meeting agendas, allocating time to items on the business agenda based on how much debate and consideration was needed and how fast decisions had to be taken on them. They separated the time to discuss short-term operations from the time to discuss long-term strategy. The main motivation was to ensure that there was enough time for the latter. In addition, Walter felt that the modes of discussion were different and shouldn't be confused. "We run our board meetings backwards from what most companies do," he says. "We spend most of the first half of the meeting on the strategy of the company and the last half on operations."

Walter has extended this approach to allocating meeting time to different levels in the organization. He expects each business unit and function to develop and share its own agenda and demonstrate how this supports the overall company agenda. Throughout Cardinal, managers now allocate their time less to tactical management and more to the main priorities for growing sustainable earnings.

ASK FOR THREE TO FIVE ALTERNATIVES . . . AND FOR BOTH THE DESTINATION AND THE PATH

In our survey of how managers spend their time, only 14 percent of executives said they were consistently presented with any alternative choices when making decisions. Not being able to compare a proposal against a good alternative proposal is likely to diminish the quality of decision making.[15] The stakes rise for challenging a decision. Managers are presented with a fait accompli: either we agree or we go back to the drawing board. But the quality of

TABLE 3.2. CARDINAL HEALTH'S COMPANY AGENDA.

Strategic Agenda	Operating Agenda	Capabilities Agenda
• Identify basis for future advantage in the evolving pharmaceutical distribution industry. • Strengthen our presence in the hospital market. • Pursue the highest value product participation strategies for both generic and biotech opportunities. • Create a leadership position at the patient point of care. • Pursue strategic growth options outside the U.S.	• Continue to lead model change with pharmaceutical manufacturers and customers. • Integrate Alaris and achieve synergies. • Deliver business and cost structure improvement. • Intensify integrated go-to-market effort with acute care (via Integrated Provider Solutions). • Execute on Pharmaceutical Technologies and Services' sterile and overall go-to-market opportunities. • Address critical Pyxis operating priorities. • Address Specialty Distribution business model issue.	• Execute on Operation One Cardinal Health profit and process improvements: shared services, strategic sourcing, cost structure, management model. • Institutionalize disciplined strategic management across the company. • Internalize our message on our "shared purpose." • Elevate the focus on leadership bench-strength development. • Set up marketing capabilities. • Improve IT data capture, integration across Cardinal Health and our customers (CRM). • Improve performance management through value-based metrics and processes/compensation more linked to multiyear metrics.

decision making is not our sole concern here. Good alternatives give the leader more options for producing good performance in the short and long term at the same time.

Alcan's former chief executive Travis Engen believes that developing high-quality options was essential to his management team's ability to navigate the tension between today and tomorrow. "I see a lot of what we have done with our planning process as creating a portfolio of options. A focus on options gives you more flexibility to produce earnings today and tomorrow to high standards."

Engen required business unit managers to present at least three alternative business strategies when asking for corporate resources. He separated the discussion of alternatives from the decision on which one to choose. This ensured that managers put all options on the table and allowed time to properly evaluate the relative merits of each option. Engen sent managers back to the drawing board if they didn't come up with alternatives. Alcan's executive development programs included a module on how to develop high-quality alternatives.

But there are two big problems with institutionalizing this requirement. First, it is hard to keep up the quality of the alternatives that managers develop. If business units have been asked to generate alternatives, they can often construct ones that show their preferred choice in the best light. This is a maneuver characterized by one corporate strategy director as "Do Nothing" vs. "Slaughter Our First Born" vs. "Alternative Gold." Even if managers sincerely try to generate viable alternatives, the options they present are often minor variants on a theme or are just about which markets to serve rather than how to serve them.

To prevent such decay, you should establish the criteria you will use to judge alternatives, reject alternatives that are not up to scratch, share good ones around the company as examples, and add to managers' appraisals the skill of "producing high-quality alternatives."

The second problem is that almost all alternatives are focused on the "destination"—what or where we want the business to be in x years' time—rather than also for the different ways we could get there. This is a missed opportunity for managing the today vs. tomorrow tension. When you have agreed on the best alternative strategy, you should then ask for alternative *paths* to achieving it.

For example, what options are there to go faster, share funding with others, reduce the investment required, and conduct pilot projects to reduce the risk? Getting managers to consider alternative paths to their preferred strategic destination can stimulate ideas for long-term performance that don't damage short-term performance as much or even at all.

ADD A MIDDLE TIMEFRAME

Finally, a very simple but potentially very effective way to reduce unnecessary tension between the short term and the long term is to spend more time considering what separates them: the medium term. Barclays abandoned the traditional two-timeframe approach of a single-year and five-year planning horizon in favor of three timeframes: long-term direction, short-term priorities, and what connected them—medium-term themes. The long-term direction described the future shape of the portfolio and the assets and capabilities of the company in five to ten years' time. The short-term priorities covered the first year ahead and were articulated as specific action plans. The medium term was a middle position between plan and vision covering the timeframe two to five years out. The top management team described its objectives for this middle timeframe as strategic themes or decision rules that would govern how to use the resources and capabilities of the short term to get to the envisioned capabilities, revenues, and profits of the long term.

Compared with considering two timeframes, such a simple device has some important benefits. It forces focus on the right path—not just the right destination. It makes the decision on long-term strategy more consequential and increases the likelihood that short-term priorities will be "strategic" rather than "tactical." Furthermore, medium-term themes are more useful for communication internally and externally; they are not caught in the dilemma of being "long on vision and short on detail" or the other way around.

Chief executive John Varley of Barclays explains that an important side-effect of this third (middle) timeframe is directing the company's attention to customer benefit: "The short term focuses minds on the results that will build a track record with investors.

The long term focuses on where you want to participate and the portfolio options you are prepared to defend. It turned out that the medium-term themes for us centered on creating value for customers—creating franchise health. This was the most helpful result of taking an explicit medium-term perspective."

Dividing the problem of today vs. tomorrow into three time-frames rather than two doesn't make it go away. But doing so should better concentrate management's attention on how to link the short term and the long term more productively.

TODAY *AND* TOMORROW

Every organization is always operating in two timeframes: trying to produce today's earnings while trying to lay the ground for tomorrow's earnings. The demands of each timeframe are different and often stand in opposition. What will help today's performance may well hinder tomorrow's; what will help tomorrow's performance may well damage today's.

Most companies have great difficulty in mastering this conflict between the short term and the long term. In our survey, only one in five executives considered their companies to be good at both growing short-term earnings *and* building for the long term. About two-thirds (69 percent) rated their companies as better at one objective than the other. And this perception matches reality. In any given year, 44 percent of companies grow annual earnings in real terms while also heading down the path to positive multiyear economic growth over the next five years. Most companies either produce results today at the expense of results tomorrow, do the reverse, or produce neither results today nor results tomorrow.

Yet despite the obvious conflict, the two timeframes are intimately interwoven and interdependent. Good performance in the short term is necessary to create the funds and, in many cases, the capabilities for building for the long term. Poor performance in the short term can quite literally be fatal for the long-term viability of a company. Equally, unless a company constantly strengthens itself for the long term, its short-term performance will eventually dry up. No manager can afford not to work at mastering this second tension between today's performance and tomorrow's. They must, as Drucker put it, have their eyes to the hills as well as their nose to the grindstone. And this, despite widespread beliefs to the contrary, is what the stock markets reward.

As a leader, you can easily become trapped between two sets of forces: external pressures for short-term progress and internal pressures for long-term investment. Many companies have trapped themselves within management practices and performance standards that shed no light on the common bond between today and tomorrow: sustainable earnings. Annual earnings growth targets; present value; planning processes that allow too much gaming; IR obsessed with casting the best light on the company to increase its current share price; management meetings shaped by the urgent, not the important—all these create an atmosphere of great and unnecessary conflict between short-term and long-term performance.

Fortunately, much can be done to limit these self-imposed constraints and create the right atmosphere in which to face the challenge of today vs. tomorrow. We have seen some examples. The focus should be to build a team, an organization, a culture—and to employ a set of management practices—so that everyone and every decision is focused on growing sustainable earnings and minimizing excess investment at the same time.

> 1. Resolved, by this council, that we build a new jail.
> 2. Resolved, that the new jail be built out of the material of the old jail.
> 3. Resolved, that the old jail be used until the new jail is finished.
>
> —Minutes from meeting of the board of councilmen, Canton, Mississippi, mid-nineteenth century

QUESTIONS TO CONSIDER FOR YOUR COMPANY

1. What is our batting average on today vs. tomorrow? How does it differ across our businesses, regions, channels, customers? How does it compare with our competitors and other companies we admire?

2. Which of our assets and capabilities have the most sustainable future life? How much of our current earnings are sustainable earnings based on these assets and capabilities?
3. How much of our investment is excess investment? How do we know? Do we have any real idea?
4. Are our efforts to grow earnings based on growing sustainable earnings? Are we avoiding the trap of trying to sustain earnings growth rather than grow sustainable earnings?
5. How good are our management disciplines at keeping excess investment to a minimum? Are we avoiding the present value trap?
6. Which ideas for what the leader can do might be most useful for us?

Ideas for What the Leader Can Do to Grow Sustainable Earnings and Minimize Excess Investment

- Strive to be correctly valued, not highly valued.
- Set goals for sustainable earnings.
- Manage the long term by managing *how* the short term is produced.
- Hold a post-earnings review.
- Pay for tomorrow's performance as well as today's.
- Invest at your long-term "oil price," not your current one.
- Allocate management time based on sustainable earnings at stake.
- Ask for three to five alternatives . . . for both the destination and the path.
- Add a middle timeframe.

CHAPTER FOUR

WHOLE VS. PARTS

No man is an island entire of itself; every man is a
piece of the continent, a part of the main.
JOHN DONNE, MEDITATION 17

Under the banner of "Empowering Ourselves for Customer Intimacy," the chief executive unveiled his much-anticipated new organizational structure. He divided the company into twelve "business units." Most of the activities and costs within the old central functions were devolved to these new units. Splitting the company into smaller parts soon released ideas for changing the way the company operated. As intended, each of the new business units began adapting its approaches to sales, marketing, and operations to the needs of its own customers and local markets. Revenue picked up.

But soon there were notable instances of poor coordination across the new business units. People started grumbling about "reinventing the wheel everywhere." A corporate program called "The Power of One" was launched. New executive roles were created with responsibility for ensuring that the most egregious duplications did not happen and for taking some of the load off the chief executive to whom all the business units had been reporting directly.

It being a truth universally acknowledged that an executive in possession of a new role must be in want of a department,[1] these roles mutated slowly into full-blown "divisions" sitting between the business units and chief executive. Disputes erupted about who was really responsible for what, leading to a general sense that "we need to work better together as a team." This feeling found final expression in a new "matrix" of central functions and business units. Impressive exhibits with three-dimensional icons were produced. People started talking about the need to "think global and act local." But, despite valiant efforts, the company became unable to function decisively and, in particular, keep its overhead costs in check. The functions seemed to be represented everywhere. So, under the rationale of the need for a sharper focus on efficiency, this matrix was abandoned, the CEO formalized the divisions into global lines of business, and the business units were told to concentrate solely on sales.

The heads of the newly denuded business units complained that with their reduced responsibilities, they were being "sent into battle with our hands tied behind our backs." After a short while, there were notable instances of customer service failure and overstandardization of the company's products. Finding new revenue became harder and harder. As a response, the CEO created new executive roles to ensure that units with similar customers coordinated their activities where necessary and shared learning in sales and marketing. These new roles, the global lines of business, and the sales units fell into regular dispute. "Our New Rules of Engagement" became a new company initiative to foster better teamwork, but better teamwork was not forthcoming. The company found that it couldn't act nimbly or decisively enough and, in particular, couldn't respond to changes within its local markets.

More activities were taken away from central control and given to the sales units. People started muttering about the burden of central overhead. "We must never lose sight of the imperative to be close to our customers," declared the chief executive as he announced his decision to split the company into many business units, each with direct control over most of its costs.

TENSION 3: WHOLE VS. PARTS

The third and final tension that gives momentum to the corporate cycle is "whole vs. parts" (Figure 4.1). This is the tension between improving the collective performance of the company as a whole and improving the individual performance of each unit within it. As is true with the other two tensions, companies find it very difficult to do both at the same time. It's hard to score a high batting average.

FIGURE 4.1. THE WHOLE VS. PARTS TENSION.

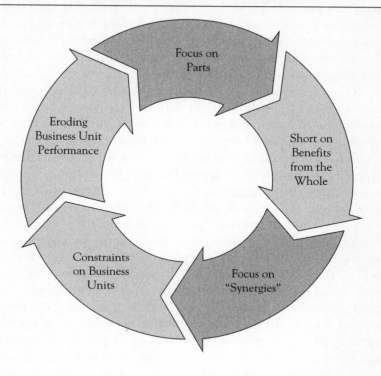

But just what does batting average on whole vs. parts mean? And what is it for a typical company? Imagine a company called MultiCo. It didn't exist on Monday, but on Tuesday it was created from three independent businesses: A, B, and C. Each business started with its own stand-alone value. On Wednesday MultiCo sets up a corporate center. MultiCo's leaders can influence company performance in two directions: vertically or horizontally. To improve performance vertically, they can try such things as setting new priorities for business units ("operating excellence," "become number one or two or get out," "destroyyourownbusiness.com"); assigning new managers to business units; establishing new goals ("20 percent of sales from international markets, 25 percent return on equity, 3 percent annual productivity growth"); changing the link between performance and pay; and so on. None of these actions rely necessarily on the existence of any other units within the company, simply on the bilateral relationship between MultiCo's corporate center and each unit—A, B, and C. When done well, such actions add to the performance of the parts, either by generating more revenue or incurring fewer costs or doing both. We call this *vertical value*—the performance added to each unit that is due solely to the relationship with its "corporate center." Of course, if that relationship gets in the way more than it helps, vertical value can be negative rather than positive.

The other direction that MultiCo leaders can influence performance is horizontally. *Horizontal value* is performance added to the parts through coordinating the actions of units outside the corporate center.[2] It is possible to create horizontal value only if there are at least two units outside the corporate center. The sorts of actions that MultiCo leaders could use to improve performance horizontally include creating shared support services units for activities like HR, finance, IT, and R&D; procuring supplies collectively; coordinating sales to common customers across businesses; creating centers of technical expertise, such as marketing or production; and sharing intellectual property and other assets, such as a corporate brand. Again, such actions can lead to a net positive effect or a net negative one. One aspect of horizontal value, though, will always be negative: the costs of the corporate center, which would not exist if MultiCo did not exist.

The total value of MultiCo, therefore, is the sum of the stand-alone values of the businesses, plus the total vertical value added to those businesses, plus horizontal value net of corporate center costs (Figure 4.2). Thus a company's batting average on the whole vs. parts tension is how often it adds vertical and horizontal value at the same time.

What we've just said may sound as if the whole vs. parts tension is just about corporate management. Absolutely not. *Every business within MultiCo is its own MultiCo.* Every business is both one business and many businesses at the same time. This is true for a large multinational trading across many countries, categories, and channels; for a multibusiness division operating within an even larger company; and even for a small subsidiary with two sales offices. There is no manager who does not have both a vertical and a horizontal influence on performance, be it positive or negative. If it is

Figure 4.2. The Value of MultiCo.

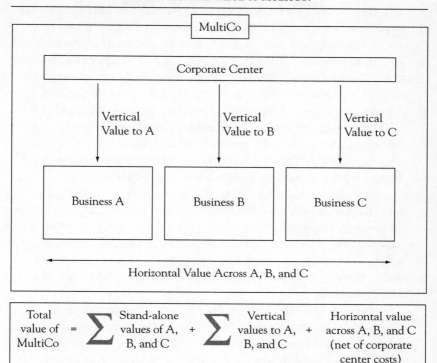

$$\begin{array}{c} \text{Total} \\ \text{value of} \\ \text{MultiCo} \end{array} = \sum \begin{array}{c} \text{Stand-alone} \\ \text{values of A,} \\ \text{B, and C} \end{array} + \sum \begin{array}{c} \text{Vertical} \\ \text{values to A,} \\ \text{B, and C} \end{array} + \begin{array}{c} \text{Horizontal value} \\ \text{across A, B, and C} \\ \text{(net of corporate} \\ \text{center costs)} \end{array}$$

possible to conceive of a managed entity as having parts, then it is possible to think of the challenge of managing that entity as being about adding vertical and horizontal value to its parts. It too faces its own whole vs. parts tension.

Omnicom and WPP

An illustration of the two directions in which companies can improve performance is found by comparing two rivals in the world of marketing communications: Omnicom Group and WPP. "I don't know of any other industry where the two leading players adopt such a different approach to 'whole versus parts,'" says Chris Jones, formerly the chairman and chief executive of J Walter Thompson (now JWT), one of WPP's main businesses. Although they compete in the same market, Omnicom makes a priority of adding value vertically; WPP makes a priority of adding value horizontally.

Both companies owe their origins to Saatchi & Saatchi, the advertising agency conglomerate, but in quite different ways. Omnicom was formed in 1986 through a voluntary merger of BBDO, DDB, and Needham Harper Worldwide to fend off a potential takeover by Saatchi & Saatchi. It is now an umbrella for fifteen hundred companies in all parts of the marketing communications business.

It describes itself as a "strategic holding company." "We have no creative people here at Omnicom," says John D. Wren, who took over as president and chief executive in 1997.[3] The company's head office takes up only one-and-a-half floors of space and houses 150 employees. It has been described as "a holding company for advertising executives who did not want to be owned by a holding company."[4] The corporate center concentrates on setting financial targets, preferring to give large amounts of autonomy to its operating units.

Omnicom does undertake activities that are intended to create horizontal value. It has shared services such as treasury and IR that individual group companies don't have to have. It has also grouped together the marketing services operations of the three original agencies into a division called Diversified Agency Services (DAS). And there's Omnicom University to train managers. But such activities are minimal when compared to the way in which its rival WPP seeks to add value.

Martin Sorrell, WPP's chief executive, was Saatchi & Saatchi's finance director. He left to pursue a series of hostile takeovers, including agencies J Walter Thompson and Ogilvy & Mather, to create a new marketing communications group. Although Sorrell started off as a financier and Wren a practitioner (running Omnicom's DAS division before becoming chief executive), Wren has taken a financial approach to the management of Omnicom as a "holding company," while Sorrell has taken a practitioner's approach to running what he calls the "parent company"—WPP.

In addition to the usual holding company activities of treasury, tax, IR, and acquisitions, WPP identifies five areas in which the parent plays an active role: talent, property, procurement, information technology, and knowledge sharing. It runs a program for graduates that places them on three one-year rotations across WPP's companies, and it centrally manages the careers of high-potential employees. Annual awards are given to recognize and promote teamwork across WPP companies. WPP stock options are granted to those who have worked within a WPP company for more than two years. The company seeks to achieve economies of scale in property management by colocating different business units in the same properties and through sharing best practice in the design of office spaces. Procurement is the subject of central programs and practices; for example, travel services across WPP are managed by the same provider. An enterprise-wide intranet provides resources for all WPP oper-

> ### Adding Value in
> ### Two Directions
>
> There are only two ways for a company to add value to its constituent parts: vertically and horizontally. Whole vs. parts batting average is how often a company adds value in both directions at the same time.
>
> *Vertical value* is performance added through better management of the unit. It does not rely on the existence of any other unit within the company, only on the bilateral relationship between unit and corporate center.
>
> *Horizontal value* is performance added through coordination with other units.
>
> Batting average on the whole vs. parts tension is how often a company adds positive vertical value and positive horizontal value at the same time.

ations. Different forums exist for what they call "knowledge communities," and there is a global unit, "The Channel," for advancing thinking on media. Proprietary WPP-sponsored market research—including a brand research study covering 180,000 interviews—is available to all WPP companies. Sorrell positions WPP as a brand itself in "holding company pitches" where corporate clients seek a single marketing communications partner to manage their corporate brands. Whereas Wren's main concern is that each of Omnicon's units perform well, Sorrell's concern is not simply performance but also how it is achieved. Accordingly, the detail at which targets are set and performance is monitored is greater at WPP.

With their different organizational models, each company is placing a different bet: Omnicom on the importance of operational freedom, WPP on the importance of operational coordination.

WHY BOTH VERTICAL *AND* HORIZONTAL VALUE

Of course, companies have to add value in at least one of the two directions in order to justify their existence. But why should they try to achieve both? Why does a high batting average matter for this tension?

Companies don't report their vertical and horizontal value so we couldn't research the link between batting average and TSR directly for this tension. But there are two good reasons to believe it is worth achieving both objectives at the same time. First, choosing only one dimension leaves competitors free to profit from and damage you on the other. Omnicom and WPP illustrate the point. Omnicom's greater emphasis on unit autonomy gives it strengths in retaining the kind of talent that values independence, appeals to those clients who want to select from competing agencies rather than choose an integrated offer, and may make it more credible to claim effective "Chinese walls" between agencies serving competing clients. In contrast, WPP's greater emphasis on coordination opens up more possibilities for achieving economies of scale in procurement, property, and other shared services; gives it an edge in holding company pitches that offer clients one partner to help manage branding consistency and costs; and makes sharing best practices easier. Yet the strength of one is the weakness of the other. Omnicom's model leaves a lot of potential horizontal value on the table—for example, duplicated back offices, less bulk purchasing clout, and missed opportunities to win holding company pitches. WPP's model runs the risk of leaving much vertical value untapped—for example, less opportunity to benefit from clients' picking and mixing agencies themselves, more internal politics, and perhaps demotivated talent. It would be hard to argue that each isn't making a major trade-off and leaving itself exposed to attack from the other.

Second, as we will see, vertical value and horizontal value behave in the same way as the objectives within the other two tensions: they depend on each other. Positive vertical value creates opportunities for positive horizontal value, and vice versa. And vertical value will eventually suffer if horizontal value is poor, and vice versa. The right aspiration is to add more to the parts than any other company could. Concentrating on only one dimension will constrain your ability to meet this standard.

MEASURING BATTING AVERAGE ON WHOLE VS. PARTS

How successful are companies at achieving this magic combination—at adding both vertical and horizontal value simultaneously? What is the typical batting average on whole vs. parts?

Management Survey: Whole vs. Parts

One-quarter of respondents said that their companies were good at improving performance both vertically and horizontally.

Almost three times as many respondents rated their company as better at adding vertical value than at adding horizontal value (46 percent vs. 17 percent).

Some 70 percent of executives rate their companies as "not very effective" to "very ineffective" at adding horizontal value; conversely, 51 percent rate their companies as "effective" or "very effective" at adding vertical value to their business units.

Not high, according to the executives in our management survey (see box). Only one-quarter of them rated their company "good" at adding value both vertically and horizontally.

It is very difficult to measure horizontal and vertical value independently, particularly for large numbers of companies and years. It is, however, possible to measure their combined effect. If the net effect of efforts on both fronts were positive, we would expect to see that the company performed better than might be expected if its parts were independently owned and operated.

We designed and conducted research to measure this. We looked at the performance of companies who were in the same sector but with multiple divisions. We calculated the ratios of economic profit to sales of single-division companies in the same sectors to help us construct estimates of stand-alone economic profits. We measured the difference between each company's actual economic profit and its economic profit when calculated as a sum of its parts on a stand-alone basis.[5] The results for 2004 are shown in Figure 4.3.

We repeated this analysis for the four years 2001 to 2004. We found the same pattern. On average across the four years, 45 percent of multidivisional companies earned economic profits higher than the sum of the stand-alone economic profits of their parts. In

FIGURE 4.3. NET IMPACT OF VERTICAL VALUE AND HORIZONTAL VALUE (2004).

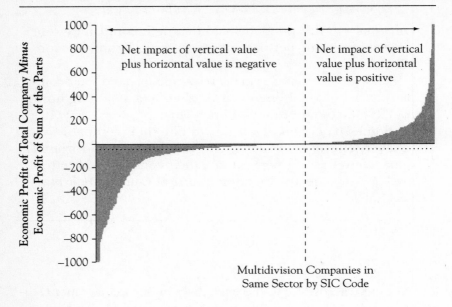

other words, the net impact of their efforts to add value, vertical and horizontal, was positive. Conversely, the net impact of vertical and horizontal value was negative for 55 percent of multidivisional companies. So for the average multidivisional company, the combined impact of their efforts to create vertical and horizontal value is negative. This is striking. However it chooses to organize itself, the multidivisional company is justified only if it can increase vertical or horizontal value in ways that could not be achieved by its businesses acting independently. The implication of this analysis is that the typical multidivisional company does not justify its existence.[6]

This analysis also tells us something about batting averages on the whole vs. parts. Some proportion of companies that operate at a premium to their parts will do so because a net positive vertical value exceeds a net negative horizontal value, or vice versa. So 45 percent must be the *maximum* batting average on whole vs. parts for multidivisional companies.

DISENTANGLING VERTICAL VALUE
FROM HORIZONTAL VALUE

But how much of this finding is the result of vertical vs. horizontal value? Is it possible to separate the two effects?

Is Horizontal Value Typically Negative?

The executives in our survey certainly believe that horizontal value is usually negative. Respondents were much more pessimistic about their company's ability to add value horizontally than vertically. Some 70 percent rated their companies either "not very effective" or "very ineffective" at adding horizontal value. This contrasts with 51 percent rating their companies "effective" or "very effective" at improving performance vertically. This pattern held true for executives at both the corporate and business unit levels.

There are good reasons to imagine that horizontal value is indeed often negative.[7] Central functions can easily become distant from the business units they are supposed to serve. As we saw in Chapter Two, attempts to achieve scale economies can trip up over the costs of complexity from scope. And, as noted, corporate center costs are a negative horizontal value in themselves.

To test the hypothesis that horizontal value is often negative, we looked at the difference between multidivisional companies in the same sector versus multidivisional companies in more than one sector (Figure 4.4). It seems reasonable to assume that the less the businesses within the company share the same industry, the less opportunity there will be for adding horizontal value. Conversely, when the company's businesses operate in the same sector, they are more likely to share similar activities and challenges, raising the odds that horizontal value can be created. Thus a company with divisions in retailing, manufacturing, and financial services is likely to have fewer horizontal opportunities than a firm with divisions in financial services alone. It seems logical to imagine, therefore, that the performance of companies playing in *more than one sector* should be a better indicator of vertical value than the performance of companies playing in only one sector. If horizontal value is typically negative, but vertical value is positive, we might expect to see fewer single-sector companies trading at a discount to their parts than multisector companies.

We found exactly the opposite. More multisector companies operate at an economic profit discount to their parts than single-sector companies. Why? One interpretation is that, despite the opinions of the managers in our survey, vertical value is more likely to be negative than horizontal value.

Is Vertical Value Typically Negative?

There are many reasons to suspect that vertical value is often negative. Corporate managers who are further from the company's customers and competitors than business unit managers and who can spend less time on any particular business might well have less knowledge on which to base targets, priorities, and guidance for each business. Business unit managers are not hesitant to share their views on unhelpful corporate interference.

FIGURE 4.4. THE IMPACT OF PORTFOLIO DIVERSITY ON
VERTICAL AND HORIZONTAL VALUE.

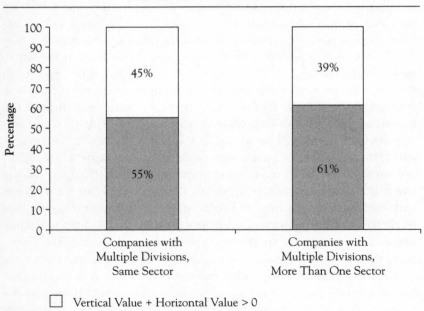

But to infer from our findings that vertical value is usually negative may be a bridge too far. It is quite possible that more portfolio concentration—less diversification—also increases the opportunity to add value *vertically*. After all, the ability to add value vertically—by setting the right goals, by challenging business unit management, and so on—might also rely on depth of knowledge and expertise in one sector. Certainly the suspicion that "corporate managers don't understand my business" itself acts as a barrier to the center adding value vertically. Our conclusion: looking at differences in portfolio diversity can't conclusively separate out the two effects.

> *The net effect of both vertical and horizontal actions is negative for the typical multidivisional company. Fifty-five percent of companies trade at a discount to the stand-alone sum of their parts.*
> *By implication, batting average on whole vs. parts—*
> *how often both vertical and horizontal value are positive—*
> *is typically less than 45 percent.*
> *Portfolio focus seems to make it somewhat easier to score a higher batting average on whole vs. parts. But it is not clear which dimension, vertical or horizontal, is made easier.*

An Alternative Hypothesis

We think that a different explanation is more likely to fit the facts: *actions to increase value vertically and actions to increase value horizontally tend to cancel each other out.* This explains why the average company trades at a discount to the sum of its parts and why so many others trade very near to it. The average company is a combination of a WPP and an Omnicom trying to add value in both directions and suffering the trade-offs in both directions at the same time. We've seen this canceling-out effect before. In Chapter Two, we saw that attempts to "balance"—focus and diversification, organic and M&A growth, profitability and growth businesses—as a means of resolving the profitability vs. growth tension are dead ends. And in Chapter Three, we saw that tools to manage the short term often cancel out those geared to the long term. As we saw for the other two tensions, it is hard to achieve "both" at the same time and much easier to achieve "either" or "neither" (see Figure 4.5). And the reason is the same here as for the other two tensions: it is very easy to lose sight of the common bond that ties together the two objectives within the tension.

COMMON BOND 3: DIAGONAL ASSETS

It is natural to think of organizational assets and capabilities as falling into two categories: those that are specific to individual businesses, such as a particular brand or a patent or technology; and those that are shared by two or more businesses and that have lower costs or greater skills than if managed by the businesses themselves, such as shared payroll processing, shared logistics, the IR department, corporate taxation, a corporate brand, and so on. In our terminology, these are respectively vertical and horizontal assets.

We saw that Omnicom concentrates on nurturing vertical assets—the specific individual strengths of its operating companies. WPP concentrates more on building horizontal assets—for example, shared properties and the brand research that each business can call on in its marketing to clients.

Our analysis implies that most companies fail to nurture assets of both types at the same time. But there is no reason to believe that this cannot be done. In fact, with appropriate management, the two types of assets can be mutually reinforcing.

HORIZONTAL ASSETS CAN CREATE VERTICAL VALUE

Efforts to add horizontal assets can create a vertical side benefit. For example, when centralizing an activity like logistics, a company might achieve lower costs than could any business acting on its own. Doing so might at the same time remove distraction and save the business time that would be better spent on managing activities where it might add more value as an individual unit. IR is another example: not only does a business save itself the full costs of an IR department by sharing them with other businesses (horizontal value), but its managers should be better able to concentrate on managing the fundamentals of the business because they don't have to spend time presenting to analysts (vertical value).

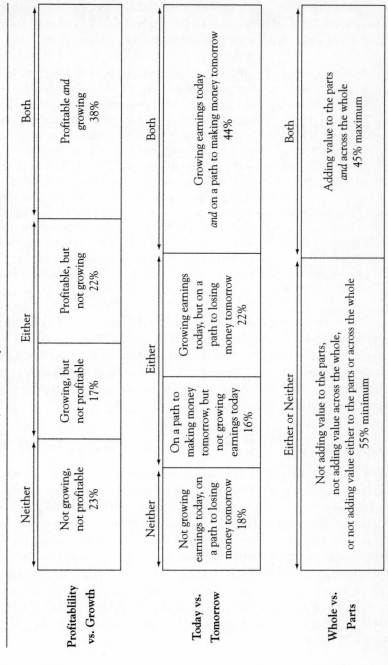

FIGURE 4.5. PROBABILITIES OF COMPANIES' ACHIEVING EITHER, NEITHER, OR BOTH OBJECTIVES—WITHIN EACH TENSION.

In some cases, such moves might also increase the businesses' standards for performance. Lewis Campbell, Textron's chairman and chief executive, tells the following anecdote:

> Two neighbors. Saturday. Beautiful day. Both look out their back door and see that the grass needs to be mowed. One decides to play golf and pay someone else to mow the lawn. The other decides to mow the lawn himself. Later in the day, each neighbor is sitting in his backyard with his wife enjoying the beautiful day and trimmed lawn. Then the neighbor who mowed his own lawn notices that he missed a patch and says to himself, "Oh well, I'll have to take care of that tomorrow." The other neighbor notices a similar missed patch in his lawn and flies off the handle, saying, "I paid him good money to mow this lawn! This just isn't acceptable."
>
> Moral of the story: everyone has more tolerance for their own mistakes than they do for others', especially when they are paying them. That's why it's sometimes better to centralize common processes and pay a third party to run them. The standards immediately go up.

Selecting the right kind of horizontal assets to build and managing them in the right way can also create vertical value, such as sharper priorities and higher performance standards. Where a business can sharpen its priorities or raise its standards by creating an effective customer-supplier relationship, horizontal assets are no enemy of vertical value.

VERTICAL ASSETS CAN CREATE HORIZONTAL VALUE

The possibilities go in the other direction as well. A good idea for improving the performance of one business may well have useful application elsewhere in the company. If transferring it is fairly painless, then what started life as a way of increasing vertical value can also end up adding value horizontally. For example, a new approach to staff scheduling may have application to other units, or a strong position in a market that results from better management of a business may create the scale for procurement savings for another business unit. When you consider it, there are a lot of opportunities for horizontal and vertical assets to beget more of each other.

THE COMMON BOND: DIAGONAL ASSETS

There is no guarantee, however, that such side benefits will actually materialize. If the corporate center charges back the costs of central logistics through an opaque transfer pricing mechanism or if the businesses suspect that the head of logistics is slacking on his job, then any vertical side benefit of sharper business unit focus from centralizing logistics will be swallowed up in argument and mistrust. If the only way that business-specific know-how can be made available to the other businesses is through a cumbersome and time-consuming committee for sharing best practices that isn't really recognized in pay or promotion, then any potential benefit will be offset by irritation and distraction from the task of managing each business's individual performance.

A third kind of organizational asset and capability is required if horizontal assets are to have vertical value and if vertical assets are to have horizontal value. For obvious reasons, we call them *diagonal assets*.

Shared logistics could be a source of horizontal value, and the sharper focus on more important points of leverage for the business that it facilitates might be a source of vertical value. But it takes trust and transparency to convert one into the other. Business-specific know-how can add vertical value and can be shared elsewhere to add horizontal value. But it takes a sense of "connectedness" and a common aspiration to create the conditions for sharing it without imposing a damaging burden of coordination. Trust, transparency, a sense of connectedness, and a common aspiration are thus examples of diagonal assets.

Diagonal assets are usually the overlooked and intangible qualities in organizations: cultural values; a sense of connectedness; behavioral norms; such technologies as an information system; physical proximity; a common language; a management philosophy; a management rotation policy; an individual who connects, perhaps even the chief executive himself or herself. These are all ways of making connections, of tying things together. They form the connective tissue in the organization linking the parts without formal structure.

In a company with strong diagonal assets, managers can achieve the two objectives of adding vertical and horizontal value

---

Diagonal Assets

Diagonal assets are capabilities and resources that help vertical assets create horizontal value and horizontal assets create vertical value. They let a company improve the performance of its parts and the whole at the same time.

Examples include cultural values, a shared sense of "how we do things around here," a common management philosophy, physical proximity between units, key people who make connections, and so on.

Diagonal assets are ways of tying things together without the need for formal structures.

Diagonal assets are company-specific because each company has different sources of horizontal and vertical value. Therefore what connects them will be unique.

A company with strong diagonal assets will find that it really can be more than the sum of its parts.

---

at the same time. A company with few diagonal assets will find many barriers to improving the performance of the parts and of the whole concurrently.

> *To improve the performance of the whole and the parts at the same time, managers must strengthen the organization's diagonal assets.*

It is helpful to think of organizational assets and capabilities as falling into three categories: vertical, horizontal, and diagonal (Figure 4.6).

HOW COMPANIES LOSE SIGHT OF DIAGONAL ASSETS

Diagonal assets are hard to pin down. Just like customer benefit (for profitability vs. growth, Chapter Two) and sustainable earnings (for short term vs. long term, Chapter Three), diagonal assets are hard to touch and feel. And because such assets and capabilities are so often intangible, they tend to be neglected. Our hypoth-

FIGURE 4.6. THE THREE TYPES OF ORGANIZATIONAL ASSETS AND CAPABILITIES.

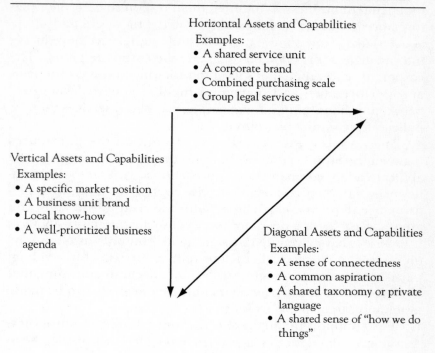

Horizontal Assets and Capabilities
Examples:
- A shared service unit
- A corporate brand
- Combined purchasing scale
- Group legal services

Vertical Assets and Capabilities
Examples:
- A specific market position
- A business unit brand
- Local know-how
- A well-prioritized business agenda

Diagonal Assets and Capabilities
Examples:
- A sense of connectedness
- A common aspiration
- A shared taxonomy or private language
- A shared sense of "how we do things"

esis for why the majority of companies trade at a discount to the sum of their parts is that they are being run in ways that erode diagonal assets; thus, their efforts to create horizontal value tend to undermine their efforts to create vertical value, and vice versa. In particular, there are two traps that companies fall into that have this effect.

THE AUTONOMY TRAP

The tools for increasing what we have called vertical value are well known and widely used. First, you split the company into as many reasonably self-standing units as you reasonably can. You then "decentralize," meaning that you set up within each unit all the functions—human resources, IT, operations, finance, marketing, and so on—that a self-standing entity would have. You call these "business units." You give them lots of authority. You set up incentives that mirror the rewards they would receive if they were stand-alone, independent businesses. You hold them responsible for their performance just as the capital markets would if they were traded separately. Finally, you remove overhead and interference by reducing intermediate layers between them and the corporate parent. The corporate center then limits itself to reviewing business unit plans and performance and managing highly selective "synergies" between business units—for example, via shared services units or policies for coordinating purchasing.

These tools create a clear line of sight on the differences between the business units within the company. They improve the ability to adapt companywide approaches according to those differences. And they create an effective context for motivating performance improvement. The benefits are clear: if you know you are responsible for a decision, you will usually care more about it; if superiors have given up decision rights, you will waste less time on internal politics; smaller teams reduce the risk of free riding; performance measurement can be more accurate, meaning that leaders can use more precise incentives; decisions can be made faster and can be made closer to the customer.[8]

The common theme here is the aim to increase autonomy. Autonomy—the right to self-government—increases the degree to which business unit managers can shape their business to its market conditions, which in turn can increase its performance, in particular its revenue growth. Lloyds TSB's former chief executive and then chairman, Brian Pitman, recalls a powerful positive consequence of the decentralization he oversaw at the bank: "It leads to new ideas. We never used to have a strategy for aircraft leasing before we had a business unit for aircraft leasing!"

But the autonomy model increases the risk of duplicated activity and normally creates larger spans of control. Perhaps most important, the more you free up the parts to act independently in pursuit of their own performance, the more they will cite "accountability" as a defense from the "interference" that adding horizontal value requires. Managers of "empowered" business units will—and do—push back against any form of interference or loss of authority and possession of any and all activities that might impinge on their perceived ability to improve the performance of their individual businesses. They are quick to equate accountability (being responsible for outputs) with authority (having decision rights over inputs). And they are quick to equate authority with possession—running their inputs themselves.

Matt Barrett, chairman of Barclays, isn't a fan of the culture of autonomy: "The whole 'Thanks and see you next year' and 'I want to do my own thing' and 'if it doesn't work you can fire me' attitude really gets me. I already know I can fire you. That's no comfort at all. It's not actually very helpful. Yes, you'll walk the plank first, but I'll be sent down it after you."

Alcan's former CEO Travis Engen argues that the concept of business unit autonomy challenges the very existence of the company itself. "What crime is there in knowing something about your business?" he says. "Why should a company exist if it doesn't know anything more about its businesses than the capital markets?"

The trap is that increasing autonomy in order to increase performance makes adding horizontal value harder. Autonomy soon creates barriers to sharing and cooperating. A culture of autonomy erodes a company's diagonal assets.

But the desire for autonomy is real. Bob Walter, chairman of Cardinal Health, would fight as hard as anyone else for his independence if he headed a business unit: "As an entrepreneur, there are certain things I honor: independence and speed of decision making and execution. How can I ask a manager running a company that we acquire to now come to a bunch of meetings and be Mr. Corporate Citizen?" This view was echoed by Dow Jones chairman Peter Kann: "The best people tend to be those that value independence, perhaps even above power. As a result, people who are attracted to the center often tend not to be as good as people in the business units."

THE CENTRALIZATION TRAP

It is generally accepted that you can effect better performance of the parts by creating more autonomy. So too is the idea that improving the performance of the whole requires *constraining* autonomy in the pursuit of a collective benefit. Hence the tools most commonly used for increasing what we have called horizontal value include combining smaller units into larger ones, centralizing the main functional responsibilities into shared units to remove duplication, limiting the authority (e.g., for capital expenditure) of the business units, standardizing policies in areas where there is an important collective benefit, adjusting business unit responsibilities and rewards to account for their membership in a wider enterprise, and adding intermediate levels of oversight and coordination to make collective benefits actually happen.

Centralization—the aggregation of functional accountability at a higher level in the company—is the common theme. It is used in an attempt to achieve economies of scale and greater skills through specialization, for instance by attracting better talent into various functions such as finance, IT, HR, and marketing than individual businesses might be able to attract on their own. Sometimes the aim of centralization is simply to reduce costs.

The centralization model suffers from a greater weight of required coordination than the autonomy, or "portfolio," model and thus creates an in-built tendency to increase the number of layers in the organization. It can blur accountabilities, as business managers can argue that their own performance is too dependent on that of the central units for their businesses to be held accountable for performance. The pressure often builds to sharpen responsibilities, act more nimbly, reduce layers, and access underexploited benefits of customizing to the differences between each business.

Textron CEO Lewis Campbell urges caution in relying on centralization. "One thing you have to watch out for is the tendency for the people running central functions to focus more on their efficiency rather than on their value to their customers—the businesses. That was a problem at one time when I was at General Motors. The assembly division became so powerful that they started telling the divisions what they could and couldn't do with their models. It was all about their efficiency rather than what the divisions wanted in order to satisfy their customers who bought their cars. Central functions can lose sight of their missions."

BP's John Browne has a similar reservation:

There is a constant quest for perfection on every axis. There is always a desire to standardize—for example, the heads of functions saying that the solution is central procurement. It may be a neater solution. But I say let's talk about the impact on decision making. We could probably purchase everything properly and save money that way. But would we be purchasing the right things? The sum of the local optimums is greater than the global optimum. It is not something that is amenable to global certainty. It is important to allow the right amount of freedom to innovate. This is a very big self-healing mechanism. I don't believe you can be insightful enough to coordinate the whole thing centrally. It is very easy to identify horizontal value analytically, but it is harder to identify what is lost vertically.

Centralization suffers from the opposite risk of autonomy. Because it relies on compulsion to achieve horizontal value, centralization can damage the motivation of individual businesses to perform better and can create too much distance between where decisions are made and where the consequences of those decisions are felt. It can also reduce the willingness of businesses to share good ideas voluntarily. Centralization can easily create diagonal liabilities rather than assets.

The Organizational Seesaw

Companies that fall into one of the two traps—of autonomy or centralization—often end up oscillating between different organizational models. Almost one in three executives in our survey said their companies tended to swing between a focus on the whole and a focus on the individual parts. One in four said their companies tended to swing between centralization and decentralization.

Companies move from one to the other with high levels of predictability: adopting one model, attempting to deal with its deficiencies by amending it to move further toward the other model, eventually abandoning large parts of it and moving completely to the other model, then trying to cope with a new set of problems, and so on. Along the way, the same pivotal activities and the same unfortunate people are routinely centralized, decentralized, and recentralized—for example, marketing, planning, and procurement.

There are those who hold that the tendency of companies to see-saw between centralization and decentralization is simply the natural evolution of their development—a form of "balancing" the two over time. We see much of this seesawing as being both unnecessary and ultimately debilitating. It signals that a company is trapped in the tension between whole (horizontal value) and parts (vertical value).

THE MATRIX SOLUTION

Some companies try to achieve a stable solution through an amalgam of organizational models. These attempts have usually been ill fated. They fall down over the difficulty of keeping accountabilities clear and the sheer effort required to keep the wheels turning. Swiss-Swedish engineering group Asea Brown Boveri (ABB) was for years frequently cited as creating a viable "matrix" that addresses the challenge. It split itself into thirteen hundred operating companies with a further subdivision of five thousand profit centers, each with an average of around thirty-five employees. Each operating company had a dual reporting line: one a country head (for example, Germany) and another the global product area (for example, transport). Both bosses had a say in performance evaluations and compensation, and in this way "strategies" for the different dimensions of the business—global and local—were developed and implemented. Whether you treat ABB as a brave pioneer or as proof that such a model is unsustainable, it is hard to deny that the resources the company required to keep the matrix functioning were enormous. Large amounts of money, IT investment, executive time, travel, and goodwill were thrown at making the matrix work. Such matrix models will always come with the challenge of overlapping accountabilities and a huge coordination task. The resources and mechanisms needed to keep things going are at best expensive; at worst they confuse accountabilities and slow the organization down. At ABB, a regional structure was eventually put in place at the top level of the company, eliminating the matrix.

This is not to say that compromise solutions cannot work. But solutions based on formal structure do not address the fundamental difficulty. Managing the tension revolves around granting autonomy and denying it. It soon becomes a case of autonomy, line of sight, and activity here, and lack of autonomy, blind spots, and an inability to act there. Companies find themselves in a familiar situation: the efforts to increase performance vertically often serve to decrease performance horizontally, and vice versa. Like adding slack to stimulate growth and removing it to increase profitability, or bringing forward investment to improve long-term performance and delaying or reducing investment to improve short-term performance, this is another instance of a common problem: using tools with exactly opposing effects to try to hit two objectives. The means to induce one are harmful to the other. Trying to achieve better performance on both rarely results in good performance on either.

Absent a solution to the two traps of autonomy and centralization, all organizational models contain the seeds of their own failure.

WHAT THE LEADER CAN DO

You have risen through the ranks from running one unit to running several. You know that what it takes to succeed in your new role will be different from what it took in your previous role. You suspect that your units are better off being run by you than not, but you know that you can do more to increase their performance both individually and collectively.

You worry about being caught between the trap of increasing autonomy to increase individual performance and the trap of centralizing authority to increase your performance as a whole. The idea of diagonal assets is interesting in concept, but feels a bit vague in practice. So what can you do to grow vertical and horizontal value at the same time—and make the whole of your business more than just its standalone parts?

CREATE MORE CONSEQUENCES FOR NOT "WEARING TWO HATS"

The ability to wear two hats—to represent one's own business and also the company as a whole—needs to be regarded as part of everyone's job. For BP's John Browne, this is part of a broader definition of accountability: "I recognize the behavior: 'Leave me alone to hit my own target; leave me alone to be accountable.' I think it comes down to how you define accountability: account-ability for what? You *are* accountable. Indeed you are the sole per-son accountable for your area because you have to bring accountability down to one person. But because you are part of a bigger team, your accountability is to perform against an objective assessment of your contribution to the team. Managers must han-dle two jobs at once. And if you signal that you expect it, they will."

There should be clear consequences for an individual's per-formance in striving to add value vertically and horizontally. At Gillette, Jim Kilts instituted a grading system designed to give feed-back to his top managers on how well they were working both indi-vidually and as a team.[9] At the end of each year, the executive team grades the quality of its decision making and its overall perfor-mance as a team. All team members grade themselves. The CEO grades each team member. Each team member grades each of the other team members. And each team member grades the team overall.

Textron's Lewis Campbell believes that acting for one and for all is greatly influenced by how pay is determined: "We now split bonuses into a personal performance rating and a company per-formance rating, and these are multiplied. So if Textron does really well, if a manager has done something on behalf of other busi-nesses that helped them and possibly hurt his business, that man-ager can get a big bonus even if it wasn't a great year for his business."

Matt Barrett of Barclays feels likewise:

Bill Marriott Sr. [the founder of hotel giant Marriott Corp.] had a good line: "You get what you stroke." Incentives matter. Not be-cause people are rats and you need to give them cheese. It's because incentives signal to the organization what matters to you, the leader. There's no point saying "Meeting central standards for customer service is terribly important" if you don't measure and pay on it. Incentives should be used to encourage behavior and to signal what you are trying to achieve. I always start with the belief that if the performance isn't there, it's because I haven't made my expectations clear enough. A manager doesn't get into the shower in the morning and think, "How can I really piss Matt off today?" I have to believe that he doesn't know he's pissing me off. So I have come to assume that if someone isn't performing, it's because I haven't been clear. Businesspeople don't try to fail—they often fail because they haven't understood what was expected of them. And incentives play a big part in setting expectations.

When he became chief executive, Barrett found that his senior executive team was used to a culture where everyone put his or her own business first. He recalls his shock tactics to make it clear that from now on everyone would wear two hats:

> When I'd been at Barclays about six months, I took the ExCo [Barclays' executive committee] out for an away day. Over dinner the night before I said, "I've got some good news: I'm disbanding ExCo." There was a stunned silence around the room. Then the question: "Why?"
>
> I said, "I'm really respectful of your time, and it's not good for any of us to have a series of bilateral meetings with an audience." They all objected. No one wanted to lose the status of being a member of the ExCo. So I said at the end, "You either persuade yourselves that your first job is the co-management of the group and your second job is managing your piece, or I'm disbanding ExCo." I wanted to create a sense of ownership on the high-value-at-stake issues wherever they sat in the organization. It really turned things around. The guys understood I was serious.

WORK TIRELESSLY TO BUILD CONNECTEDNESS

Setting managers' expectations that their role is to add value horizontally as well as vertically—to wear two hats—is the starting point. Leaders need also to actively cultivate "connectedness." This is the single most important factor in getting a company to act as many parts and as one whole at the same time. Connectedness—a sense of shared identity or belonging to the company—is a prime example of a diagonal asset.

As is true of several other topics we have covered in this book, the art of developing a strong sense of connectedness is worth much greater attention than we can give here. But we highlight some of its most important elements: acceptance that accountability is different from autonomy; norms of behavior and a cultural identity for the company; doing real work together; and physical proximity.

"First, leaders need to break the myth that accountability = authority = control," says ABN AMRO's chairman Rijkman Groenink. "It's imperative to instill both a common as well as an individual sense of accountability across the different echelons of an organization. If you don't, as a large company, you can never be anything other than your parts. Take as an example our drive to ensure regional businesses extract the benefits of coordinating between their own consumer, commercial and wholesale operations which had been working in silos. In one country, it worked, in another the going was much tougher as the predominant culture was to say, 'I've got accountability' [read control], which translated into a reluctance to cross to the other side."

Matt Barrett has some characteristically forceful views on the subject:

> The argument that you have to own all the resources is absolute horseshit. One time I was with a group of managers making that argument, so I asked them, "What do you think is the bank's most crucial technology?" People started suggesting mainframes and stuff like that. I let it run. After about half an hour, they said "The telephone—we'd be absolutely stuffed without it; we couldn't survive." Then I asked, "Where's the back office of the telephone? Or light, heat, and power—where's the back office? So you're telling me that the bank's most crucial technology that we absolutely depend on, and that we'd be stuffed without, we don't control? So why do you want to control the other things?" The issue is that while it works, while you pick up the receiver and get a dial tone and the service levels are good, you couldn't care less. What it comes down to is that people want more autonomy and less interference. They want to live in some Elysian Field of no constraints. But no one is in that field.

Setting out and living by behavioral norms that are unique to your company is important to creating the sense of identity that underpins connectedness. At BP there are strong norms, including those of mutual trust, of admitting early when one faces difficulties ("no surprises"), of seeking assistance when needed, of responding positively to requests for help, and of keeping promises about performance. According to John Browne, "You have to work on the behaviors that are critical. For example, it is a standard of behavior here that managers have to consult before making an important decision. You must develop your people according to the culture you want. How people behave depends on the signals you give them."

Cadbury Schweppes has invested considerable effort in identifying and sharing the cultural traits that it expects of its managers. They boil down to the "3 A's": accountable, adaptable, and aggressive. The company links these traits to job descriptions, performance plans, pay, and promotion. Chairman John Sunderland says, "Big companies are like oil tankers: when you turn the levers in one direction it takes a while for the course to correct; but overcorrection is always the risk. To manage the risk, you need to bring people with you on the journey. A strong and shared culture helps you steer the ship, especially when you are trying to navigate towards competing objectives."

Creating a distinct company identity is an essential ingredient for connectedness. Distilling the essence of that identity and publicizing it can help. But if you want people to feel connected with each other, there is no substitute for getting them to do real work together. Franz Humer, chairman and CEO of Roche, feels that what most strengthened his leadership team's sense of connectedness was the decision to work together as a team on high-priority issues that crossed divisional boundaries. His executive team undertook an exercise over several months of agreeing on a "corporate agenda" for the company that identified the top opportunities for the company over the next few years. Humer then assigned different divisional heads the task of leading individual items on their corporate agenda. "It has helped to have everyone at the top of the company work on one common view of the future and how we are going to get there. This is as important as having one common set of incentives. The parts can be on different roads, but they need to be roads that go roughly in the same direction."

Similarly, for Travis Engen, Alcan's former CEO, the shared pursuit of good performance on environment, health, and safety (EH&S) has been important to tying the company together. "Improving EH&S improves productivity, and getting it wrong is very costly—so it's important to performance. But beyond that it helps build morale and create pride in the company. EH&S always scores highest on importance in employee surveys. It's part of doing right by society and being seen to do so. Having all of us working on it binds the company together."

In building connectedness, physical proximity can't be underestimated. Dow Jones's Peter Kann recalls: "When I became publisher for *The Wall Street Journal Asia* early in my career, it was very 'siloed': news, production, ad sales, circulation never talked to each other even though everything they did had an effect on each other. I was the first to bring together all of these into one room of a warehouse in Asia. It worked, and I brought this model back with me to the United States." Likewise, Xerox's Anne Mulcahy argues that "touch-based leadership"—direct contact with and closeness to the different constituencies within the company—is critical to getting the most out of everyone.

A strong sense of connectedness, however fostered, is perhaps *the* primary diagonal asset. Without it, leaders will find it very hard to convert the expectation that their managers "wear two hats" into a reality.

IF YOU CAN'T CHANGE THE PEOPLE, CHANGE THE PEOPLE

The ultimate sanction in the search for connectedness is to remove the people who don't perform to the behavioral standards expected of them. General Electric's well-known solution to the tricky problem of what to do with those managers who produce financial results but don't exude the values and norms of the company is simple: fire them.

How do you deal with managers who say (in effect), "Just tell me what you want and I'll give it to you, but leave me alone"? Travis Engen is clear: "I find someone else." John Sunderland shares that view: "Sometimes you need to change the people: you often find that people new to the job will accept the new rules much more easily than the incumbents."

Nothing in our experience of watching companies wrestle with making the parts and the whole more valuable at the same time would say to do anything different. Mastering the tension of whole vs. parts may require you to have in your manager population a greater proportion of people who value achievement and affiliation and fewer of those valuing power and control than in the general population. Todd Stitzer of Cadbury Schweppes is clear about what he expects of his managers: "People need to be able to work across business units and functions without ego. The people who succeed are those who earn authority rather than demand it."

To conclude that an individual has become a diagonal liability rather than an asset—and that there is nothing you can do about it—should be the last resort. But there is no more powerful way to make clear your expectations for how the team should work together than by changing its composition.

TELL YOUR CUSTOMER BENEFIT STORY

A compelling story of how the company is going to give more benefits to its customers than will competitors is another important diagonal asset. Properly constructed, a sincere belief in a higher-order purpose can create a sense of mutual belonging that has relevance to each part of the company. To Andrew Cosslett, CEO of InterContinental Hotels Group, this is an overlooked need that leaders must address. "There is a great unspoken imperative in leadership, and that's engagement. People need to know why we are here and how we are going to win. Asking them to be motivated by hitting financial goals just doesn't cut it. They need a higher-order quest. Without a compelling story, leadership becomes exhortation."

Most people don't get excited about advancing the interests of shareholders. Roberto Goizueta, chief executive of Coca-Cola during one of its most successful eras—from 1980 until his untimely death in 1997—was famous for saying that he thought about how to improve shareholder value from the time he woke up until the time he went to bed. Not many other people do. "Shareholder value" or financial goals simply do not travel well down organizations. Higher-order purposes give more meaning to people's efforts than does making money for owners, or even for themselves.[10]

When Cosslett ran the U.K. chocolate business of Cadbury Schweppes, his message to his troops was that their quest was to give consumers more "moments of pleasure"—the consumer benefit that the firm's confectionery products provided. At InterContinental, Cosslett evangelizes the mission of increasing benefits to both of its customers—hotel owners (because most of InterContinental's hotels are franchised) as well as hotel guests: "In addition to guest pleasure, we have to be clear how we are going to grow the value of hotels to their owners. It has to be part of the strategy—that we are doing things in their best interests. At my first management conference as the new CEO, I said there will be no flip charts and no PowerPoint presentation. I just told stories. And I started off by bringing in twenty owners onto the stage and making people have breakfast with them. The message was 'Now we are going to listen to these people.' Our job is to work with our hotel owners—our customers—to make them more successful."

Cosslett has made an internal brand out of his story about how InterContinental will win: "360."

> I was looking for something that would organize people's efforts. I was sitting at my desk doodling around our goal of adding sixty thousand beds within three years. And there it was: 360—a circle. It works on so many different levels. It's about bringing the globe together for travelers. It's about bringing our hotel owners inside the circle—really listening to them and understanding their needs. It's about making a 360-degree change in your own individual behavior. It's about a collaborative culture, and so on. Three-sixty is not about the number—it's about connecting people with what we are in business to do. And it has consequences. For example, it gives us more license to seek common brand standards. People understand that we have to meet certain brand standards because people travel everywhere and expect some consistency.

Barclays chief executive, John Varley, argues that creating a sense of purpose around providing benefits to customers helps leaders in their efforts to overcome the political challenges of acting as one company as well as many businesses.

> Our customers certainly look to us to be one organization as well as many. I'll give you an example. We hosted a lunch for a number of important corporate banking clients. One household-name chair-

man came over with about five or six other chairmen and CEOs. He was an important corporate client and we had a good corporate relationship with him. What became clear was that we had got things badly wrong in serving his family on the personal banking side. He made his views quite plain and it was clear that the corporate relationship was on the point of being irretrievably lost because of his personal relationship with us. Managers understand the logic of acting as one company or as many if it is based on what is important to customers. So, an important way of managing this tension, as well as the others, is to insist that we all spend more time with customers. I have set myself the challenge of having customer contact every day. The message is: "if I can do it, so can you."

Telling the "right" story is an art rather than a science. It should be generic enough to be espoused by different parts in different ways but specific enough to be meaningful, motivating, and unifying. It should be about specific customer benefit, not generic "customer focus." And naturally it is not just a "story"—it has to be a genuine and factual view about how the company will win in its market. Any such story has a half-life. But a compelling story or sense of purpose around customer benefit can be a diagonal asset for the company: it binds the whole together without undermining the parts, and it motivates the performance of the individual parts without constraining horizontal value.

CENTRALIZE WHEN YOU DECENTRALIZE . . . AND VICE VERSA

The leaders of most large companies arrive at a stage where they feel the need to decentralize: to break the company up into smaller pieces. The motivations are various. Often leaders feel that such changes will increase the metabolic rate of the company, make it more adaptable to its external environment or better able to exploit differences across its products and markets.

In 2000, Matt Barrett used decentralization as a central plank in improving the performance of Barclays. He broke the bank's five divisions into twenty-three business units, appointed general managers for each of them, and gave them greater responsibilities for developing and implementing "strategy." The heads of divisions became "span breakers" between the CEO and the business units, with the role of acting on behalf of the chief executive in overseeing the business units rather than acting as the head of a fully formed and staffed organizational unit. Barrett says his intention was "to transform the company from a fleet of five aircraft carriers, with all the attendant inflexibility and immobility that goes with big ships, into a flotilla of twenty-three motorboats that are very agile, very maneuverable."

But this wasn't the usual decentralization initiative: Barrett also centralized at the same time. He consolidated head-office functions at the divisional and subdivisional levels into a single "group head office." He brought in new heads of the central functions with a mandate to raise groupwide standards in their areas. The executive team agreed on a single, overarching long-term goal for economic profit for the company that cascaded to each business unit. They launched an extensive exercise to develop and disseminate a single company strategy. The strategy included "decision rules" within which each business unit had to operate, for instance ensuring that their strategies aligned with the new corporate direction or with the corporate brand. A new "management model," with common standards, a common language, and a common step-by-step method, was introduced; it formed the basis for much-expanded executive development programs. Corporate managers dedicated much time and effort to developing new cultural values for the company. If this was decentralization, you might have been forgiven for mistaking it for centralization.

Barrett's motivations for the changes were various: to increase his line of sight on the company; to reap the benefits of focus enjoyed by the "monoline" competitors, such as specialist credit card companies; to capture economies of scale; and to build capabilities. "At the same time that I decentralized, I strengthened the corporate center. Your ability to decentralize is a function of your capabilities and expertise. You have to preserve the standards, controls, policy, values. Big companies are corporations, not confederations. Federal governments know what activities are reserved to them. They keep control of fiscal policy, monetary policy, environment, defense. Companies must keep a firm hold of strategic planning, cultural values, controls, and the measurement of performance."

In our experience, the most successful decentralization efforts have been those, like Barclays', where there is a lot of concurrent centralization—for example, decentralizing decision authority but at the same time centralizing goals, culture, strategy development standards, and top manager development. Appropriately managed, such changes are consistent with achieving vertical and horizontal value at the same time.

Financial services group BBVA has recently looked to "empower" its regional businesses in Europe and the Americas, but has decided to, at the same time, strengthen the group's central control in certain areas. According to José Ignacio Goirigolzarri, president and chief operating officer: "We come from a past of acting within a single harmonized model for going to market. There arrives a moment when you realize that increasing diversity will improve performance. But in this process we have decided that there are two things that make BBVA worth more than just the sum of the parts: our ability to continuously create revenue synergy across the group which rely on our brand and on our systems of know-how transfer; and the cost synergies we derive from our four shared services: compliance and prcedures, funding, IT, and people. We will, if anything, be increasing our grip in these areas. The local CEO received support and needs to be aligned with the Group in any of them. To make decentralization work, very strong leadership from the center is needed."

BP's John Browne agrees: "When there's a performance crisis, centralizing is the immediate response, and when things are going very well, uncontrolled decentralization is the response. You have to be in the middle. I'm afraid it's the old tight-loose point—it's terribly old-fashioned, I know. If you can pick the things you are tight on and what you are loose on, and stick with it, that's the answer."

BP goes to great lengths to define what the company will be tight on and what it will be loose on. It delegates "powers and limitations" to its business units. These are tight on such things as corporate reputation, the BP brand, financial targets, and cultural standards for behavior. It is loose on much else.

The implication is that the most successful centralization will be one with a lot of concurrent decentralization. For example, a company that creates shared services units for certain well-specified services such as payroll processing or logistics might also grant a *greater*—not a lesser—degree of freedom to the businesses to seek out and use alternative suppliers of those services outside the company.

There are tremendous stresses in putting this principle into practice, and the argument between decentralization and centralization is never ending. But for that argument to be more fruitful, the question should be not which one to choose but how to embrace both at the same time.[11]

Act Both "Top-Down" and "Bottom-Up"

The principle of seeking creative tension between the whole and the parts also applies to a company's processes, not just its organizational structure.[12] Cardinal Health complements the more traditional "bottom-up" planning processes—whereby each business unit proposes a plan, and the company's plan is largely the sum of its business units' plans—with a "top-down" process that sets strategic direction for the company as a whole and, in so doing, for the individual parts. The executive committee identifies a series of issues and opportunities that cross or transcend the business units and calls them "horizontals." For instance, the company's approach to unbranded generics is relevant to several of its businesses. Generics are therefore an ongoing focal point for companywide ("top-down") activity that complements and reinforces the efforts of any business within Cardinal where generics are important. Accordingly, Cardinal is able to add value to its businesses through both the more traditional bottom-up, business-by-business processes and these top-down "horizontal" issues and opportunities.

As the leader, you should ask yourself which has the upper hand in your company's processes: bottom-up or top-down? In the search for better-performing parts and a better-performing whole, having a strong element of both is crucial.

Ask Whether You Should Standardize Rather Than Centralize

Considered by some to be the first conglomerate, New England textile maker Textron started to diversify in 1953 by buying a maker of car-seat cushioning material. Today it earns $10 billion in revenue making products ranging from helicopters and aircraft to golf cars, cable installation systems and lawnmowers. Textron takes a very different approach to the task of adding horizontal value than the traditional "centralize" option.

Says CEO Lewis Campbell,

> The issue we face is that the corporate center wants every business unit to be the same, but every business unit wants to be different. I want to keep every business unit focused on customers and to be state-of-the-art on common activities, for example: payroll, health care, six sigma, supply chain management, talent development, IT, receivables, accounts payable. This can be done either by centralizing or through "commonizing"—adopting the same language, textbook, tools, and so on, without actually creating a central function. Every business has "core" and "context" processes and activities. Context processes are common across all the businesses, like getting the paychecks out on time. Core processes are specific to the customer value added equation in each business. They drive the value of that business. I look for the group to add value to the context processes by either centralizing them or "commonizing" them and to focus the business units on becoming customer satisfaction machines.

Textron has applied both approaches—centralizing and standardizing—to these "context" processes. It has centralized a number of functions, taking all responsibility for them away from the business units. Thus it has made payroll processing a central function and outsourced others. For example, it reduced the number of data centers from eighty-eight, which were internally operated, to two, which are now operated by a third party. It also cut the number of health insurance plans from 154 to just one.

In its manufacturing processes, however, Textron takes the "standardize" approach to adding horizontal value. It uses common "enterprise management processes" such as Six Sigma, Lean Manufacturing, and integrated supply chain management. A Textron "transformation leadership team" reports to Campbell and meets quarterly to share best practices in these areas. Each business has a representative from the business for each process.

Textron seeks to build what it calls a "networked enterprise": a portfolio of businesses with no shared customers, costs, or competitors, but with shared enterprise management processes. Says Campbell, "We're now at a stage where we can take specialists in many of our enterprise management processes out of any business and drop them into another business, and they can be immediately effective."

The whole concept of centralization is changing, according to Roche's Franz Humer: "The old functional definition of centralization had a location in mind. In a globalizing world perhaps the word 'centralizing' is no longer applicable. Particularly with IT developments, you can run things 'centrally' but not in the center."

Centralizing standards rather than functions doesn't make the problems of central functions disappear at the stroke of a pen. And there is an inevitable tendency for the organizational vehicles that are charged with facilitating common approaches to morph into functions. Thus, what started out as a temporary assignment gathers organizational momentum and seeks to establish itself on a more permanent basis. As Campbell says, "You have to be careful that the resource you set up centrally to drive this is shut down once the state of the art has been picked up by the business units. This is harder to do than it seems."

Textron's approach may be the only realistic one given its portfolio of businesses. A central manufacturing function really wouldn't make sense. Yet standardization rather than centralization might actually have the most benefit for portfolios that are *less* diverse than Textron's.

USE DIAGONAL ASSETS TO GUIDE YOUR ACQUISITIONS AND PORTFOLIO DIVERSITY

When facing the challenge of making acquisitions pay off, leaders of most large companies look through the lens of horizontal value. They ask themselves how they can lower costs and increase revenues through combining activities. Financial buyers—such as private equity firms—look through the lens of vertical value. They ask how they can improve the management of the business they acquire to exploit an "undermanagement bargain." It will be no surprise to learn that we think the right question to ask is how a company can do both at the same time.

As we noted in Chapter Two, the odds of acquisitions are in favor of sellers rather than buyers. Neither synergy as classically meant (horizontal value) nor undermanagement (vertical value) is likely to be sufficient to make M&A pay. To beat the odds, you need to create new horizontal *and* vertical value through your acquisitions. This means that diagonal assets are critical to making growth by acquisition work. We are convinced that the reason successful acquisitions by corporate buyers are so rare is that the focus is on synergy rather than on diagonal assets.

Textron guides its acquisitions by concentrating on its diagonal capability of continuously improving manufacturing. Lewis Campbell says, "The ability to 'commonize' some processes, centralize others, and focus the businesses on their core processes gives you the basis for tangible benefits from making acquisitions. So instead of being woolly about 'synergies,' we can be specific about how we, Textron, will add value to the company we are acquiring."

To be a true diagonal asset, such capabilities have to be better than those available on the open market. If Textron is only as good at Six Sigma, Lean Manufacturing, and supply chain management as anyone else, there is no true source of advantage and no compelling rationale for ongoing growth through acquisition.

This is where portfolio diversity—the extent of your company's participation across markets—may come in. There may be an advantage to more portfolio concentration if it increases the chances that what management claims to be diagonal assets really are. For instance, operational improvement might be a generic capability. But operational improvement in defense industries or in asset-intensive businesses might not. Says Campbell, "If you have businesses that have the same operational characteristics in terms of customers to be served, products to be made, employees to be paid, and receivables to be managed, you have more potential to manage the tension between whole and parts."

Conversely, if your diagonal assets don't apply to all your businesses, then you should consider divesting. For Reuters, its information management capability—combining data and news—is a good example of a diagonal asset. It allows what has horizontal value (it is much cheaper for many businesses to share the costs of developing news and data) to be easily converted into vertical value—for data and news to be combined and priced in different ways by different businesses for their own individual benefit.

It is a real diagonal asset when the information has strong economic benefits to the business. This was not clearly the case with one of Reuters's businesses: Instinet, a regulated electronic marketplace for equities. Reuters judged that Instinet did not reap enough benefit from the overall company's information management capability. It was divested. CEO Glocer argues, "You need to ask yourself whether you can identify a particular reason why $2 + 2 = 5$."

Diagonal assets are a company's best source for making the whole worth more than the sum of the parts. They should therefore be the guide for both acquisitions and decisions on portfolio diversity. The concept of synergy that guides many, perhaps most, corporate acquisitions is by its very nature slanted toward considering the overlap between company operations and the opportunity to create horizontal value. True synergy comes from exploiting and extending diagonal assets.

WHOLE *AND* PARTS

Companies often overlook the assets and capabilities that help them convert horizontal value into vertical value, and vice versa. But it is these diagonal assets that are central to the ability of a company to meet the daunting challenge of being more than simply the sum of its parts.

Managers lose sight of diagonal assets because they fixate on formal structure: creating autonomy or centralization in their organizational designs. If a company uses these approaches alone, horizontal and vertical value soon end up substituting for each other: vertical value is increased by increasing autonomy; horizontal value is increased by decreasing autonomy. This is a sure recipe for staying trapped in the whole vs. parts tension.

But there is something troubling about the conventional wisdom that sits behind these two approaches: that autonomy is the only route to adding vertical value and that centralizing—which constrains autonomy—is the only route to adding horizontal value.

It seems odd to believe that owners and overseers of business units can add vertical value to them only by increasing their autonomy—that is, by replicating the conditions of not being owned and overseen in the first place. By implication, ownership brings no vertical value. This seems doubtful. Although increasing autonomy is certainly one path to make the parts produce better results, there is no reason to believe that it is the *only* path. If instead of increasing autonomy, companies dedicate themselves to developing and enforcing standards in areas where they have an inherent advantage in owning the businesses they own, they can create vertical value in ways that cannot be achieved outside the company. The company may bring experience in setting standards for performance that create the right behavior. It may be better at selecting, developing, and assigning people. Or it may have insight into how best to achieve performance—for example, how to develop effective strategies. These three standards—for performance, for people, and for strategy—can be powerful tools for increasing vertical value well beyond what businesses could achieve if they were independently owned or owned by another company.

This could explain the performance of highly successful diversified companies—such as GE, Berkshire Hathaway, and KKR—with limited opportunities (and appetite) for adding value horizontally. The main advantage of this alternative path to increasing vertical value is that it does not at the same time act as a barrier to increasing performance horizontally. It does not create the differentiated cultures and the "accountability excuse" that come with the autonomy model and that block a company's ability to generate horizontal value.

Increasing the autonomy of the parts is usually seen by the corporate center as the *only* path to vertical value. In a similar way, they see constraining the parts' autonomy as the *only* path to improving horizontal value. Goold and Campbell have termed this "parenting bias"—the belief that synergy between business units will be captured only by forcing them to cooperate.[13] In truth, as they argue, business units have every reason to forge links with each other when those links will make their own business more successful. After all, they regularly team up with outside suppliers, customers, or joint venture partners. They'll even cooperate with direct competitors if it's in their interest. The authors cite the example of the music industry, in which the four leading companies often share the same CD-manufacturing plant in countries with sales too small to support four separate plants. If there are genuine mutual benefits to such cooperation and few obstacles to sharing, appropriately motivated and capable business units will seek them out.

Increasing the business units' motivation for performance and removing obstacles to their cooperation may well be a better approach to adding value horizontally than forcing coordination through centralization and in effect constraining their autonomy. This means relying less on organizational structure—such as hierarchy, intermediate layers, centralizing functions, and the pooling of authority—and more on diagonal assets such as connectedness, cultural norms, and common aspirations for performance.

QUESTIONS TO CONSIDER FOR YOUR COMPANY

1. Is our company worth more than the stand-alone sum of its parts? What explains the discount or premium?
2. What are the most important assets and capabilities that we have as a company: vertical, horizontal, and diagonal?
3. How good are we at improving performance vertically without undermining it horizontally? Are we avoiding the trap of increasing autonomy to increase individual business performance?
4. How good are we at improving performance horizontally without undermining it vertically? Are we avoiding the trap of centralizing to increase collective business performance?
5. Which ideas for what the leader can do might be most useful for us?

Ideas for What the Leader Can Do
to Strengthen Diagonal Assets

- Create more consequences for not "wearing two hats."
- Work tirelessly to build connectedness.
- If you can't change the people, change the people.
- Tell your customer benefit story.
- Centralize when you decentralize . . . and vice versa.
- Act both "top-down" and "bottom-up."
- Ask whether you should standardize rather than centralize.
- Use diagonal assets to guide your acquisitions and portfolio diversity.

Chapter Five

Breaking the Corporate Cycle

If you chase two rabbits, both will escape.
RUSSIAN PROVERB

Silence and look out, we shall catch both hen and chicks.
SPANISH PROVERB

In writing this book, we asked twenty chairmen and chief executives of some of the world's largest and best-known companies about the three tensions, and about the management practices they found helpful and not so helpful in overcoming them. All of them recognized the three tensions as familiar, if not very welcome, friends. Many talked of the pressures from their various constituencies that made the tensions even more acute. These included the differing concerns of business unit and functional managers ("the quest for perfection on every axis"), the pressures from the board ("Now that we're producing tons of cash, they're putting a lot of pressure on me to make acquisitions, and I'm finding myself having to resist"), and the scrutiny from regulators ("Sarbanes-Oxley brings a centralizing tendency that's causing enormous tension").

Most of all, they felt pressure from the investor community for results today. Tom Glocer of Reuters recounted a particularly telling example:

We recently announced what we called Core Plus—a strategy to get
us into a new growth phase. The stock was trading around 390, and
after the announcement the stock fell to 350. It came back later to
over 400 as investors started to see the sense in the strategy. But
there was a short-term fall. I had an extraordinary meeting with
one fund manager. It was obvious he was very angry. He shouted at
me: "Why did you go and do this? You're going to ruin my quarter!" I explained why we were confident the strategy would be in
the interests of growing the value of the company. He then said,
"Look, I have no doubt at all that the strategy is in the best long-
term interests of Reuters and its shareholders. My problem is that
my investors judge me quarterly." I was dumbfounded that he was
that explicit.[1]

Some leaders felt certain tensions more keenly than others. ("I
worry about profitability/growth and short term/long term but
not really about whole/parts." "Profitability and growth isn't much
of a tension for us at all." "There comes a size where the main issue
is parts versus whole." "I think the three are in the right order of
hierarchy: profitability and growth comes first.") Consistent with
the pressure for results that they feel from investors, the tension of
today vs. tomorrow was the topic of as much as half of their comments. This was followed by parts vs. whole, with profitability vs.
growth just behind. Some felt that the tension that matters most
depends on the industry ("The tensions for a car company are different from those for a bank") or on a company's life stage ("Prof-
itability/growth and short term/long term are much more relevant
to start-ups"). One wondered aloud how best to cope with a company whose different businesses face different tensions.

Several chief executives pointed to other "tensions," such as
between change and constancy, between short-term share price
and growth, between risk and return, and between near-term success and continuous improvement. "Life is all about tensions" was
a comment from more than one. They talked of tensions between
"living life for today and living for tomorrow," between "not spoil-
ing your children and not brutalizing them," and even between
"marrying an ugly spouse and being jealous."

Most saw mastering tensions as *the* critical capability of leadership ("You have to be able to walk and chew gum at the same

time.") But no one saw any easy answers. Most agreed that in concept "the answer" is simple, but that "simple in concept" doesn't mean "easy in practice." A few thought that in seeking an answer we were chasing after the philosopher's stone or the Holy Grail.

Our portrayal of the corporate cycle (Figure 1.1) as the combined effect of the three tensions provoked broad recognition: "This is *exactly* what happens"; "I recognize this behavior completely." Many added their perspectives on the leadership behaviors and management practices that pull companies into the cycle. Some pointed to the tendency to swing the pendulum away from one's predecessor[2] ("Business leaders are worse than politicians in blaming the previous incumbent") or the difficulty that leaders have in letting go of methods that have worked in the past ("It's not just the tools that cause cyclical behavior—it's managers who can't let go of tools that worked for them in the past") or the scarring effect of previous mistakes ("What one considers the most important objective is often shaped by past near-death experiences").

THE CORPORATE CYCLE REVISITED

We have seen that some of the causes of the corporate cycle are unavoidable: competitive forces, the economic cycle, the typical life span of a business from start-up to maturity, the many different orientations of managers, and the political behavior inside any organization. These forces are powerful enough as they stand. But our focus has been on what is avoidable. The difference between the unavoidable and the avoidable is the difference between a great batting average in theory and a great batting average in practice.

Over the last three chapters we have discussed six traps—two per tension. Any one of them can catch and hold a company in the corporate cycle. They encourage companies to lose sight of the common bonds that make opposing objectives achievable at the same time. What makes the traps so troublesome is that they all stem from sensible practices. Combine these with the unavoidable laws of economics and forces of human nature, and the effect can be insidious (Figure 5.1).

FIGURE 5.1. THE CORPORATE CYCLE REVISITED.

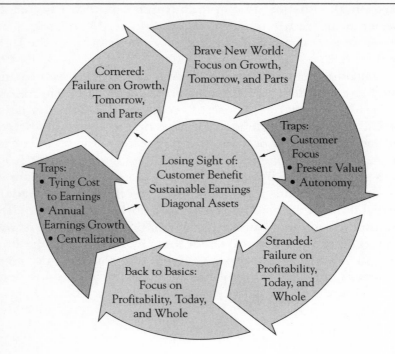

For companies trapped in the cycle, the Brave New World phase means going for growth, by building for tomorrow and freeing up their individual parts. The obvious path to more growth is increasing "customer focus." But this behavior leads the unsuspecting to lose sight of customer benefit—to suffer from "benefit blindness." Sooner or later—without enough customer benefit—the costs needed to "push" revenue growth mount up, and without enough scope for high prices, profitability is undermined.

As they invest in the hope of future rewards, managers are lulled into incurring excess investment—perhaps because they have convinced themselves of the "hockey stick" forecasts or because they have invested when the coffers were full and earnings targets met, rather than because the investment case was robust. Sooner or later, investment returns are sufficiently disappointing to shut down the flow of funds.

As they increase the autonomy of their parts—particularly to stimulate new revenue growth—leaders unwittingly erect barriers to increasing the performance of the whole. The opportunities to reduce duplication and increase coordination build up as fast as the diagonal assets needed to capture them are eroded. Sooner or later, the benefits from greater autonomy are overwhelmed by the costs and missed opportunities.

Poor profitability, weak short-term performance, and lack of one-company benefits shift the weight of priority toward a Back to Basics phase. In the bid to become more profitable, managers peg costs back to earnings. In the previous good times, bad costs had been allowed to build up; in these bad times, all costs are cut—both good and bad. Sooner or later—without enough good costs to support customer benefit—it becomes harder to grow revenues.

As companies try to improve short-term performance, they are tempted to sustain earnings growth by borrowing from the investment that is needed for the future and to squeeze earnings from an aging business model. Sooner or later, managers cross the line from eliminating excess investment to cutting investment that is vital for building tomorrow's business. They let "sustain annual earnings growth" become more important than "grow sustainable earnings."

As companies centralize to capture "synergies," with regard to reducing costs in particular, they create motivational issues for individual parts of the business. The missed opportunities to adapt company approaches to individual markets become glaringly obvious, but the centralized structure makes them hard to capture. Sooner or later, the benefits from centralization are overwhelmed by the costs and missed opportunities.

Stagnant revenue growth, lack of investment for the long term, and underperforming parts shift the weight of priority back toward a new phase of Brave New World—a renewed focus on growth, investing in the future, and improving the individual parts. The Back to Basics phase may have cornered the company, but it has at least filled the coffers enough to fund the next phase of the cycle. . . .

In the corporate cycle, the central conundrum for leaders is that the most effective means they have to improve performance on one objective make performance on the other objective harder to achieve. The strongest tools are also the most divisive.

This is not to say that all companies are trapped so completely in the cycle. Different companies run different risks. But any of the traps hidden within familiar management practices can pull a company into the cycle (Figure 5.2).

CHASING TWO RABBITS

Given the challenge presented by the corporate cycle and the three tensions within it, managers tend to opt for one of two schools of management: one that chooses certain performance objectives over others, and another that calls for "balance."

THE "CHOICES" SCHOOL OF MANAGEMENT

The proverb tells us that if we chase two rabbits, both will escape. So too does much intuition about management. It is not surprising that, faced with the tensions, many business leaders feel the need to make some choices about what performance objectives to put first. If you inherit the leadership of a company that is growing rapidly but that has low standards for profitability, you are tempted to choose profitability improvement as "the number one priority for this company." If the company has a history of excellent results year to year, but faces some potential challenges to its viability in the long term, it would be negligent not to want to give higher priority to building for—and investing in—tomorrow's performance. If the company has strongly performing business units but no history of coordinating across them to anyone's benefit, you might well want to make adding one-company benefits more of a priority. Current performance often shapes current priority.

It is also natural to consider which performance objective within a tension is more valuable than the other. To choose priorities—based on your particular starting point and on what is most

FIGURE 5.2. THE HIDDEN TRAPS THAT KEEP COMPANIES IN THE CORPORATE CYCLE.

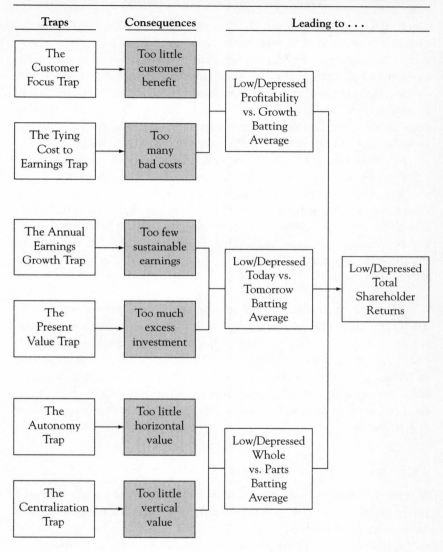

valuable to your business at any point in time—would seem to follow common managerial sense.

Our survey confirmed that most companies do indeed make choices among which performance objectives to put first (Figure 5.3).[3] In fact, only one in three companies place equal emphasis on both objectives within each of the three tensions; the rest prioritize. About 60 percent put profitability improvement ahead of revenue growth, or the reverse; 70 percent emphasize current performance over building for tomorrow's performance, or the reverse; 72 percent put individual performance of the parts ahead of benefits across the whole, or the reverse. Many, perhaps most, companies belong to the "choices" school of management.

Yet everything we have seen suggests that choosing between objectives is traveling hopefully and not a real solution to breaking the corporate cycle and mastering the three tensions. Good performance on one objective does *not* naturally result in good performance on the other. If anything, the odds are in the other direction: it is easier to end up with "either" or "neither" than with "both."

The problem with choosing one performance objective over another is that putting one objective first is a sure way to put the other one last. To choose some objectives over others is to give the corporate cycle another push. Prioritization of *tasks*—for example, marketing over innovation, training over pay, expanding in China over expanding in India—is often good management. Prioritization of *objectives* risks being part of the problem rather than part of the solution.[4]

THE "BALANCE" SCHOOL OF MANAGEMENT

If management cannot be reduced to a science of choices among performance objectives, is it perhaps best thought of as the art of balancing among them?

If incentives, culture, organizational structure, operating procedures, management information, and other tools and technologies—and the people who are best suited to whatever is the task at hand—all divide neatly along the lines of different performance objectives, why not divide, conquer, and then balance? Why not, for example, organize businesses into two camps: those to manage

FIGURE 5.3. THE NORM IS TO CHOOSE.

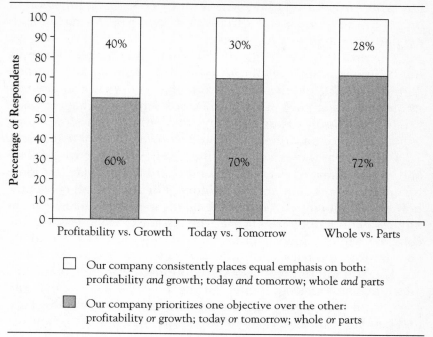

Source: Management survey commissioned with the Economist Intelligence Unit, Mar. 2005. Scope: 191 responses.

for growth and the long term; and those to manage for profitability and the short term? Staffing, pay, structures, processes, and culture could then be designed specifically to maximize performance on a smaller, more coherent set of performance objectives, without having to worry about the other performance objectives at the same time. The many different performance objectives can then be achieved at the total company level by achieving some in one part of the business and the others in other parts.

This approach appeals to many deeply held management intuitions that we have covered earlier: that companies naturally have growth stages and profitability stages; that some people are "explorers" of the future and others are "exploiters" of the present; that the needs of short-term performance are fundamentally inconsistent with those for building long-term success; that dedication to one objective is always likely to result in better performance than juggling several objectives at once.

The problem is that "divide, conquer, and balance" is simply not coherent at the level of the bedrock of a company: its culture. A culture of risk taking and experimentation does not square easily alongside a culture of standardization and best practice; a culture of execution sits unhappily with a culture of vision; and a culture of autonomy does not fit well with a culture of teamwork.

Certainly at the extremes of the business life cycle—start-up and exit or managed decline—it seems hard to argue against some form of divide, conquer, and balance. For the typical company, however, the attempt to coordinate highly specialized management models all under one roof brings with it some troubling issues. The company's internal mechanisms for ensuring productive "dividing, conquering, and balancing" will always be fraught with difficulty.

And you will remember that we found no evidence that a balanced business leads to higher batting averages: balance between organic and M&A growth, between portfolio focus and diversity, and between exposure to high-growth and high-margin businesses had no or limited effect on batting averages.

Moreover, there is something worrying about the whole philosophy of balance. It can be a bit too quick to lower performance standards: to let "growth businesses" off the hook of worrying about becoming profitable faster, to let profitable businesses claim that their markets are "mature," to excuse short-term performance because investment means that earnings targets will not be hit anyway, to put too little pressure on investment plans to produce results now as well as later, to let local considerations override companywide ones, and to let "acting as one company" excuse underperforming parts. To balance objectives is to limit the achievement of one in order to achieve a bit more of the other. It is to average down, to have a little less growth in order to have a bit more profitability, to serve the interests of the long term a little less well in order to squeeze out a bit more for the short term, to accept a bit less value horizontally to get a little more value vertically. Balance can easily become the enemy of "both." The challenge of achieving many objectives simultaneously does not go away by creating balance: it is just masked in a cloud of aggregation.

Between these two schools of management—choice or balance— leaders face a dilemma: either potentially achieve good performance on one objective along with poor performance on the other, or live with less performance on both objectives than desired or possible. To choose is to risk never catching more than one rabbit—and then only for a while. To balance is to risk chasing both rabbits at the same time, only to catch neither. To catch both hen and chicks, leaders need to adopt a different approach.

CATCHING BOTH HEN AND CHICKS: NOT CHOICE OR BALANCE, BUT BOTH

These are important arguments against either choosing among or balancing across objectives. But there is a more important point. We have seen that the objectives in each tension are connected. They are all dependent on each other. To achieve and sustain high levels of performance on one objective, you need to achieve and sustain high levels of performance on another. Poor performance on one objective will eventually drag down performance on the other. Less of one ultimately begets less of another; more of one can mean more of another. This is because opposing objectives share a common bond.

Given this interdependence among objectives, the practice of management does not have to be a science of choice or an art of

---

Three Imperatives for
Breaking the Corporate Cycle

1. Make Batting Average Matter
2. Strengthen the Common Bond Within Each Tension
3. Pick Your Lead Tension

balance. It can be a science and an art of "both." The alternative to choosing on the one hand and balancing on the other is to make good performance on one objective fully consistent with good performance on the other.

We see three imperatives for putting this into practice: making batting average matter; strengthening the common bond within each tension; and picking a lead tension.

MAKING BATTING AVERAGE MATTER

Batting average is the great overlooked measure of corporate success. Earnings, earnings per share, economic profit, "free" cash flow, P/E ratio, EBITDA, return on capital—all these and more are widespread in use. Who has ever heard of batting average? Yet what distinguishes batting average from all other measures is that it is a better proxy for TSR than any of them.[5]

It is fanciful to imagine that companies can approach perfect batting averages on all three tensions; there are too many unavoidable forces acting against companies and too many unavoidable conflicts between objectives for that to be possible. But it is not fanciful to commit to increasing your company's batting average and, along with it, your returns to shareholders. A first-class baseball player might have a lifetime batting average of just over .300. At that level, a company CEO would struggle to be average. Companies in the top quartile by TSR hit batting averages of .500 or more. This is a more reasonable ambition: achieving multiple objectives at the same time not all of the time, but more often than not.

Batting average, like any other single measure, is no panacea. First, it is not always easy to measure. It is much easier to measure for the tension on profitability vs. growth than for the other two tensions. It is hard to measure *current* batting average for today vs. tomorrow, as it requires a forecast. And, as we saw in Chapter Four, it is hard to measure at all for whole vs. parts.[6]

And although batting average is very often a good proxy for TSR, it isn't always. It measures the frequency of hitting two objectives at the same time; it does not measure the *degree or level* to which each objective is hit. We call that *slugging average*. A company that has a profitability vs. growth batting average of 50 percent but average revenue growth of 5 percent and an average economic profit margin of 4 percent has a lower slugging average—and therefore is highly likely to earn lower TSR—than a company with the same 50 percent batting average but 10 percent revenue growth and an average economic profit margin of 8 percent.

But even with both those qualifications, batting average is a useful addition to the business leaders' armory of tools. It can be measured at many levels of the company: the company overall, each business unit, even down to individual product line. Knowing it for the individual parts of the company at a level lower than competitors know theirs is a source of considerable insight that they will not have.

Even when it is not appropriate to use batting average directly, it can be adopted indirectly. Most measures, goals, and incentives consider the *net effect* of two performance objectives. For example, "profit growth" is the net effect of profitability and revenue growth. It does not discriminate very effectively between times when profitability and revenue were achieved together or not—it is blind to batting average. So a goal for profit growth is much less likely to result in both high profitability *and* high revenue growth than a goal for profitability and a *separate* one for growth. Likewise, a pay scheme that awards an annual bonus each year based on current performance is much more likely to support both the short term and long term if some or all of the bonus is vested in some form, possibly shares, that changes over time according to multiyear performance rather than just current-year performance. Teasing apart targets and pay schemes in this way is not the same as directly linking them to batting average, but at least it makes them much more consistent with batting average.

Making batting average matter in an organization is not simply about finding ways to measure it, either directly or indirectly. It is also about ensuring that there is no hidden bias for one objective over another. No one in the organization should be in any doubt that trade-offs between objectives are unwelcome and last resorts. The leader's broken record—with its frequently repeated questions and comments—is vital to making this happen. For example, John Sunderland frequently used the phrase "I want the penny and the bun" when he was chief executive of Cadbury Schweppes. (The expression "You can't have the penny and the bun" is variously claimed to be of English, Welsh, or Scottish origin. It literally means that you can pay the baker for your bun and have the bun but not the penny it costs, or you can hold on to the penny and give up on having the bun. But you can't have both.) His managers were in no doubt that if they brought forward a proposal express- ing a choice—for instance between more earnings today and more investment for performance tomorrow—Sunderland would chal- lenge them to explain why both objectives were not possible at the same time. Consistent with this outlook, he is also the chief executive we refer to in the mud hut anecdote at the beginning of this book.

STRENGTHENING THE COMMON BOND WITHIN EACH TENSION

Adopting batting average as a measure of success and making it part of your broken record can take you a long way. But of course, if this is all you do, it becomes mere exhortation. As Barclays chief executive John Varley put it: "Demanding both without clarity about how to achieve both will confuse the organization. You have to translate messages about where to focus to get both. Otherwise it won't work."

At the root of managing for "both" is the idea that managers should manage the *relationship* between objectives, not the objec- tives themselves. What does this mean? The analogy of a rela- tionship between people is useful: a mutually rewarding relationship—with a spouse or partner, child or parent, friend or colleague—comes from thinking through the eyes of the other and acting in the interests of both. To make compatible the two objective in a tension, each objective must "look through the eyes of the other" and each must "act in the interest of both": growth should be managed for profitability and profitability for growth; today's performance should be managed to increase tomorrow's performance, and vice versa; the parts should be managed to increase the performance of the whole, and the whole should be managed to increase the performance of the parts. If objectives are managed as relationships, they can often be avoided as choices or things to be balanced.

What this entails is managing not the objectives themselves but the common bonds between them: *customer benefit, sustainable earn-*

The Common Bond Within Each Tension

Profitability vs. growth	*Customer benefit*—the reward that customers receive through their experience of choosing and using a product or service
Today vs. tomorrow	*Sustainable earnings*—earnings that are not based on borrowing or lending between timeframes
Whole vs. parts	*Diagonal assets*—organizational resources and capabilities that help vertical assets to have horizontal value and horizontal assets to have vertical value

---

ings, and diagonal assets. In fact, if we have one thing to say in this book, it is this: do not lose sight of customer benefit, sustainable earnings, and diagonal assets; and do not let your team and organization lose sight of them either.

All too often, leaders have very poor line of sight into these three common bonds. They simply cannot see how one objective relates to the other. They therefore overlook the connections between them when they make decisions, and there is more conflict between objectives than necessary. We've already seen many examples of this, such as the lack of visibility into customer benefit leading to poor decisions on how to grow revenue or reduce costs, planning processes that reveal more about the "gaming" capabilities of the executive team than they do about the company's sustainable earnings, and false certainty about the benefits of centralization because the company's diagonal assets are not well understood.

There are ways to measure the common bonds. Measuring change in market share and price relative to competitors or measuring the strength of customer advocacy will get much closer to assessing the level of customer benefit than traditional measures of customer satisfaction.[7] A well-constructed post-earnings review will yield an estimate of the sustainable vs. transitory earnings in any given year. Managers' ratings of how much "connectedness" they feel or the number of voluntary interactions by managers across different business units can indicate whether a company's diagonal assets are strong or weak. And if you can measure it, you can set targets for it.

But attempts at direct measurement and targeting can go only so far. As we have seen, the three common bonds are elusive. Customer benefit changes by individual customer, by context—even by time of day. Whether earnings are sustainable—whether the assets that underpin them have a future life—depends on competitive and technological events that you cannot know in advance. How much—or even where—your company's total investment is "excess" is therefore also unknowable with 100 percent precision. There is no parallel universe in which one component of any investment can be removed *ex post facto* to see whether it was in fact needed. And you won't find diagonal assets on an organizational chart or on a balance sheet. You can't touch any of the common bonds.

That doesn't mean they aren't vital to the management of every business. It's just that there's no point in being overly forensic about them. They are elusive and must largely be managed indirectly rather than directly. That's why so much judgment is needed in running and leading a business; why explaining a company's success is so hard to pin down; why the corporate exemplar ("secrets of their success") school of management is so fraught with risk. And it is why the "tools" that business leaders use to manage and improve performance need to be assembled with great care.

New Ways of Using Old Tools

The many different means that business leaders have of achieving better results can be sorted into one of five categories of "management tools": the standards the company expects for itself, the strategies it adopts to achieve those standards, how accountabilities and formal structure are organized, company processes and routines, and people and culture (Table 5.1).

The idea of "both" as a school of management is a useful way to think about how to use and combine these different management tools in ways that will stimulate better performance.

TABLE 5.1. MANAGEMENT TOOLS.

Standards	Strategy	Structure	Process and Routines	Culture and People
Goals and targets	Vision and mission	Accountabilities and "decision rights"	Planning	Pay, rewards, and recognition
Measures	Target customers	Role and task definition	Budgeting	People selection criteria, policies, and processes
Selection of peers, benchmarking	Segmentation	Business unit boundaries	Investment management process	Induction, training, and development
Prioritization	Intended differentiation	Corporate center scope, staffing, and role	Business processes	Communication
"Broken records"	Pricing policy	Shared service units	Performance monitoring, routine management information	Values and norms
Questions the leader asks	Operating and technology choices	Coordinating devices (for example, task forces)	Management time and agenda	Shared beliefs
	Corporate portfolio boundaries		Committee structure	Stories
	Mergers, acquisitions, alliances		Approval criteria (for example, alternatives)	

"Twinning" tools within the same type (for example, standards) but with opposing biases—using them in pairs—can make a much more effective combined tool. A volume goal becomes more productive when used alongside a profitability goal. Decentralization can work more effectively when it is twinned with centralization, and vice versa. Accountability for one objective can be twinned with accountability for its counterpart. There is a large supply of possible combinations that can have the same result: the potential to unite opposing objectives.

A second technique is to juxtapose or offset tools of one type favoring one objective with tools of another type favoring the other objective. For example, where they pay on results today and promote on results over years, companies are using pay to motivate short-term performance and promotion to motivate long-term performance. The "harder" tools of measures and incentives can be used to encourage individual units to perform better, while the "softer" tools of culture and values can be used to encourage performance of the whole.

There are many potentially powerful combinations of tools that come from these two simple techniques of twinning and juxtaposition. To make a management tool more effective, we have found it useful to ask whether it would help toward achieving a higher batting average to "twin" it with another tool that has an opposing bias or to manage it alongside other tools in a larger juxtaposition.

We considered the five main management tools and these techniques of twinning and juxtaposition when we assembled the ideas for what the leader can do to tackle each tension (Table 5.2). These are consistent with using old tools in new ways to keep a company's attention and energies trained on each common bond—and to reduce the chances that those bonds fall into the company's blind spot. There are many alternative sets of tools that might achieve a similar effect.

This approach to combining tools goes against the grain of a deeply held view that everything should "point in the same direction"—that standards need to be aligned with strategy, which needs to be aligned with structure, processes, and culture. Everything needs to reinforce everything else.

The real aim should be to create *coherence* in the pursuit of multiple performance objectives rather than alignment. If you pay

Alignment vs. Coherence

Alignment means "arranging things in a straight line." Much of management theory and practice says that managers should seek alignment (or fit) between management tools. For instance, incentive plans, goals, monitoring routines, and business unit boundaries should all be designed with the same performance objective in mind—perhaps faster revenue growth or building for the future. That way, tools become mutually reinforcing because signals to employees about what matters are not mixed.

However, the pursuit of alignment can very easily result in a company being overly focused on managing performance on one side of a tension. It can also make it difficult for companies to adapt to changes in their external environment. For this reason, alignment within organizations is a cause of the corporate cycle rather than a solution to it.

Rather than alignment, *coherence*—a logical ordering—is a better organizing concept for assembling management tools. Coherence calls for a clear logic in how various management tools are combined (see Figure 5.4), even if they are not aligned to all point in the same direction. Unlike alignment, coherence is much more tolerant of deliberate, constructive conflict between tools. For example, a highly decentralized organization structure combined with a highly centralized set of common planning standards and routines will create conflict. But with the right capabilities for managing the conflict, that combination of tools will be much more likely to help in the management of—in this case—the whole vs. parts tension.

managers on short-term performance and promote them on long-term performance, then pay and promotion criteria are not "aligned," as they are aimed at different objectives. However, in the pursuit of a higher batting average on today vs. tomorrow, they are highly coherent.

Figure 5.4. Summary of Ideas for What the Leader Can Do.

	Profitability vs. Growth	Today vs. Tomorrow	Whole vs. Parts
	Grow Customer Benefit and Shrink Bad Costs	*Grow Sustainable Earnings and Minimize Excess Investment*	*Nurture Diagonal Assets and Avoid Diagonal Liabilities*
Standards	Grow productivity in good times and bad.	Strive to be correctly valued, not highly valued. Set goals for sustainable earnings.	
Strategy	Ask how to grow your market, not just your market share. Ask what would grow benefit for your customer's customer. Segment one level lower than the competition. Prefer market strength to market attractiveness.	Invest at your long-term "oil price," not your current one.	Use diagonal assets to guide your acquisitions and portfolio diversity.
Structure	Define your business boundaries by customer benefits, not just products.		Centralize when you decentralize . . . and vice versa.

	Natural Focus: Strategy (Business Model)	Natural Focus: Process and Routines (and Standards) (Management Model)	Natural Focus: Culture and People (and Structure) (Organizational Model)
Process and Routines	Map costs to customers' willingness to pay. Apply both an operating and a structural perspective to costs.	Manage the long term by managing how the short term is produced. Hold a post-earnings review. Allocate management time based on sustainable earnings at stake. Ask for three to five alternatives for both the destination and the path. Add a middle timeframe.	Act both "top-down" and "bottom-up." Ask whether you should standardize rather than centralize.
Culture and People	Make "grow customer benefit" your broken record.	Pay for tomorrow's performance as well as today's.	Create more consequences for not "wearing two hats." Work tirelessly to build connectedness. If you can't change the people, change the people. Tell your customer benefit story.

Two Opposites Don't Always Make One Harmony

Although combining tools with opposing biases can help achieve many objectives at the same time, managers should guard against the hope that doing so is automatically the answer. Management tools can be constructed to take into account all three tensions simultaneously, but in practice there are many dilution and canceling-out effects. For example, an annual bonus that is based on growth and profitability will be more powerful in influencing behavior than one that is based on growth, profitability, short-term profits, long-term profits, individual performance, and team performance.

You are asking for trouble if you try to create collections of tools with opposing biases to manage all three of the tensions. The result will be an organization tied up with checks and balances. The risk is that offsetting tools of one bias with others of the opposing bias only gums up the organization. That is why it is important to pick a lead tension.

PICKING A LEAD TENSION

You may have noticed that each of the three tensions is a complete equation for future growth in economic profits. The sum of future economic profits can be divided by revenue growth and profit margin. Or it can be divided by current profits and future profits. Or it can be divided by each part of the company plus what is added (or subtracted) across the company as a whole. The three tensions are not three different things. They are three different perspectives on the same thing (see Appendix A for a fuller and more technical elaboration of this important point).

Each of these lenses on future economic profits raises different questions and prompts managers to come up with different answers. To look through the lens of profitability and growth is to ask what the company does for its customers and how its activities are configured to support what it does for its customers—it is to ask *why* the company performs as it does. Examining the company from the perspective of the tension between today and tomorrow is to delve into *when* it produces performance. The perspective of whole vs. parts gets to the heart of *where* the company produces performance; it encompasses how the company is subdivided into its parts, its corporate or multibusiness strategy, and the rationale for its existence as an entity in the first place. The three tensions are the why, when, and where of future economic profits.

All three tensions act on all companies all the time. Business performance is constantly under threat from all three sides. So shouldn't leaders work on all three tensions at the same time all the time?

Well, no. Although all three are about the same thing, each tension lends itself to different tools with which to accomplish the same overall task. The tension between profitability and growth focuses the mind on the company's *business model:* it prompts questions of "strategy." The tension between short term and long term points managers at the company's *management model:* it prompts managers to think about the company's processes and routines for managing performance and investment. The tension between the whole and its parts steers leaders to consider the company's *organizational model:* its structure, culture, and people. And all three tensions naturally raise questions about the company's standards. Of course, all five management tools are relevant to the management of each tension. It's just that some perspectives sit more naturally with some tools than with others. And whether the focus that is generated by worrying about one particular tension is productive for a company depends on what is really at issue; is it the business, management, or organizational model?

The Diagnosis Is Critical

An added complexity is that the three tensions are not independent of each other. Poor performance on one can create poor performance on another. There are lines of cause and effect between the tensions, which means that some tensions can be more important to get right than others.

For example, the wrong targets can lead a company to focus too much on short-term earnings and to lose sight of sustainable earnings. The result: cutting good as well as bad costs. This in turn can lead to poor growth and, ultimately, falling profitability. Thus a problem on the today vs. tomorrow tension can manifest itself as a profitability vs. growth problem.

The reverse is also an ever-present risk. A problem in achieving a reasonable profitability vs. growth batting average can lead to difficulty in sustaining short-term earnings into the long term; a company that becomes more and more reliant on increasing margins to produce earnings growth will soon be unable to overcome the tension between short-term earnings and long-term profits.

Similarly, a problem of whole and parts can manifest itself as a different tension. For example, decentralization can lead to excessive autonomy of the parts and then to unnecessary duplication of costs that are not needed for customer benefit. This in turn can lead to poor profitability, undermining options for growth and creating a major tension between profitability and growth. Equally, a problem of whole and parts can create a problem in the today vs. tomorrow tension: a culture of business unit autonomy can act as a barrier to open interactions with the corporate center, making it difficult for the senior team to see *how* performance is being produced and whether short-term earnings are coming at the expense of investment needed for long-term performance.

Because the tensions interact in complicated ways, it is often difficult to disentangle cause from effect and problem from symptom. The tension where performance is most obviously wanting may not be the one to which you should pay the closest attention.

Coca-Cola

The recent position of Coca-Cola serves to illustrate the challenge. Most assessments of Coke's position today lead with the tension between today's performance and tomorrow's. Coke's management, as we have seen, has found itself missing progressively lower ambitions for annual volume and earnings growth. Its preoccupation has been to restore earnings growth. It could be that improving Coke's performance on this tension is the right answer: that they should worry first and foremost about growing sustainable earnings and minimizing excess investment.

But if you look behind Coca-Cola's performance, you will find that the company has also generated more of its earnings growth from profitability than from revenue growth, whereas PepsiCo's source of earnings growth came more from both. Coke's real issue may well be that the ability to grow the customer benefit of carbonated soft drinks is limited. The relative price of this category versus other categories may be an indicator: "Starbucks can charge $2 for a cup of coffee, and they [Coca-Cola] can barely sell a 12-pack of Cokes for $2" was the verdict of one commentator.[8] Slow market growth in the carbonated drinks market is perhaps another indicator. Mounting concerns about obesity are another. The symptom of Coke's problem might be its struggle to reconcile performance today with performance tomorrow. But if Coke is experiencing a transition in the nature of customer benefit, the real issue for the company may well be how to master the tension between profitability and revenue growth and Coke should give priority first and foremost to growing customer benefit.

Alternatively, it could be that Coca-Cola is too centralized around the head office in Atlanta, causing bloat, inflexibility, and second-class citizenship for the noncarbonated drinks business or local operations. This has perhaps made it difficult for the company to adapt to changes in its environment, particularly in customer benefit. So perhaps the tension between whole and parts is the root tension, and it is to strengthening diagonal assets that the company should look.

We don't presume to know or to judge. But Coca-Cola's situation illustrates the point that a symptomatic tension may not be the same as a root tension. In any event, we are confident that the company's most valuable line of inquiry into how to improve performance is to ask on which of customer benefit, sustainable earnings, or diagonal assets the company should concentrate its efforts.

Determining the Right Lead Tension for Your Company

Our discussion suggests that you should pick a lead tension so as to narrow down your efforts to improve performance. Managers need to think through their company's problems and unravel the underlying causes and effects.

The first question to ask is "What is our performance on each tension? What is our batting average?" This is a question that is amenable to numbers and to peer comparison. As in the Coca-Cola example, plenty of interpretation will always be needed to determine which one tension represents the best bet as a lead tension.

But the diagnosis cannot finish here. If, for example, you decide that profitability vs. growth should be the company's lead tension, there is still a question of which side of the tension—profitability or growth—is the real problem. The company that finds that it is growing but not achieving sufficient profitability would be excused for thinking that it had a profitability problem, not a growth problem. This might indeed be true if its real issue was too many bad costs. But if the reason has more to do with the type of

growth—pushing revenue growth when there is not enough customer benefit—lack of profitability may be signaling an issue with
growth, not profitability. The company that is finding it hard to
achieve the short-term performance it wants may be suffering an
"execution" problem. Equally it might be suffering from trying to
push too hard on a business model that hasn't enough long-term
potential in it or because it is investing too much. The company
that is not adding enough horizontally across its businesses might
conclude that it should find new ways to do so; but if a prevailing
culture of autonomy is the reason it is failing to add horizontal
value, the company may need to change how it seeks to add vertical value rather than horizontal value.

Because the two objectives in each tension interact, it is sometimes hard to discern which objective is more at issue than the
other. The objective within a tension that feels most pressing may
not be the one to press on most.

The diagnosis of where the problem really lies—of which is the
critical "half" of a particular tension—is not straightforward. You
must know how well the company has performed on the three
common bonds—customer benefit, sustainable earnings, and diagonal assets—and which of these is the main issue. To help you
think about these questions in your company, we summarize in Figure 5.5 some of the indicators of the root causes of low batting
averages.

When Not to Pick a Lead Tension

There are two circumstances in which picking a lead tension may
not be a good idea.

When There Is a Financial Crisis. First, picking a lead tension may
well be a luxury for a company in the grip of a financial crisis.
To "right the ship," it may be necessary to swing the business
toward the extremes: profitability, today, and the whole. In other
words, the imperative becomes to position the company in
the right place *within* the corporate cycle before trying to break
out of it.

Reuters, the business information company, met such a crisis
in 2001. It was one of those occasions when everything hits the
company at once. Reuters had a very high fixed cost base with

expensive information systems configured to operate best with many individual users. It was overly reliant on the cash foreign exchange and equity markets. Volume from foreign exchange had fallen due to the introduction of the euro and competitor systems. Reuters's main client industry—investment banking—went into recession in early 2001. The Internet hit the company much more quickly than management had expected; it was a new lower-cost technology for producing a similar customer benefit. Initially these changes were gradual; then they picked up pace. The number of individual users fell away dramatically; Reuters's profit decline was even more dramatic. Cash flow was drying up fast.

Chief executive Tom Glocer, who took over in 2001, went into what he describes as "triage mode." He centralized the company around customer groups, replacing the powerful regions of the previous structure. He pulled IT together around fewer computer platforms. And he oversaw a dramatic reduction in the cost base, taking £900 million (about $1.6 billion) out of annual costs. Reuters has recently just emerged from twelve quarters of falling earnings.

Reflecting back on the experience, Glocer says,

> Reuters had been trading on fumes for years. Success was masking a loss of relationship with—and understanding of—what our clients were doing, their partnerships, and how they were making money. It used to be clear: customers wanted real-time news and information for foreign exchange trading. As we started to branch out, we lost touch with what our customers were doing. I used to ask our salespeople, "How many of you can explain to me what a prime broker does? Do you realize that a significant portion of large banks' profits are coming from that?" It was a classic case of costs that were once good turning bad because customer benefit changed. Then, in a crisis everything becomes clear, and competing priorities fall away. The need and the bias to act are so great. I knew I had to centralize and get the costs into big buckets and get people to ratchet them down.

When Slugging Average Matters More Than Batting Average. Another circumstance in which picking a lead tension may not be the best course of action is when a company already has a high batting average. Then the priority may well be increasing slugging average

FIGURE 5.5. DIAGNOSIS FOR YOUR COMPANY.

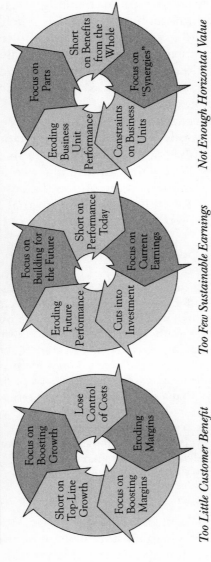

Too Little Customer Benefit

- Low or falling share or price relative to competitors
- Falling market growth; struggles for share
- Low or falling customer loyalty
- Reductions in volumes per line; increasing complexity

Too Few Sustainable Earnings

- Increasing reliance on margin rather than revenue (or increasing reliance on revenue rather than margin) to achieve earnings growth
- Difficulty in hitting earnings targets without delaying investments

Not Enough Horizontal Value

- Few voluntary interactions between business units or between units and the corporate center
- Strong separate cultural identities across business units or functions
- High unit costs relative to peers on activities where there are usually economies of scale

Too Many Bad Costs

- High unit costs relative to competitors or best in class
- Cost disciplines that change dramatically between good and bad times
- Changes in prices linked to changes in costs
- Cutting discretionary spending in the last quarter of the year
- Low or falling investment vs. competitors and vs. earnings growth

Excess Investment

- Investment following earnings; investment at same times and on same things as competitors
- "Hockey stick" forecasts

Not Enough Vertical Value

- Interactions between center and businesses solely about financial outcomes
- Increasing number of layers in the organization; high percentage of time spent on coordination rather than decision making
- A culture of blame and finger pointing

Overall

- Swinging between growth push and productivity push
- Giving priority only to costs in difficult times and only to growth in boom times

Overall

- Swinging between a focus on strategy and a focus on execution

Overall

- Swinging between decentralization and centralization
- Constant inconclusive debates about accountability vs. authority vs. possession

without reducing batting average: achieving an even higher rate of profitability and growth, even more earnings today and profits tomorrow, and even more horizontal and vertical value. In these circumstances, working on all three common bonds at the same time may be a better approach than prioritizing them.

BREAKING THE CORPORATE CYCLE

The ability to master the three tensions and break the corporate cycle they form is worth a lot for company owners. Small amounts of improvement in batting average translate into large returns for shareholders.

But it is not only shareholders whose interests are served by breaking the corporate cycle. A company that is growing will find that it is better able to provide fulfilling jobs and career opportunities for its people than a company that is not growing. A company that is profitable will be better able to pay higher wages and benefits than one that is not. But only a company that is both growing *and* profitable will be able to serve both sets of interests. A company that performs well on current earnings may find that its current shareholders benefit; but if it does so at the expense of longer-term earnings, those who invest in it for their long-term pensions will suffer. Only if it can do both at the same time can it serve both sets of interests. If the local business is thriving, its local community can thrive as well. But if the parent company performs poorly, the national community will receive less in tax revenue. Conversely, the good performance of the parent company is of no consolation to the local community if the parent's subsidiary has to be shut down. Good performance of the parts and of the whole at the same time is the only way of meeting both local and national community needs at the same time. Winning the battle for "both" is the route to good performance for all stakeholders, not just shareholders.

The "choice" school of management is not well equipped for this battle. In the face of today's pressures on leaders and the stock market's current mood, it is natural to want to focus on certain performance objectives over others—growth over profitability, for example, or current earnings over long-term health—depending on how well a company is currently performing. Yet our research tells us that emphasizing one performance objective over another—except in special cases such as start-ups, exits, or performance crises—is not the right route to better performance. Good performance on one objective does not automatically result in good performance on others. If anything, the odds are in the other direction: it is easier to end up with "either" or "neither" than "both." Furthermore, by prioritizing between objectives, many companies actually end up swinging between them.

And "balance," as we have seen, can easily become the enemy of "both." This is because it has nothing to say about the relationship between performance objectives: the common bonds that tie them together.

Our advice, therefore, is to neither balance nor prioritize between objectives but to *prioritize between tensions.* Leadership teams should debate and carefully pick the right lead tension for their company. And they should focus their organization's energies on strengthening the common bond that unites its two sides.

This is no easy panacea. What a company's lead tension should be is as much a matter of judgment as of analysis. And the three common bonds are hard to measure. You can't touch or feel them. But no matter how difficult, working hard to strengthen the common bond in your company's lead tension is the only truly reliable route to improving your company's performance for all its stakeholders.

CHAPTER SIX

THE NEXT BIG THING

If an idea's worth having once, it's worth having twice.
TOM STOPPARD

It's déjà vu all over again.
YOGI BERRA

In Greek mythology, the Straits of Messina were a channel between two cliffs an arrow's shot apart. Monsters lived on each side: six-headed Scylla, who lashed out at any ship that passed too close; and Charybdis, who would suddenly swallow the surrounding sea down into a vast whirlpool. Unable to avoid crossing the straits, Odysseus steered his ship away from Charybdis nearer to the side where Scylla waited. He lost six of his companions, one to each of Scylla's heads. Had he chosen to steer clear of Scylla, he might have lost his entire crew. Scylla and Charybdis have become an enduring metaphor for a dilemma: a choice between equally unpalatable options.

A mark of progress in any human endeavor is the resolution of what was formerly thought a dilemma: avoiding both Scylla and Charybdis. Our ancestors living in mud huts faced the stark dilemma between no daylight and no heat. Punch a hole in the side of your hut, and you let the daylight in, but also the cold. Block up all the openings, and you stay warm, but sit in darkness. Glass made it possible to let in the light but not the cold, to avoid the need to choose between the two objectives.

Popularized in the eighteenth century, crop rotation moved farming beyond the dilemma of low yields and unhealthy soil. Because different crops take from and give back to the soil different nutrients, careful crop rotation avoided depleting the overall health of the soil without the need for setting it aside as fallow.

It took the arrival of anesthesia to overcome the dilemma in surgical medicine between causing terrible pain and failing to save lives.

Since the arrival of modern monetary and fiscal techniques, what was considered by many economists to be an unavoidable choice between low inflation with high unemployment and low unemployment with high inflation has now been consigned by many to an honorable mention in the history of the subject.

Glass, crop rotation, anesthetics, and macroeconomic techniques all moved their respective disciplines beyond unpalatable and seemingly intractable choices between desirable objectives. Building, farming, medicine, and economics have now moved on to other frontiers, with new dilemmas to overcome.

But such progress has so far eluded the discipline of management. Business objectives that have not fundamentally changed for thousands of years still present themselves to managers today as either-or choices. All too often, success on one dimension of performance—profitability vs. growth, today vs. tomorrow, whole vs. parts—comes at the cost of failure on the other. Avoiding Charybdis makes falling prey to Scylla more likely.

We've shown that most companies today don't yet succeed in hitting multiple objectives at the same time most of the time.[1] And, as we have seen, we cannot put all the blame on the unavoidable laws of economics or forces of human nature. As a discipline, management seems stuck in the era of the mud hut.

MANAGEMENT FASHION

Commenting on the phenomenon of fashion in management ideas has itself become fashionable. There are even business school courses dedicated to it. Much thought has been invested into what causes new management ideas to be adopted so enthusiastically. Some prefer explanations based on demand: for example, that such ideas are simple and attractive solutions to difficult problems, or that the desire not to be left behind encourages mass adoption of any credible new idea. Others point to explanations based on supply: for example, better marketing techniques.

Equal attention has been placed on what causes many of these ideas to be rejected so completely after being adopted so enthusiastically. For some it's that many new ideas are simple and attractive solutions to complex and unattractive problems; they are literally too good to be true. For others it's that they were designed with "planned obsolescence" in mind. Yet others point to problems with how ideas are adopted—failures of implementation. Much advice is offered on how to tell the difference between an authentic innovation and a passing fad, with many commentators pointing to one particular telltale characteristic of a fad: the wide gulf between claims for results (large) and ease of understanding (small).

It has also become something of a sport to point out that there's nothing new under the sun, that so-called new ideas are often old ones with new labels, and in some cases not even with new labels. Benchmarking became all the rage in the late twentieth century, now ranking in the top three of most adopted management tools.[2] But the ancient Greeks would have taken some convincing that the idea of benchmarking was more than two thousand years into their future. In "The Economist," written in the fourth century B.C., Xenophon advocated this to those wishing to improve the productivity of their estates: "He has only to look at his neighbor's land, at his crops and trees, in order to learn what the soil can bear and what it cannot."[3]

That most modern of words—"empowerment"—is spoken as if it were a recent invention made possible by advances in information technology. Yet the word comes to us from the mid-seventeenth century, and Peter Drucker pointed out that no modern manager would have been as empowered as a local manager was in the East India Company in the early eighteenth century. Lest you think that we have exempted ourselves from this general rule, we note that the concept of "tensions"—or more precisely the "tension of opposites"—can be traced to the ancient Greek philosopher Heraclitus. He even had a word for the tendency of things to swing back and forth from one extreme to its opposite— *enantiodromia* (a term unlikely to become a buzzword). Even the phrase "There is nothing new under the sun" is at least three thousand years old. It's a fun game if you have the time.

A swing in fashion or a new twist in an old debate can be mistaken for something genuinely new, especially to those who weren't there the last time around. The increased pace of adopting "new" management ideas bears witness to a rapidly changing context as companies attempt to deal with changes in information technology, ever-increasing global competition, greater speed and lower costs of communication, and all their attendant implications. But this change in context should not blind managers to the underlying nature of the challenges of business leadership. The three tensions and the corporate cycle they form have always been with us. Here too there is nothing new under the sun. The context in which a modern company operates could not be more different than what the Ancient Greeks faced, but the essence of the challenge is the same. An ever-changing context can mask a never-changing challenge. And it is this confusion of context and challenge that leads to false hopes for a "next big thing" in management.

THE CYCLE OF MANAGEMENT IDEAS

But this analysis overlooks a more fundamental question: Is there a *pattern* to the emergence, adoption, eclipse, and reemergence of management ideas? Our answer is yes. There is in fact a striking pattern to the fashion in management ideas: they swing with the three tensions.

In our research for this book, we compiled a list of popular management ideas: theories, concepts, tools, and techniques. We then categorized them according to their *primary use,* as opposed to their *original intent*—the purpose originally conceived for them. For example, the primary use of "diversification" is revenue growth, so we put it into the Growth category; we put "vision and mission statements" into the Tomorrow bucket. The categorization reflects the nature of the "bias" that the idea brings. For example, diversification has a growth bias; vision and mission statements have a bias toward the long term. We then used a number of sources to estimate when each idea was at the zenith of its relative popularity.[4] In Figure 6.1, we summarize popular management ideas since 1900.

FIGURE 6.1. A CRUDE HISTORY OF POPULAR MANAGEMENT IDEAS SINCE 1900.

Year	Profitability	Today	Whole	Growth	Tomorrow	Parts	Theme
1900							
1905	Scientific management						Back to Basics
1910		Time and motion study					
1915			Mass production				
1920							
1925	Return on Investment						
1930		Budgeting					
1935							
1940							
1945							
1950			Corporate strategy				
1955				Diversification; vertical integration		Decentralization, Theory Y, strategic business units, portfolio management	Brave New World
1960				Marginal costing	Strategic planning		
1965				Experience curve, growth-share matrix			
1970					Scenario planning, zero-based budgeting		
1975							

1980	Downsizing, flattening, de-layering	Kaizen, Japanese management	Kaizen, Japanese management			Back to Basics
1985	Activity-based costing, Total Quality Management, Business Process Re-engineering, Economic Value Added	Payback, Just in Time, time-based management	Management buyouts, leveraged buyouts, restructuring			
1990	Value Based Management			Core competence	Vision and mission, strategic intent	
1995				e-revolution, chaos, corporate venturing	Empowerment, intrapreneuring	Brave New World
2000	Six Sigma, ISO 9000, supply chain integration, outsourcing	Execution, Lean Manufacturing	Learning organization, knowledge management, globalization, outsourcing			
2005						Back to Basics

The rough sketch is as follows: ideas with a growth bias have tended to alternate in popularity with ideas that have a profitability bias; ideas with a long-term bias have tended to alternate with ideas more oriented to the short term; ideas with a bias toward the individual parts of companies (or vertical value) have tended to alternate with ideas that focus on the whole of companies (or horizontal value). Furthermore, there have been clear periods when the emphasis is on management ideas to help companies find their brave new world and other periods when the ideas are primarily about getting back to basics. The fashion in management ideas follows the rhythm of the corporate cycle.

This view that there are clear patterns to the fashion in management ideas is a huge simplification. Mapping management ideas to their primary use is an inherently subjective undertaking. An objective assessment of the chronology of relative popularity is extremely difficult to make on a consistent basis over a hundred-year period. We certainly wouldn't claim that ours is perfect. But taking all that into account, there is still too much evidence of a pattern here for this to be mere coincidence.

When we came into John Browne's office for our discussion with him, the first words out of his mouth were "Have you seen those recent articles saying revenue is all that matters again? It's amazing how these cycles come around. It's hardly surprising it's so easy for all of us to lose the plot." As we stand in 2007, we are coming out of a Back to Basics phase in the cycle of management ideas—one that has lasted since the end of the dot-com boom in 2000. On current course and speed, "the next big thing" will be a new Brave New World stage. Yesterday's pariahs—growth, the long term, and parts—are fast becoming become today's saviors. Then, inevitably, they will be eclipsed once more. It seems that rather than offering help to business leaders in breaking the corporate cycle, management ideas are trapped inside it.

Why is this? Why does popular management thinking follow the corporate cycle rather than help companies escape from it? Some might argue that, like seagulls following a trawler, management ideas simply follow the corporate cycle. At any stage of the cycle, as companies wrestle with one set of priorities, they create demand for management tools and concepts of a particular bias. If those ideas are not sufficiently designed—or used—with the other objective in mind (for example, growth *with* profitability, profitability *with* growth), they only help companies get to the next stage of the cycle rather than break out of it. Those ideas are then naturally abandoned with the same enthusiasm as they were adopted in the first place, to be replaced by new management ideas with an opposing bias.

Another view is that the cycle of ideas creates reciprocal momentum to the cycle of corporate objectives and priorities. Credible, topical, and interesting management concepts create demand, and change how companies behave. Because no one wants to miss out on the latest idea, there is always great potential for widespread adoption. It may even be that the cycle of ideas acts to synchronize where companies sit within the corporate cycle at any point in time. And all these processes are aided and abetted by the overall economic cycle. They, in turn, may even contribute extra momentum to that cycle.

A YOUNG DISCIPLINE

Management as an explicitly recognized discipline—and profession—is still relatively young—barely one hundred years old, if that. The cycle of ideas reflects both high demand for the next big thing and a lack of consensus on the basic rules for the discipline of management. Without such consensus, it is difficult for different contributions to management theory and practice to build on each other constructively and to create a coherent body of useful knowledge over time—the ultimate sign of a disciplined profession.

The "rules" in any discipline cover (at least) three things: its purpose, its scope, and its method. There will always be debate about all three, but there needs to be a minimum level of consensus. In management, that minimum level has not yet been reached.

NO AGREEMENT AS TO PURPOSE

First, there is no true agreement on what management's overall purpose should be. Perhaps the two most influential thinkers of the last century, Alfred Sloan and Peter Drucker, set the tone for what has been a fault line of disagreement about management's purpose ever since: whereas Sloan thought that "the primary object of the corporation . . . [is] . . . to make money"[5] for its owners, Drucker argued that it should be "to create a customer."[6] Other more modern versions of this debate center on "shareholder vs. stakeholder" and on a company's "commercial vs. social" responsibility.

The purpose of business is all these things, and more. A business does economic things: pays employees, provides a return to owner capital, pays taxes, funds pensions, and more. It also does social things: provides goods and services that people need and want, creates meaningful and rewarding employment, contributes to local communities, and more. It can do these economic and social things well or badly. Asking for the single purpose of a business is akin to asking for the purpose of a multipurpose tool (think Swiss Army "knife"). It depends on who is using it to do what. As a result of this ambiguity, business leaders and theorists tend to develop their own basket of performance measures: TSR, growth, corporate social responsibility, customer satisfaction, productivity. There is no single definition for good business performance. Consequently much of what constitutes debate within the field of management theory and practice is more talking at cross purposes from different definitions of business purpose and performance. In the world of management thinking, everyone is the referee of his or her own game.

THE WRONG SCOPE

Second, the scope of much management thinking does not match the scope of the practical performance challenges that business leaders face. Much of it is fragmented by objective (one book on growth, one on operations, another on shareholder value, another on corporate social responsibility, and so on) or fragmented by tool (one book on performance measurement, one on strategy, one on organizational structure, another on information technology, and so on). All too often, the result is a set of partial and unrelated ideas for the conscientious (and busy) business manager to follow—and reconcile with all the other partial and unrelated ideas he or she is offered. By contrast, as we have seen, the principal concerns of business leaders are not so fragmented: not how to grow, but how to grow without damaging profitability; not how to become more profitable, but how to do so without taking the eye off growth; not how to achieve more performance today, but how to build for long-term performance at the same time; not how to make the corporate center improve performance across the company as a whole, but how to do so without undermining its individual parts; not how to do any *one* of these, but how to do *all* of them at the same time.

Perhaps the most seductive management ideas are the ones that seem to be a single management tool for hitting many objectives (for example, process reengineering) or that in effect offer a single dominant or higher-order objective (for example, "grow yourself to greatness"). But the unfortunate truth is that multiple means are needed to hit multiple objectives. No economist would be taken seriously if he were to argue that governments can meet all their macroeconomic objectives (low inflation, high employment, strong GDP growth, and so on) through fiscal policy alone. Equally unpersuasive would be the argument that if you worry about one objective—keeping employment high—the other objectives will automatically take care of themselves. Governments need a combination of fiscal, monetary, trade, and regulatory policies to manage the multiple objectives of low inflation, high employment, and strong GDP growth. This is because macroeconomic objectives are interrelated; for example, all things being equal, success in raising the employment rate may risk causing demand to outstrip supply and thus too much inflation. Further, macroeconomic tools interact with each other; for example, trade policy is highly interdependent with monetary policy via exchange rates.

These same interactions—between objectives and between tools—occur in business every day. Single-objective or single-tool prescriptions are no match for multiple, interdependent objectives. Yet popular management thinking is full of such "solutions."

No Consensus on Method

If the minimum level of consensus has not yet been achieved for the purpose and scope of management, neither has it for what constitutes a robust method. For instance, the search to codify "exemplar" performance has recently emerged as a next big thing in popular management thinking. Management thinkers often proceed by finding successful companies (by whatever definition), identifying common themes that explain their success, then drawing conclusions about the causes of exemplar performance that are applicable to other companies.[7]

But many such studies make us want to believe that relatively simple comparisons can reduce the enormous complexity of explaining business success to a few handy prescriptions. Alfred Sloan had it right when he said "It is not easy to say why one management is successful and another is not. The causes of success and failure are deep and complex, and chance plays a part."[8] Perhaps this is why some business leaders, though flattered to be on the list in best-selling "secret of success" books, in private are not persuaded that the cited recipe for their success really is the reason for their spectacular performance.

To search for the causes of high performance by identifying "exemplar" companies and their "secrets to success" may well be to search down a blind alley. The interactions among management tools, among performance objectives, and among tools and objectives, and how all of that fits with the external environment are so complex that only large data sets are able to isolate correlation between variables in order to test or confirm a theory of performance. Large data sets are the antithesis of shortlists of exemplars; complex relationships are the antithesis of secrets of success. The important distinction between objectives and tools, the existence of positive and negative "complementarity" between objectives, substitution effects between tools, and lagging effects— all these produce a world so complex that simple recipes, heroic chief executives, and exemplary companies are bound to appeal . . . and bound to disappoint. The main result of the search for exemplar performance is for the fashion in management ideas to spill over into a fashion for companies and their leaders. And, inevitably, today's corporate heroes turn into tomorrows' fallen angels.

It is hardly surprising, then, that without sufficient consensus on these critical foundations—purpose, scope, and method—much of modern management thinking is pulled into the corporate cycle rather than acting as a force for breaking it.

THE NEXT BIG THING

The talent for overcoming tensions and the performance compromises they embody is perhaps the most valuable talent for an organization to have. But today it is a talent for the few. The challenge for management as a professional discipline is to make this a talent for the many. In doing so, a stronger consensus on its purpose, scope, and method is essential.

But so too is a final ingredient: adopting a different attitude toward the search for "the next big thing." It is not the need for undiscovered new tools that holds management back; it is the need for a deeper understanding of how existing tools—standards, strategy, structure, process, and culture—are best combined. The problem with many management innovations is not that they are intrinsically unhelpful to the search for good performance; the problem is that they are only as effective as the company they keep—that is, how they are deployed in combination. Much work is needed to produce new insights into how the many tools currently available to managers can be combined to help them perform well on the full combination of their performance objectives.

But that's good news. It means that the next big thing isn't in front of us: it's already all around us.

APPENDIX A

MARKET VALUE AND BATTING AVERAGE

An important underpinning of this book is the link between a company's market value and its batting average—its success in overcoming tensions between objectives.

There are four links in the chain between market value and batting average (see Figure A.1): from market value to economic value; from economic value to economic profits over time; from economic profits over time to the three tensions (profitability vs. growth, today vs. tomorrow, and whole vs. parts); and, on each tension, from economic profits over time to batting average.

This appendix summarizes and simplifies those links. Although financial knowledge is not required, this is intended for those who prefer the technical side of life. Readers who want to explore more about valuation and the management of economic value are encouraged to consult *The Value Imperative*, written by our Marakon colleagues James McTaggart, Peter Kontes, and Michael Mankins (Free Press, 1994), in particular appendixes A and B, from which we borrow.

DEFINITIONS

Market value is the market price of a company's common shares multiplied by its number of common shares outstanding. For example, the market value of FedEx on March 31, 2006, was $34.5 billion, the product of a share price of $113 and 305 million shares

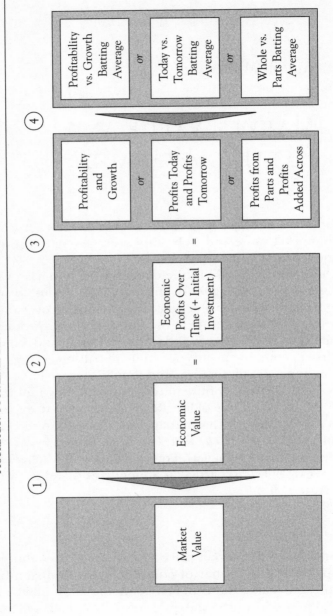

FIGURE A.1. FOUR LINKS BETWEEN MARKET VALUE AND BATTING AVERAGE.

outstanding. The measure we use for change in market value is *total shareholder returns (TSR)*. This expresses the change in the value of a shareholder's investment as a company's share price changes, and it includes dividends to complete the calculation. For example, on March 31, 2001, the share price of FedEx was $42. At this price, $100 invested in FedEx bought about 2.4 shares. If investors reinvested the dividends FedEx paid over the next five years, by March 31, 2006, their initial $100 investment would have been worth $275, a 22 percent compound annual growth rate. The annual TSR for FedEx over the five years was therefore 22 percent.

Economic value is the sum of all future cash flows expected from a company, discounted at its cost of capital. Cash flow equals net profit after tax, less reinvestment in the business.

Economic profit is the amount earned over and above all costs, including notional capital costs. Thus it is net profit after all operating costs, depreciation, tax, and a notional charge for the cost of capital. For example, a company with $100 million in revenue, operating costs before tax of $80 million, a 25 percent tax rate, $120 million of capital, and a 10 percent cost of capital will have an economic profit of $3 million. The calculation is as follows:

	Revenue	$100M
less	Operating costs	$80M
equals	Operating profit before tax	$20M
less	Tax (25% × $20M)	$5M
equals	Operating profit after tax	$15M
less	Capital charge (10% × $120M)	$12M
equals	Economic profit	$3M

Batting average is the frequency with which a company achieves the two performance objectives within a tension that make up economic profits over time (for example, positive revenue growth and a positive economic profit margin) at the same time. For example, a company that achieves both real revenue growth and a positive profit margin in three out of five years has a batting average of 60 percent on that tension. The concept applies to each tension.

We have used batting average to measure the degree to which a company is trapped by—as opposed to the master of—the three tensions and thus how far it has broken out of the corporate cycle. If a company has a batting average of 50 percent or more on a particular tension, it is more the master than the slave of that tension.

THE LINKS

For each of the four links in the chain between batting average and market value, we summarize here the nature of the link and the evidence for it. We also touch on some important caveats.

LINK 1: THE LINK BETWEEN MARKET VALUE AND ECONOMIC VALUE

Valuation theory argues that market value is determined by economic value—the discounted sum of expected future cash flows—and that this is as true for the value of bonds as for the value of equities.

The evidence that market value gravitates to economic value is as overwhelming as it is neglected in the day-to-day management of companies. Figure A.2 shows the correlation between market value per share (share price) and estimated economic value per share in December 2005 of the 1,267 companies for which Value-Line provides long-range consensus forecasts of economic profits (which we used to calculate economic value). No other measure comes close to this level of correlation. Changes in economic value give the most complete explanation of changes in market value.

LINK 2: THE LINK BETWEEN ECONOMIC VALUE AND ECONOMIC PROFITS

Although economic value is usually expressed as the sum of discounted future cash flows, it can also be expressed in a different way: as the sum of all discounted future economic profits added to current capital.

From an equity value perspective, equity cash flow (ECF) is defined as

ECF = Earnings − Δ Equity Invested

and Economic Value (EV) = $\displaystyle\sum_{t=1}^{\infty} \frac{\text{Equity Cash Flow}_t}{(1+K_e)^t}$

If B = Equity Invested and K_e = Cost of Equity Invested, then ECF can be defined in terms of economic profits as follows:

$$
\begin{aligned}
ECF &= E - \Delta B \\
&= E - B_{t-1} \times K_e + B_{t-1} \times K_e - \Delta B \\
&= EP + B_{t-1} \times K_e - \Delta B \\
&= EP + B_{t-1}(1 + K_e) - B_t
\end{aligned}
$$

This specification of Equity Cash Flow can be substituted into the valuation equation:

Economic Value (EV) = $\displaystyle\sum_{t=1}^{\infty} \frac{EP_t + B_{t-1}(1 + K_e) - B_t}{(1 + K_e)^t}$

Simplifying this equation, we show that the economic value of a company is equal to the present value of its future stream of economic profits plus the beginning equity investment:

$$
(EV) = \sum_{t=1}^{\infty} \frac{\text{Economic Profit}_t}{(1+K_e)^t} + \sum_{t=1}^{\infty} \frac{B_{t-1}(1+K_e)}{(1+K_e)^t} - \sum_{t=1}^{\infty} \frac{B_t}{(1+K_e)^t}
$$

$$
= \sum_{t=1}^{\infty} \frac{\text{Economic Profit}_t}{(1+K_e)^t} + B_{t=0} + \sum_{t=1}^{\infty} \frac{B_t}{(1+K_e)^t} - \sum_{t=1}^{\infty} \frac{B_t}{(1+K_e)^t}
$$

$$
= \sum_{t=1}^{\infty} \frac{\text{Economic Profit}_t}{(1+K_e)^t} + B
$$

Therefore, the economic value of a company (or its business units) can be determined not only by discounting its future cash

FIGURE A.2. THE CORRELATION BETWEEN ECONOMIC VALUE AND MARKET VALUE.

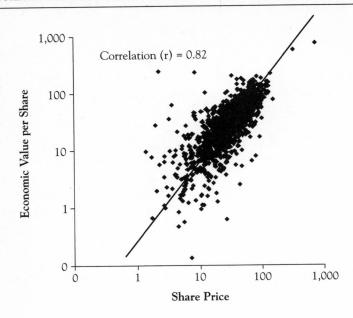

flows at the cost of capital but also—and equivalently—by discounting its future economic profit at the cost of capital and adding the company's (or business units') current amount of capital invested. Economic profits are thus a measure of value creation: economic value less today's capital investment.

LINK 3: THE LINK BETWEEN ECONOMIC PROFIT OVER TIME AND EACH OF THE THREE TENSIONS

Each of the three tensions in this book can be considered a complete equation for economic profits over time. Economic profit over time can be divided by economic profit margin and revenue growth; by economic profits today and economic profits tomorrow; and by the economic profit added to or subtracted from each part of the company plus the economic profit added or subtracted across the company as a whole—what we have termed vertical value and horizontal value, respectively. The three tensions are not three different things. They are three different perspectives on the same thing: economic profits over time and therefore economic value.

As illustration of this equivalence, imagine a hypothetical company that has two business units and has created horizontal value across them through joint marketing and procurement initiatives. Its cumulative economic profit over the three years is 100. This result can be reached in three different ways, X, Y, and Z, according to each tension (Figure A.3). (Strictly speaking, we should express this as a present value of discounted economic profits, but we have tried to keep it simple for this illustration.)

LINK 4: THE LINK BETWEEN ECONOMIC PROFIT OVER TIME AND BATTING AVERAGE

Batting average measures the frequency of hitting both objectives within a single tension at the same time. It does not measure the degree or level to which each objective is hit. We have referred to that as slugging average. Thus a company that has a profitability vs. growth batting average of 50 percent but average revenue growth of 5 percent and an average economic profit margin of 4 percent has a lower slugging average—is producing lower levels of economic profits—than a company with the same batting average of 50 percent but 10 percent revenue growth and an average economic profit margin of 8 percent.

In mathematical terms, economic profits over any period of time are a function of slugging average, not batting average. If slugging average were all that mattered to the assessment of future economic profits, we might expect to find no relationship between batting average and TSR.

But this is not what we have found. In our database of more than one thousand companies, the correlations with TSR over the twenty years of batting average for positive economic profit margin vs. positive nominal revenue growth and batting average for positive annual economic profit growth vs. positive cumulative economic profit over the next five years are 0.69 in both cases. (As noted in Chapter Four, we have been unable to measure batting average for the third tension—whole vs. parts—on a systematic basis for large numbers of companies and years.) These levels of correlation are usually considered to be consistent with a strong

FIGURE A.3. EACH OF THE THREE TENSIONS IS A COMPLETE EQUATION FOR ECONOMIC PROFIT OVER TIME.

Business Unit A

	Yr 1	Yr 2	Yr 3
Revenue	60	60	60
less:			
Operating costs	30	40	40
Tax	9	6	6
Capital charge	6	6	6
Economic profit	15	8	8
Cumulative economic profit years 1–3	31		

Business Unit B

	Yr 1	Yr 2	Yr 3
Revenue	40	50	60
Operating costs	20	20	20
Tax	6	9	12
Capital charge	4	4	4
Economic profit	10	17	24
Cumulative economic profit years 1–3	51		

Horizontal Value Between A and B

	Yr 1	Yr 2	Yr 3
Revenue	15	15	15
Operating costs	5	5	5
Tax	3	3	3
Capital charge	1	1	1
Economic profit	6	6	6
Cumulative economic profit years 1–3	18		

Total Company

	Yr 1	Yr 2	Yr 3
Revenue	115	125	135
Operating costs	55	65	65
Tax	18	18	21
Capital charge	11	11	11
Economic profit	31	31	38
Cumulative economic profit years 1–3	100		

Weighted average total company economic profit margin × Cumulative total company revenue = 27% × 375 = 100

Year 1 total company economic profits + All future years' economic profits = 31 + (31+38) = 100

Economic profits Business Unit A + Economic profits Business Unit B + Economic profits from horizontal value across A and B = 18 + (31+51) = 100

(X) Profitability vs. Revenue Growth Perspective

(Y) Today vs. Tomorrow Perspective

(Z) Whole vs. Parts Perspective

positive association. By comparison, the correlation between TSR and economic profit growth—a measure of slugging average—was less than 0.5.

(*Please note:* In the text, we have departed from these technical definitions of batting average in two ways. In the tension of profitability vs. growth, we have used *real* revenue growth instead of nominal revenue growth as our measure of growth. And we have used annual *earnings* growth instead of annual economic profit growth as our measure of short-term performance in the today vs. tomorrow tension. We felt that these departures would make more sense to most managers. After all, companies that are shrinking in real terms don't tend to think that they are growing, and annual growth in earnings is a considerably more widespread measure of short-term performance than annual growth in economic profit. In any event, the correlations with TSR are similar under both our technical definitions of batting average and the definitions we use in the text. Over the twenty years, the less technical definitions give correlations with TSR of 0.63 for batting average of positive economic profit margin vs. positive real revenue growth and of 0.72 for positive annual earnings growth vs. positive cumulative economic profit over the next five years.)

We conclude from this that economic profits that come with high batting averages are generally expected by the capital markets to continue to grow more securely into the future than equivalent levels of economic profits that come with low batting averages. Batting average is, in other words, an indicator of the *sustainability* of economic profits into the future and, therefore, of change in economic value and market value. It is both level *and* sustainability that matter to economic value and, therefore, market value and TSR.

It is important to note that our claims are limited. These are not perfect correlations, and they are not as high as the correlation between economic value and market value. We do not argue that batting average is a better proxy for market value than economic value. Batting average is, after all, a retrospective measure, and economic value and market value are both prospective. And it takes no account of the *level* of economic profits, or slugging average. We simply argue that the existence of a positive correlation between batting average and TSR implies that batting average is an indicator of the sustainability of economic profits, which is highly valued by the capital markets.

Companies should take from this that they should work on both batting *and* slugging average. Of course it will usually be the case that the higher the batting average, the higher the slugging average.

Appendix B

Our Research Methodology

This appendix describes how we have tackled the research in the book in order to make it as robust as possible.

Main Company Database

At the heart of our research is a database of the financial performance of more than one thousand public companies over a twenty-year period: 1983–2003. Our main selection criterion for companies was the availability of robust data. We included companies on which our information source (Datastream World Market Index) had operating and capital market performance information in every year of the twenty-year period. We selected 1,072 companies out of the total of about 6,300 public companies that Datastream tracks.

For each company, we captured annual financial performance information (in local currency and U.S. dollars) on revenue, earnings, dividends, shareholders equity, market value, earnings per share (EPS), cost of equity capital, and total shareholder return (TSR). We included exceptional items in our profitability measures because we wanted to measure a company's total performance. It turns out that exceptional items are all too common. We checked whether excluding such items altered the results in any material way. It did not.

The main nonfinancial data in the database are the country in which the company is domiciled and its Standard Industrial

Classification (SIC) codes. The database also includes local GDP growth for each country in each year.

From these financials, we have examined nominal and real performance across a number of measures, such as revenue growth, economic profit margin, annual earnings, and cumulative economic profit. We used this data to measure company performance against the tensions and to search for patterns between different variables.

The distribution of companies in the database by geography and industry is illustrated in Table B.1.

MANAGEMENT SURVEY

We commissioned a survey of management opinions from the Economist Intelligence Unit (EIU). EIU conducted an online survey in March 2005 over a period of two weeks and received 193 responses. The survey was completed by senior management in a wide variety of roles: 44 percent "C-level" executives, 27 percent directors, 21 percent managers. They represented companies across a broad range of industries and company sizes, and were fairly evenly spread across regions: 29 percent were from the United States, 30 percent from Western Europe, 31 percent from the Asia Pacific region, 10 percent from the rest of world.

We can't and don't claim that such a survey is strictly statistically representative of the business management community as a whole. The survey population is, after all, relatively small and is based on self-selection. But we do believe it to be a useful indicator of management perceptions of the three tensions.

PROFITABILITY VS. GROWTH ANALYSIS

BATTING AVERAGE

We defined *profitability* as positive economic profit margin and calculated it as economic profit divided by revenue. We defined *growth* as positive real revenue growth calculated as annual revenue growth less local GDP growth. *Profitability vs. growth batting average* was the proportion of years in which a company achieved a positive economic profit margin *and* had positive real revenue growth.

TABLE B.1. OVERVIEW OF THE DATABASE.

Geographical Mix			Industry Sector Mix		
Country	Number of Companies	% of Total	Industry	Number of Companies	% of Total
United States	370	35	Consumer goods	111	10
Japan	257	24	Manufacturing	92	9
United Kingdom	101	9	Construction and property	90	8
Germany	51	5	Retail	70	7
Canada	50	5	Utilities	69	6
France	36	3	Banks	68	6
Italy	21	2	Chemicals	62	6
Sweden	21	2	Natural resources (other than oil)	62	6
Finland	20	2	Automotive	52	5
Australia	17	2	Entertainment	50	5
Netherlands	17	2	Oil and gas	40	4
Denmark	14	1	Insurance	39	4
Singapore	13	1	Pharmaceuticals and biotech	36	3
South Africa	12	1	Computer hardware and software	35	3
Switzerland	12	1	Diversified industrials	31	3
Spain	11	1	Transportation	30	3
Hong Kong	10	1	Telecommunications	27	3
Malaysia	8	1	Publishing, printing, and photography	26	2
Belgium	7	1	Business supplies	24	2
Norway	7	1	Financial services (excluding banks and insurance)	21	2
Ireland	5	0	Health care	19	2
South Korea	4	0	Electrical equipment	18	2
Mexico	3	0	All companies	1,072	100
New Zealand	3	0			
Austria	2	0			
All companies	1,072	100			

PORTFOLIO DIVERSITY ANALYSIS

We used SIC codes as a proxy for the degree to which a company had a diversified business portfolio. SIC codes are four-digit codes assigned by the U.S. government to identify the primary business of a company. The first two digits identify the major industry grouping, the third digit identifies the industry group, and the last digit identifies industry. Datastream provides a maximum of ten SIC codes per company at the four-digit level. Of the 1,072 companies in our database, 800 had SIC code information for every year in the thirteen-year period from 1991 to 2004. We defined the degree of diversification as the average number of distinct SIC codes that a company had at the three-digit SIC code level over the thirteen-year period. We looked at the analysis at a three-digit level. The average company has 2.9 SIC codes at the three-digit level. We checked a representative sample of companies to determine whether the three-digit level at which to measure diversity is skewed by companies with very small proportions of their revenue in other industries. It is not.

Comparing a company's profitability vs. growth batting average to its number of SIC codes yielded no material correlation. We also looked at the change in level of diversification over time and how that related to change in batting average and TSR. We found no meaningful relationships.

ACQUISITIVENESS ANALYSIS

We based our measure of acquisitiveness on data from 562 companies for ten years, from 1995 to 2004. We selected these companies on the basis of data availability. We defined a company's acquisitiveness in any one year as the sum of the market value of its acquisitions in that year as a percentage of its market value at the start of the year. To get to an overall acquisitiveness score, we calculated the average acquisitiveness over the ten-year period. Companies' acquisitiveness includes public deals of more than $100 million and excludes private deals. Comparing each company's acquisitiveness to its profitability vs. growth batting average, we found no correlation.

PORTFOLIO EXPOSURE ANALYSIS

We based this analysis on the full 1,072-company database. We calculated batting average by industry to compare this to industry attractiveness. We ranked the industries by multiplying compound average growth in revenue over twenty years by average twenty-year economic profit margin.

TODAY VS. TOMORROW
ANALYSIS OF CONSECUTIVE EARNINGS GROWTH

We defined *consecutiveness* as the number of consecutive years of positive EPS growth in the twenty-year period. Thus a company that achieved positive EPS growth in all twenty years would score nineteen on consecutiveness. And a company that grew EPS in six years out of the twenty years, but never in two years in a row, would score zero on consecutiveness.

Many companies have negative EPS in any given year. Therefore, to count as achieving positive EPS growth, a company had to achieve positive earnings growth and finish with positive earnings. This eliminated companies that had negative earnings at both the start and end of the period but whose earnings became less negative.

Because more frequent achievement of positive EPS growth would be expected to lead to higher TSR, we isolated the impact of consecutiveness on TSR performance by observing different EPS growth "cohorts." For example, we observed companies achieving positive EPS growth in ten out of twenty years as a separate cohort from companies that achieved positive EPS growth in twelve out of twenty years. Within a cohort, we then compared a company's TSR to the consecutiveness of its positive EPS growth. We found that within EPS growth cohorts, the average TSR decreased as the number of years of consecutive EPS growth increased. We assessed different definitions of consecutiveness: for instance, the maximum number of consecutive years of positive EPS growth that a company achieves. The results of this analysis were not materially different from other methodologies.

BIAS ANALYSIS

We deemed a company "biased" if its financial performance behaved in a particular way more often than would be expected by chance alone. For example, although the average company might be expected to grow earnings and be on the path to multiyear economic profit growth six years out of fifteen (a batting average of 40 percent), a company that did that for nine years or more would be biased toward that type of performance. A company that did so for seven years would not be sufficiently out of the normal range of behavior to warrant being deemed biased toward that type of performance.

We calculated the minimum number of years required to deem a company biased over the twenty-year period at a level of 95 percent statistical significance. This is the measure for how likely bias is to be intentional as opposed to random. Whereas batting average lets us understand the benefit of achieving both short-term and long-term performance at the same time more often, bias analysis enables us to understand the benefit of achieving the other three possible outcomes: positive annual earnings growth without positive cumulative economic profit over five years; positive cumulative economic profit over five years without positive annual earnings growth; and neither positive annual earnings growth nor positive cumulative economic profit.

The picture that emerged was that the frequency of achieving positive cumulative economic profits was more important to TSR than the frequency of achieving annual earnings growth. Out of the total company database, over the twenty years,

- 184 companies were biased toward achieving both positive earnings growth and positive cumulative economic profit over five years; they achieved the highest average annual TSR: 21 percent.
- 22 companies were biased toward achieving positive cumulative economic profit over five years without positive earnings growth and achieved 12 percent average annual TSR.
- 105 companies were biased toward achieving positive earnings growth without positive cumulative economic profit over five years and achieved 6 percent average annual TSR.

- 651 companies were not biased toward a particular outcome. They achieved 11 percent in average annual TSR.

It should be noted that these TSR figures are higher than the whole twenty-year database because the measurement ended in 1999, near the peak of the high share prices of the dot-com boom. We checked whether a different ending date would have changed the direction of the results. It would not have done so.

BATTING AVERAGE ANALYSIS

For our measure of today's performance, we used earnings growth in that year. For our measure of tomorrow's performance, we used cumulative economic profit over five years. A year's performance counted toward a company's batting average if both earnings growth and cumulative economic profit over the next five years were positive. Thus, whether the performance in 1998 counts toward overall batting average depends on earnings growth from 1997 to 1998 and cumulative economic profit from 1998 to 2002. As mentioned in Chapter Two, we chose to use a five-year period because it coincides with many companies planning horizons and is close to the average tenure for chief executives of public companies in the United States and the United Kingdom. We checked whether the results would have been different with periods of six or seven years and they would not have been.

Because a material number of companies have negative earnings in any given year, we adjusted the measure of a company's performance today. To count as positive performance today, a company needed to achieve positive earnings growth and finish with positive earnings. This eliminated companies with negative earnings at both the start and end of the period but whose earnings became less negative. Although mathematics might lead you to think otherwise, we didn't think a reasonable person would regard going from a larger to a smaller loss as "positive earnings growth."

Because the measure of performance tomorrow was cumulative economic profit over five years, we could observe only fifteen years of performance out of the twenty-year period for which we have data. Consequently, we compared fifteen years of batting average performance to fifteen years of TSR performance to maintain consistency between timeframes.

REINVESTMENT ANALYSIS

We defined *reinvestment rate* as the proportion of earnings not paid out in dividends to shareholders each year. It is therefore calculated as: $1 - $ (dividends / earnings). The reinvestment rate was calculated over twenty years; in other words, reinvestment rate = $1 - $ (sum of annual dividends over twenty years) ÷ (sum of annual earnings over twenty years). We excluded companies with either very high reinvestment rates (above 100 percent) or very low reinvestment rates (below 0 percent), which produced a sample set of 738 companies. We found no correlation at all between twenty-year reinvestment rate and twenty-year TSR performance. We considered three alternative measures of reinvestment rate. None showed a meaningful positive correlation with TSR. The alternative measures we considered were (1) the change in shareholder equity in relation to earnings; (2) the change in shareholder equity in relation to sales; and (3) the change in shareholder equity in relation to shareholder equity.

WHOLE VS. PARTS

ANALYSIS OF THE SUM OF THE PARTS VS. THE WHOLE

Most analyses of whole-company performance vs. the performance of the sum of the parts are based on market values. That is, they compare the actual market value of the company with a sum-of-the-parts valuation constructed from industry valuation multiples. We applied a similar methodology to economic profit as well as conducting the more usual market value approach. We based our analysis on a bespoke database of companies over four years (2001–2004). The number of companies varied between 1,735 in 2003 and 1,992 in 2002. The set represents all publicly traded companies in the Datastream World Market Index database, with information on market value, earnings, shareholder equity, TSR for the company overall, and SIC code and revenue data by division. We excluded companies that had a discrepancy of more than 1 percent between the aggregate divisional revenues and total company revenue.

We categorized companies into three types based on the number and type of SIC codes:

- *Single-division company.* Companies with one division and one SIC code. There were between 618 and 971 single-division companies in the database, depending on the year.
- *Multidivisional company.* Companies with multiple divisions, all of which have the same SIC code—that is, are within the same industry sector. There were between 364 and 855 companies in this category.
- *Multibusiness company.* Companies with multiple divisions and multiple SIC codes—that is, with divisions in different industry sectors. There are between 294 and 472 companies within this category, and it includes multi-industry conglomerates.

We categorized single-division companies into industry segments based on their three-digit SIC codes. We consolidated companies across similar SIC codes to ensure that most industry segments included at least five companies. For example, we grouped single-division companies in 2004 into eighty-two industry segments, of which 90 percent had at least five companies. For each industry segment, we calculated the average market value–to–revenue multiple and economic profit–to–revenue multiples for each industry segment. We excluded companies with market value–to–revenue multiples greater than 10 and economic profit–to–revenue multiples greater than 1. We found that the multiples of single-division businesses did not vary materially with business size or market value. We determined the sum-of-the-parts value (or economic profit) for a multidivisional company in each year by multiplying each division's revenue by the industry average market value–to–revenue multiple (or economic profit–to–revenue multiple) and aggregating the resulting value (or economic profit) across divisions.

NOTES

Chapter One: The Corporate Cycle

1. A 2005 study by our firm, Marakon Associates, found average CEO tenure in the top 100 public companies in the United States and the United Kingdom by market capitalization to be 6.7 years. In any case, the batting average results for today vs. tomorrow are not very sensitive to whether multiyear performance is measured over five, six, or seven years (see Appendix B).

2. The term *institutional imperative* was coined by Warren Buffett ("Letter to the Shareholders of Berkshire Hathaway Inc.," 1989, which can be accessed at www.berkshirehathaway.com/letters/1989.html). According to Buffett, the institutional imperative exists when

   > For example: (1) As if governed by Newton's First Law of Motion, an institution will resist any change in its current direction; (2) Just as work expands to fill available time, corporate projects or acquisitions will materialize to soak up available funds; (3) Any business craving of the leader, however foolish, will be quickly supported by detailed rate-of-return and strategic studies prepared by his troops; and (4) The behavior of peer companies, whether they are expanding, acquiring, setting executive compensation or whatever, will be mindlessly imitated.

3. Correlation does not necessarily mean causation. It is in theory possible that the causation goes in the other direction than the one we infer: that higher returns to shareholders lead to higher batting averages. In practice, any effects in this direction are likely to be comprehensively outweighed by the effects in the other direction. In general, when we cite correlation and imply causation, we have tried to make this kind of practical judgment.

4. Economic value can either be calculated by discounting expected future cash flows or by discounting expected future economic

profits and adding them to current capital. See Appendix A for details on the equivalence of these two approaches.

Chapter Two: Profitability vs. Growth

1. We define organic growth as revenue growth achieved through existing operations as opposed to through acquisition.

2. Quoted in Constantios C. Markides, "To Diversify or Not to Diversify," originally published in *Harvard Business Review,* Nov.-Dec. 1997 and reprinted as part of a collection of articles on growth strategy in *Harvard Business Review: On Strategies for Growth.* (Boston: Harvard Business School Press, 1998), p. 83.

3. The rank order was developed by multiplying average compound annual growth in revenue for the years 1983–2003 by average economic profit margin over the same period.

4. It can also happen if the (good) costs necessary for customer benefit are simply too high—if they could never attract enough revenue to allow economic profitability to reach positive levels. Passenger air transport comes to mind as a possible example.

5. In his book *The Modern Firm* (Oxford, UK: Oxford University Press, 2004), John Roberts of the Stanford Business School points to Nokia as a good example of a company that practices "high commitment" human resource management that does not rely on strong individual incentives to motivate performance.

6. A fuller description of Nucor's story can be found in chap. 4 of *The Innovator's Dilemma,* by Clayton M. Christensen (Boston: Harvard Business School Press, 1997).

7. Theodore Levitt, "Marketing Myopia," *Harvard Business Review,* July-Aug. 1960, pp. 45–56.

8. We also discussed with Jones the idea of a customer benefit "litmus test"—questions to ask yourself to judge whether your company actually is focusing on customer benefit. He suggested the following questions:

   • Can our people describe in simple and convincing terms what the principal benefit of what we are selling is? Not what it is or what it does, but what its benefits are?

   • Do we really know and worry about who else is providing a comparable benefit to that provided by our products? This is a different question than Who are our direct competitors? The direct competitors for boxes of chocolates are other companies making boxes of chocolates; but if you are going to a dinner party, then comparable benefits to those provided by a box of chocolates can be found in a bunch of flowers or a bottle of wine.

- Is our pricing explained by our customer benefit? Or rather is it explained by the price direct competitors set or what is needed to meet financial targets?

- Do we segment our market by benefit rather than by considerations of demography, propensity, usage, and attitude, or any other consideration?

9. "Closing the Delivery Gap" by James Allen, Frederick F. Reichheld, Barney Hamilton, and Rob Markey of Bain & Company, 2005, and which can be accessed at www.bain.com/bainweb/pdfs/cms/hot-Topics/closingdeliverygap.pdf.

10. Six Sigma, pioneered by Motorola, is a method of increasing performance by reducing variations in the quality of processes. It was originally conceived as designing a way of working in which there would be no more than 3.4 defects per million outputs. Today, the standard for process variation is more often considered to be the point at which it is not cost-effective to pursue fewer defects. Lean Manufacturing was invented by Toyota in the 1950s to eliminate waste and reduce cycle time. The technique focuses managers' attention on the "seven wastes": overproduction, waiting time, transportation, overprocessing, inventory, motion, and scrap. Most of the U.S. companies we interviewed currently use some sort of Six Sigma or Lean Manufacturing practice, or "Lean Six Sigma."

Chapter Three: Today vs. Tomorrow

1. It is natural to ask whether there is a difference between this tension and the tension of profitability vs. growth. Growth and the long term and profitability and the short term are the natural associations to make. But different connections are possible, indeed widespread. Companies need long-term investment to achieve profitability as well as growth. Ask anyone who deals with factory reconfiguration. And, as sales managers will tell you, the revenue line in the short term is not a done deal. Both revenue growth and profitability improvement can be called on to increase performance in either timeframe. In our experience, most leaders do think of longer-term investment as being for growth. We think it is vital that they think of longer-term investment as being for building higher profitability as well. Gillette's Jim Kilts suggested that one way to think about the difference is that batting average on today vs.

tomorrow is about how often a company meets its operating plan *and* strategic plan each year, from year to year.

2. No doubt this is partly because the market decided that PepsiCo's earnings were more likely to last than Coca-Cola's. PepsiCo has, after all, reduced its reliance on traditional soft drinks by expanding into new categories, such as salty snacks, sports drinks, water, juices, and breakfast cereals, and has been more active in addressing concerns about health. Coca-Cola remains reliant on soft drinks for 80 percent of its revenue, compared with around 20 percent for PepsiCo, and is not perceived as having adapted as much or as well to changes in consumer attitudes and concerns. But the main reason for the reversal of fortunes may simply be that the market has revised downwards its previously unrealistic assessment of the likelihood of Coca-Cola's earnings growth lasting into the future.

3. Carol J. Loomis, "The 15% Delusion," *Fortune,* Feb. 5, 2001, pp. 102–108.

4. See Appendix B for how we defined *bias* in this analysis.

5. Charles F. Knight, "Emerson Electric: Consistent Profits, Consistently," *Harvard Business Review,* Jan.-Feb. 1992, pp. 57–70. Delving into Knight's record at Emerson, you find that a target for annual earnings growth was only one tool in an overall management approach of detailed planning and follow-through. Knight estimated that he devoted half his time to planning. He insisted that managers forecast for five years the components of their sales growth, not just the overall number—for instance, industry growth, changes in share, price increases, and revenue from new products and from international sales. These components were then tracked over time. Other important components of the model seem to have been a standard of continuous annual cost reduction and a culture of open and frank communication. Such practices perhaps helped the company distinguish between earnings that would be sustainable and those that would not. But even Emerson's run came to an end in 2001, when its earnings fell for the first time since 1956. A full treatment of Knight's leadership of Emerson can be found in Charles F. Knight and Davis Dyer, *Performance Without Compromise: How Emerson Consistently Achieves Winning Results* (Boston: Harvard Business School Press, 2005).

6. Warren Buffett, "Letter to the Shareholders of Berkshire Hathaway Inc.," 2000, which can be accessed at www.berkshirehathaway.com/letters/2000.html.

7. Owen Lamont, "Cash Flow and Investment: Evidence from Internal Capital Markets," *Journal of Finance,* 1997, *52,* 83–109.

8. See Appendix A for further detail on valuation.
9. Warren Buffett, "Letter to the Shareholders of Berkshire Hathaway Inc.," 1998, which can be accessed at www.berkshirehathaway.com/letters/1998.html.
10. In theory there could be a third explanation: lower reinvestment rates mean higher dividend rates, which signal to the capital markets management's confidence in future earnings. In practice, we judge that this explanation is only likely to have relevance to shorter time periods than the twenty years over which we have measured TSR. We assume that TSR over long periods are reasonably reflective of changes in economic value.
11. A revised definition of investor relations adopted by NIRI Board of Directors in March 2003 is very much in keeping with the spirit of striving to be correctly valued: "Investor relations is a strategic management responsibility that integrates finance, communication, marketing, and securities law compliance to enable the most effective two-way communication between a company, the financial community, and other constituencies, which ultimately contributes to a company's securities achieving fair valuation." See www.niri.org/about/mission.
12. Mark C. Scott, *Achieving Fair Value.* (Chichester, UK: John Wiley & Sons, 2005). The book draws on research by The Ashridge Strategic Management Centre.
13. Robert S. Kaplan and David P. Norton, *The Balanced Scorecard* (Boston: Harvard Business School Press, 1996).
14. See the article by our colleague Michael C. Mankins, "Stop Wasting Valuable Time," *Harvard Business Review*, Sept. 2004, pp. 58–65.
15. See Michael M. Mankins, Peter W. Kontes, and James McTaggart, *The Value Imperative.* (New York: Free Press, 1994), pp. 227–229.

Chapter Four: Whole vs. Parts

1. With apologies to Jane Austen. ("It is a truth universally acknowledged, that a single man in possession of a good fortune must be in want of a wife"—*Pride and Prejudice.*)
2. Under some definitions, the concept of synergy can be the same as horizontal value. But many managers think of synergy as "something added to the parts by managing them in a group." That "something added" can be vertical or horizontal, so we have avoided using the term "synergy" as a synonym for horizontal value.
3. Gary Silverman, "Omnicom Lets Its Agencies Do the Talking," *Financial Times*, March 15, 2005.

4. See note 3 above.

5. We also conducted sum-of-the-parts analysis based on market values rather than economic profits. Our results were the same in direction, only even more pronounced. On average over the four years, 67 percent of multidivisional companies in the same sector traded at a discount to the sum of their parts; 33 percent traded at a premium. And, also in the same direction, we found that multibusiness companies in more than one sector traded even more often at a discount than at a premium: 77 percent vs. 23 percent.

6. Michael Porter of Harvard Business School found that the majority of acquisitions turn into disposals within six years, suggesting that significant benefits have not been forthcoming from either increasing vertical value or adding horizontal value. Analysis of many management buyouts and spin-offs has shown that they perform better on average *after* leaving their corporate owners, suggesting that there had been limited or even negative vertical and horizontal value added when under combined ownership. Some may argue that the rationale for the multibusiness company extends to external development—the ability to improve company performance by making better decisions about adding and subtracting businesses to the portfolio. However, unless such activity adds vertical and horizontal value to existing businesses, or adds businesses to which vertical and horizontal value can be added, it isn't worthwhile.

7. This hypothesis that horizontal value is often negative is supported by other research. For example, the returns on private equity funds often outperform those for public companies. Given that private equity companies generally don't seek to add horizontal value whereas publicly traded companies do, this suggests that horizontal value tends to be negative.

8. See John Roberts, *The Modern Firm* (Oxford: Oxford University Press, 2004), in particular Chapter Five.

9. Michael C. Mankins, "Stop Wasting Valuable Time," *Harvard Business Review*, Sept. 2004, pp. 58–65.

10. We take the view that the correct focus for a higher-order purpose as a motivational tool is customer benefit. Some commentators, however, argue that the exact content of the higher-order purpose matters less than its efficacy in motivating. For example, in *Built to Last* (3rd ed.) (New York: Random House Business Books, 2000), p. 67, Jim Collins and Jerry Porras stated the following:

> Some companies, such as Johnson & Johnson and Wal-Mart, made their *customers* central to their ideology; others, such as Sony and Ford, did not. Some companies, such as

HP and Marriott, made concern for their *employees* central to their ideologies; others, such as Nordstrom and Disney, did not. Some companies, such as Ford and Disney, made their *products or services* central to their core ideology; others, such as IBM and Citicorp, did not. Some companies, such as Sony and Boeing, made audacious *risk taking* central to their ideology; others, such as HP and Nordstrom, did not. Some companies, such as Motorola and 3M, made *innovation* central to their ideology; others, such as P&G and American Express, did not. In short, we did *not* find any specific ideological content essential to being a visionary company. Our research indicates that the *authenticity* of the ideology and the extent to which a company attains consistent alignment with the ideology counts more than the *content* of the ideology.

11.   This is far from being a new idea. Alfred Sloan, the chief executive who guided General Motors through most of the first half of the twentieth century, attributed business success to "a reconciliation of centralization and decentralization" (*My Years with General Motors* [New York: Doubleday, 1963]), p. 429. He characterized the multidivisional structure with which he is associated as operating according to the principle of "centralized policy and decentralized operations." Also, in the 1960s, Paul Lawrence and Jay Lorsch of Harvard Business School conducted an influential empirical study linking performance and organizational design (*Organization and Environment* [Boston: Harvard Business School Press, 1967]). They measured degrees of "integration" and degrees of "differentiation" within companies. They found that companies with the strongest performance had high levels of both at the same time.

12.   A company's processes are the activities that accomplish its work: filling an order, developing a new product, developing and approving plans, and so on. A company's organizational structure is how accountabilities and authorities are defined.

13.   Michael Goold and Andrew Campbell, "Desperately Seeking Synergy," *Harvard Business Review,* Sept.-Oct. 1998, pp. 131–143. The authors argue that executives tend to overestimate the potential for synergy. Most relevant to our subject, they discuss "parenting bias"— the belief that synergy will be captured only by cajoling or compelling business units to cooperate. The authors advocate becoming more precise on the nature of the "parenting opportunity" as well as holding the default assumption that when it makes good commercial sense to do so, the business units will cooperate voluntarily.

Chapter Five: Breaking the Corporate Cycle

1. Some of our interviewees mused on how private companies seemed to manage to avoid many of these additional forces that make the tensions harder to deal with. Sir Brian Pitman, formerly chief executive and then chairman of Lloyds TSB, noted that through the growth of private equity investment, the money invested in private companies is now starting to exceed that invested in public companies: "For private companies, there's not the same scrutiny on pay or governance. They can sell off dud businesses where earnings per share would go down in the short term, but they will make more money over the long run. They don't have the risk of being run by the press or the investors." One could certainly make the case that the external pressures on public companies make it harder rather than easier for them to resolve the three tensions.

2. To the extent that this "swinging the pendulum" phenomenon is unproductive, allowing CEOs to become chairmen may be less of an issue for good governance than might otherwise be imagined. Such moves may create a natural brake on the pendulum.

3. We asked the following question: "Which of the following statements most closely reflects senior management's approach to running your company?" We provided these choices: "They consistently prioritize improving the stand-alone performance of the business units over achieving synergies between business units"; "They consistently prioritize achieving synergies between business units over improving the stand-alone performance of the business units"; "They swing from a focus on synergy and a focus on stand-alone performance"; "They consistently place an equal emphasis on both." Roughly 70 percent said that their company prioritized. Within those saying their company prioritized, around 40 percent said that their priorities tended to change over time—that their company tended to emphasize one objective and then later emphasize the other. The rest said that their company tended to choose their priorities and stick with them. Where a consistent choice was made, it was more likely to be profitability over growth and parts over whole—in both cases by a factor of about two to one. There was no such favoritism on the today vs. tomorrow tension: those making a choice to put current performance first were almost exactly matched by those putting future performance first.

4. There are of course many occasions when managers must determine the relative priority of different performance objectives. In our view, the criterion on which such choices should be made is by

appeal to likely impact on economic value—in other words, on future economic profits.

5.   We are not offering batting average as a more accurate alternative proxy for TSR than economic—or cash flow—value. Changes in economic value are the best prediction of long-term TSR. But, for all its virtue, economic value is not an easy operating measure for managers to use. It is complicated: most people find it hard to discount cash flows from now until infinity in their heads! Economic value is always a measure of future performance and as such is not a great one to use for rewarding *achieved* performance. See Appendix A for more on this point.

6.   On the whole vs. parts tension, where it is hard to measure batting averages directly, the proportion of years when the value of the company trades at a premium to the value of the sum of its parts on a stand-alone basis is not a bad proxy. For example, if a company trades at a premium in five out of ten years, it could be deemed to have a batting average of 50 percent on whole vs. parts. Trading at a premium is, of course, no *guarantee* that both horizontal and vertical values are positive (rather than, for example, that vertical value is negative but horizontal value is positive and more than offsets the negative).

7.   For example, in his book *The Ultimate Question* (Boston: Harvard Business School Press, 2006), consultant Fred Reichheld advocates for the use of a "Net Promoter® Score," which measures the proportion of customers who are promoters less the proportion who are detractors.

8.   Dean Foust with Nanette Byrnes, "Gone Flat," *BusinessWeek*, Dec. 20, 2004, pp. 77–82.

Chapter Six: The Next Big Thing

1.   Another hero of Greek mythology—Jason—is credited with navigating through the Straits of Messina without falling prey to either Scylla or Charybdis. Our finding has been that a business leader today is more likely to be an Odysseus than a Jason.

2.   *Bain & Company Management Tools and Trends 2005*, by Darrell Rigby and Barbara Bilodeau, which can be accessed at www.bain.com/ management_tools/home.asp.

3.   Xenophon, *The Economist* (Whitefish, MT: Kessinger Publishing, 2004), p. 76.

4.   To assess relative popularity over the last twenty years, we used the information service Factiva to search for share of press mentions in

six popular business readings: *Financial Times, Harvard Business Review, MIT Sloan Management Review, The Economist, The Wall Street Journal,* and *BusinessWeek.* We were able to count the number of articles in each publication in which there was at least one mention of specific words (for example, "decentralization"). Our assessment of relative popularity before the 1980s drew from many sources (see Selected Reading).

5.   Alfred P. Sloan, *My Years with General Motors* (New York: Doubleday, 1963), p. 64.

6.   Peter F. Drucker, *The Practice of Management* (Oxford: Butterworth-Heinemann, 1955), p. 310.

7.   This approach is entirely different from the method of testing hypotheses against observations. It often makes an assumption that the hypothesis method does not: that similarity is more important to determining causality than difference. This assumption is incorrect. Imagine if we were trying to understand the secret of successful middle-distance running. Suppose that we identified the ten fastest middle-distance runners in the world and what was similar about them. We might well find that a higher percentage of them wore lucky charms than less successful runners. Are lucky charms then a cause of faster middle-distance running? Probably not. Using the hypothesize-and-observe method, we might have surmised that successful middle-distance running has more to do with such factors as cardiovascular endowment, length of femur, training regime, diet, altitude of childhood home, and psychological motivation. On these factors our top runners might actually have been quite different—some having long femurs and living in the mountains, others having short femurs and growing up by the sea but having unusually strong motivation and a great training method. Yet all these factors could actually be valid parts of the recipe for successful middle-distance running. Although the idea is sometimes hard to accept intuitively, similarity is in fact no more of a validation than difference.

8.   Sloan, 1963, p. 429.

Selected Reading

Chapter Two: Profitability vs. Growth

Barwise, Patrick, and Sean Meehan. (2004). *Simply Better.* Boston: Harvard Business School Press.

Charan, Ram. (2004). *Profitable Growth Is Everyone's Business.* New York: Crown Business.

Hammer, Michael, and James Campy. (1993). *Reengineering the Corporation.* New York: HarperCollins.

Mankins, Michael C. (2002). "Growth Traps: Lessons from the Go-Go '90s." *Forethought, 2*(1), 16–20.

Peccei, Matteo. (2004). "Want to Grow the Top Line? Manage Costs Better." *Journal of Business Strategy, 25*(3), 35–38.

Chapter Three: Today vs. Tomorrow

Bossidy, Larry, and Ram Charan. (2002). *Execution.* New York: Random House Business Books.

Christensen, Clayton M. (1997). *The Innovator's Dilemma.* Boston: Harvard Business School Press.

Drucker, Peter F. (1955). *The Practice of Management.* Oxford: Butterworth-Heinemann.

Grove, Andrew S. (1996). *Only the Paranoid Survive.* New York: HarperCollins.

Hamel, Gary, and C. K. Prahalad. (1994). *Competing for the Future.* Boston: Harvard Business School Press.

Kaplan, Robert S., and David P. Norton. (1996). *The Balanced Scorecard.* Boston: Harvard Business School Press.

Knight, Charles F. (1992, Jan.-Feb.). "Emerson Electric: Consistent Profits, Consistently." *Harvard Business Review,* pp. 57–70.

Levitt, Theodore. (1960, July-Aug.). "Marketing Myopia." *Harvard Business Review,* pp. 45–56.

Mankins, Michael. (2004, Sept.-Oct.). "Stop Wasting Valuable Time." *Harvard Business Review,* pp. 58–65.

Marsh, Paul. (1990). *Short-Termism on Trial.* London: Institutional Fund Managers Association.

Mintzberg, Henry. (1994). *The Rise and Fall of Strategic Planning.* New York: Free Press.

Chapter Four: Whole vs. Parts

Chandler, Alfred D., Jr. (1969). *Strategy and Structure.* Cambridge, Mass.: MIT Press.

Collins, James C., and Jerry I. Porras. (1994). *Built to Last.* New York: Random House Business Books.

Goold, Michael, and Andrew Campbell. (1998, Sept.–Oct.). "Desperately Seeking Synergy." *Harvard Business Review,* pp. 131–143.

Goold, Michael, Andrew Campbell, and Marcus Alexander. (1994). *Corporate-Level Strategy.* Hoboken, N.J.: Wiley.

Handy, Charles. (1974). *Understanding Organizations.* London: Penguin Books.

Lawrence, Paul R., and Jay W. Lorsch. (1967). *Organization and Environment.* Boston: Harvard Business School Press.

Roberts, John. (2004). *The Modern Firm.* Oxford: Oxford University Press.

Sloan, Alfred P. (1963). *My Years with General Motors.* New York: Doubleday.

Chapter Five: Breaking the Corporate Cycle

Dodd, Dominic, and Ken Favaro (2006, Dec.). "Managing the Right Tension." *Harvard Business Review,* pp. 62–74.

Mankins, Michael M., Peter W. Kontes, and James McTaggart. (1994). *The Value Imperative.* New York: Free Press.

Pascale, Richard Tanner. (1990). *Managing on the Edge.* New York: Touchstone.

Chapter Six: The Next Big Thing

Furham, Adrian. (2004). *Management and Myths.* Basingstoke, England: Palgrave Macmillan.

Hindle, Tim. (2003). *Guide to Management Ideas* (The Economist Series). (2nd ed.) New York: Bloomberg Press.

Magretta, Joan. (2002). *What Management Is.* New York: Free Press.

Micklethwait, John, and Adrian Wooldridge. (1997). *The Witch Doctors.* New York: Random House.

ACKNOWLEDGMENTS

We are grateful first and foremost to past and present clients of Marakon Associates. In particular, we thank those who helped us directly with this book by sharing their thoughts and advice: Matthew Barrett, chairman, and former group chief executive, Barclays plc; Norman Bobins, president and chief executive officer, LaSalle Bank Corporation; Lord Browne of Madingley, group chief executive, BP plc; Lewis B. Campbell, chairman, president, and chief executive officer, Textron Inc.; Andrew Cosslett, chief executive, InterContinental Hotels Group plc; Travis Engen, retired president and chief executive officer, Alcan; Tom Glocer, chief executive, Reuters Group plc; José Ignacio Goirigolzarri, president and chief operating officer, Grupo BBVA; Rijkman Groenink, chairman of the managing board, ABN AMRO; Dr. Franz B. Humer, chairman and chief executive officer, Roche Holding Ltd.; Peter R. Kann, chairman and former chief executive, Dow Jones & Company; James M. Kilts, former chairman, chief executive officer and president, the Gillette Company; Anne M. Mulcahy, chairman and chief executive officer, Xerox Corporation; Blake W. Nordstrom, president, Nordstrom Inc.; Sir Brian Pitman, former chairman, Lloyds TSB Group plc; Todd Stitzer, chief executive officer, Cadbury Schweppes plc; Sir John Sunderland, chairman, Cadbury Schweppes plc; John Varley, group chief executive, Barclays plc; Robert D. Walter, chairman and founder, Cardinal Health Inc.; and Richard F. Zannino, chief executive, Dow Jones & Company. Leading a large organization is enough of a full-time job without being interviewed about it as well . . . and by people who are supposed to be advising you in the first place.

We learned a great deal from the comments of those unfortunate enough to be cornered into reading earlier drafts: Bob Buday, founding partner of the Bloom Group; Jose Giral, former chief executive of Xabre and current director of the Center of Management Research, National University of Mexico; Chris Jones, senior advisor to Marakon Associates and former chairman and chief executive, J Walter Thompson (now JWT); Peter Kann, Dow Jones & Company; John Roberts, professor of economics, strategic management, and international business at the Stanford Graduate School of Business; and David Womersley, professor of English Literature at St. Catherine's College Oxford.

We risked some beautiful friendships by inviting Marakon colleagues to review our work: Mike Baxter, Brian Burwell, Alastair Campbell, David Fondiller, Mason Kissell, Ron Langford, Michael Mankins, James McTaggart, Richard Steele, and Matt Symonds. Thank you for your ideas and support. We are also grateful to Peter Klein, former senior vice president of strategic planning and business development, the Gilette Cmpany, and Mark Reckitt, group strategy director, Cadbury Schweppes, for their helpful ideas and guidance.

Charles Whatling led the research for this book with a team at Marakon: Osanna Avanesova, Janice Barclay, Xavier Brice, Rachael Elliott, Hadrian Green, Tom Hay, Anna Hemsley, Dmitri Ivanov, Nishant Lalwani, Chris Moon, Jatin Rajput, Mie Soerensen, Daniel Thomson, and Rajal Upadhyaya. Special thanks go to Tom Hay for taking on so much. Jason Hanford, who heads Marakon's research unit, and his team patiently fielded a stream of requests. We are indebted to you all for your work over the last three years.

At Jossey-Bass, Susan Williams showed great support for this book from the early stages. We thank her and her team for all of their hard work. Special thanks go to Elizabeth Forsaith and Michele Jones.

Our thanks are due to the researchers at the Economist Intelligence Unit who helped us design and conduct our management survey and with whom Marakon has collaborated on other surveys referenced in the text. We express our appreciation to Dow Jones and speakers at their Wall Street Journal Europe/CNBC Europe CEO Summit in 2003 on "leadership dilemmas." The conference prompted us to develop our thoughts into this book.

We have dedicated this book to William ("Dr. Bill") Alberts, much loved cofounder of Marakon Associates. There would be no

Marakon if it weren't for Bill, and we could not have written this book without Marakon. We regret we didn't finish it in time for him to read it.

Finally, we would like to thank Dominic's wife, Kate, and Ken's wife, Lisa, for their unfailing support and for the time we took from being with them and our families to finish this project.

All these people have made this a better book than it would have been without them. Its shortcomings are our own invention.

October 2006

DOMINIC DODD
London, England

KEN FAVARO
New York, New York

About the Authors

The authors are from Marakon Associates, the firm called by *Fortune* magazine "the best-kept secret in consulting" and by *The Economist* "a consultancy that has advised some of the world's most consistently successful companies." Since the 1980s, the authors have advised, among others, the top management of ABN AMRO, the Boots Company, BP, British Telecom, BBVA, Cadbury Schweppes, Cardinal Health, the Coca-Cola Company, Dow Jones, DuPont, Eastman Kodak, Hoffman-La Roche, LaSalle Bank, Lloyds TSB, Prudential plc, and Tyco.

Their work has covered all aspects of business leadership, including goals, corporate strategy, business unit strategy, mergers and acquisitions, organic growth, productivity, organizational structure, resource allocation, performance monitoring, executive remuneration, and culture.

DOMINIC DODD is a senior advisor at Marakon Associates. Since joining the firm in 1989, he has been a managing partner, a founding member of the firm's London office, and Marakon's worldwide head of marketing and communications. He holds a B.A. honors degree in philosophy, politics, and economics from Oxford University. He lives in London with his wife, Kate, and their son, Thomas.

KEN FAVARO is co-chairman of Marakon Associates. He served two terms as Marakon's chief executive from 2000 to 2006. Since joining the firm in 1984, he has served as the regional managing partner for Europe, worldwide practice leader, and chairman of Marakon's partner development committee. He earned a B.S.C.E. and an M.B.A. from Stanford University, both with honors. He lives in New York with his wife, Lisa, and their children, Nicolas, Alexander, and Cristina.

INDEX

cycle, 167–183; "choices"
approach to management used by,
162, 164, 165*f*, 183; on dealing
with pressures, 157–159; dilemmas
continually faced by, 184–185;
making batting average matter,
167, 168–170; management tools
available to, 172–173*t*, 174–175*t*,
176; managing common bonds
between each tension, 167,
170–176; picking a lead tension,
167, 176–183; summary of ideas
for managing tensions for, 175*t*.
See also Companies; Management;
Questions by leader
Lean Manufacturing technique, 62,
63, 65, 153, 219*n*.10
Lean Six Sigma technique, 62, 65
Lending: excess investment and,
82–83; recommendations on corporate, 83
Levitt, T., 20

M

M&A (merger and acquisition): conducted by logic rather than emotion, 54; dilemmas presented by
challenges of, 24–25; low success
rates of, 24; organic growth vs.
growth by, 22; Porter's findings
on acquisitions that turn into disposals, 222*n*.6; using diagonal
assets to guide your, 152–154. *See
also* Acquisitiveness
Management: "balance" approach
to, 164–167, 183; "both"
approach to, 167–183; "choices"
approach to, 162, 164, 165*f*, 183;
cycle of ideas on, 187, 188–189*f*,
190–191; making batting average
matter as imperative for, 167,
168–170; phenomenon of fashion in, 185–187; picking lead tension as imperative for, 167,
176–183; popularity of specific
ideas in, 226*n*.4; strengthening

common bonds within each tension as imperative for, 167,
170–176; as young discipline,
191–194. *See also* Leaders; **Process
and routines**
Management discipline: lack of
agreement as to purpose within,
191–192; lack of consensus on
method within, 193–194; mismatch of scope between ideas
and practice within, 192–193
Management tools: benchmarking,
173*t*, 186; categories and uses of,
173*t*; cautions regarding effective
use of, 174; coherence as organizing concept for, 176; new ways of
using old, 172, 173, 195; summary of ideas for use of, 175*t*
Marakon Associates, 107, 217*n*.1
Market: market share vs. growing
your, 54–56; preference for
strength over attractiveness in,
59–62. *See also* Stock market
Market exposure, 28–29
Marriott, B., Sr., 140–141
Marriott Corp., 140
Mars, 55
McDonald's, 55
"McFlurry" milkshake initiative
(Cadbury), 55
Measures: earnings per share (EPS),
75*f*, 85–87; myth of price-to-earn-
ings (P/E) ratio, 72–73; total
shareholder returns (TSR),
12–17, 75–78, 145, 221*n*.10,
225*n*.5. *See also* **Batting average**;
Earnings; **Standards**
Meeting agenda, 108
Microsoft Network (MSN), 41
Miller Brewing, 24
Mises, L. von, 86
Moments of pleasure, 146
Motorola, 35
Mulcahy, A., 62–63, 91, 98, 144
MultiCo (fictional), 117–119*f*
Munger, C., 86